BLAZING THE WAY

AF250227

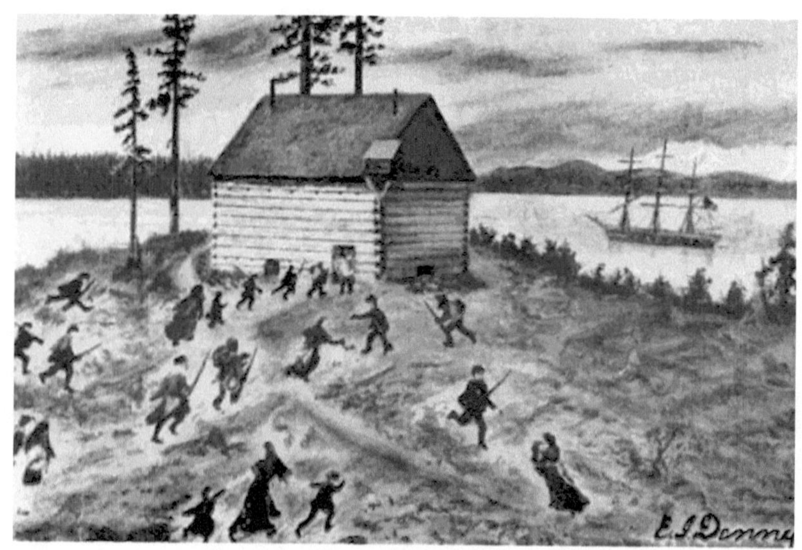

FORT DECATUR, JANUARY 26, 1856

BLAZING THE WAY

—OR—

True Stories, Songs, and Sketches of Puget Sound and Other Pioneers

EMILY INEZ DENNY

WITH ILLUSTRATIONS BY THE AUTHOR
AND FROM AUTHENTIC PHOTOGRAPHS

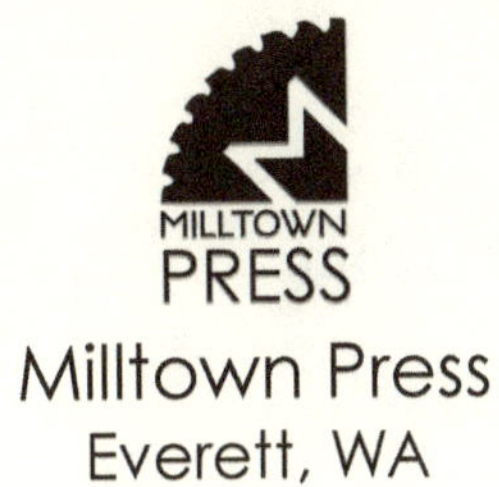

Milltown Press
Everett, WA

Copyright ©2021 Milltown Press

All rights reserved

Library of Congress Control Number: 2021941813

Cover painting by Emily Inez Denny, courtesy of Museum of History & Industry, Seattle

Printed and bound in the United States of America

First Milltown Press edition: July 2021

First published 1909 Rainier Printing Company, Inc.

ISBN 978-0-578-93382-5

Milltown Press
3616 Colby Ave #136
Everett, WA 98201

www.milltownpress.com

I-9 8 7 6 5 4 3 2 1

To My Dear Father and Mother,
Faithful Friends and Counselors,
Whose pioneer life I shared,
This book is affectionately dedicated
By The AUTHOR

A star stood large and white awest,
Then Time uprose and testified;
They push'd the mailed wood aside,
They toss'd the forest like a toy,
That great forgotten race of men,
The boldest band that yet has been
Together since the siege of Troy,
And followed it and found their rest.
—Miller

Index

PART III

INDIAN LIFE AND SETTLERS' BEGINNINGS

Illustrations

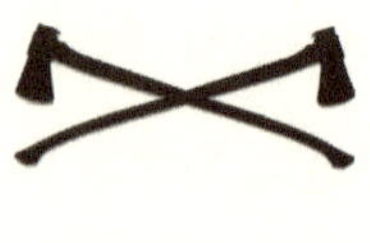

FOREWARD

THERE WAS no difficulty in choosing the first book we would publish at Milltown Press. I've long been fascinated by the peculiar and delicate relationships between the Coast Salish peoples of the Pacific Northwest and their European visitors—from the early days of the fur trade to the mass settlement of Americans following Manifest Destiny. I've researched the history of the Puget Sound region for writing projects and academics. The stories and illustrations in *Blazing the Way* are the most comprehensive overview of early pioneer life on Puget Sound that I have found.

When I first read about the Denny party landing at Alki on that miserable November day—all of their worldly possessions deposited onto the rocky beach, in peril of being swallowed by the rising tide; falling rain soaking them to the skin and no shelter but a roofless, half-built house; the women and children huddled on a drift log, weeping, as a group of Natives watched—I thought about how hopeless and helpless they must have felt

Then I thought of the modern-day Alki, lined by luxury condos and packed on a sunny day by crowds of Seattleites biking, jogging, cruising in convertibles, or coming together at an eatery for a salmon dinner and cocktails with Seattle's skyscrapered skyline looming across the bay. I wondered what the Denny party would have thought of this. They hoped to build a community of up to 1,000 settlers, and now, a mere 170 years later, there are more than three-quarters of a million souls living in the city. It's hard to fathom how this place changed so drastically and so rapidly from the wilderness it was on that day they arrived. The stories told in *Blazing the Way* help us to understand the experiences of the early settlers, their relationship to the land and the Natives, and their journey to create a community.

Emily Inez Denny grew up hearing the stories of the early days. She was born at the same time as the City of Seattle and she grew with her, as with a sister. Who better to write this story? She herself was a trailblazer, living life on her own terms during the strict Victorian era when woman's sole respectable role was to support a husband and raise a family. Instead, she was educated, never married, and spent her life as an artist and activist for women's rights, as well as creating this important work for the historical record.

I hope to honor her by redesigning this book and making it accessible to a new generation of readers who are curious about the origins and early days of the City of Seattle and those delicate relationships that were forged in the beginning. Happy reading!

Mary Senter
Publisher, Milltown Press
May 30, 2021
Everett, WA

BLAZING THE WAY

I N THE early days when a hunter, explorer or settler essayed to tread the mysterious depths of the unknown forest of Puget Sound, he took care to "blaze the way." At brief intervals he stopped to cut with his sharp woodman's ax a generous chip from the rough bark of fir, hemlock or cedar tree, leaving the yellow inner bark or wood exposed, thereby providing a perfect guide by which he retraced his steps to the canoe or cabin. As the initial stroke it may well be emblematical of the beginnings of things in the great Northwest.

I do not feel moved to apologize for this book; I have gathered the fragments within my reach; such or similar works are needed to set forth the life, character and movement of the early days on Puget Sound. The importance of the service of the Pioneers is as yet dimly perceived; what the Pilgrim Fathers were to New England, the Pioneers were to the Pacific Coast, to the "nations yet to be," who, following in their footsteps, shall people the wilds with teeming cities, a "human sea," bearing on its bosom argosies of priceless worth.

It does contain some items and incidents not generally known or heretofore published. I hope others may be provoked to record their pioneer experiences.

I have had exceptional opportunities in listening to the thrice-told tales of parents and friends who had crossed the plains, as well as personal recollections of experiences and observation during a residence of over fifty years in the Northwest, acknowledging also the good fortune of having been one of the first white children born on Puget Sound.

Every old pioneer has a store of memories of adventures and narrow escapes, hardships bravely endured, fresh pleasures enjoyed, rude but genial merrymakings, of all the fascinating incidents that made up the wonder-life of long ago.

Chronology is only a row of hooks to hang the garments of the past upon, else they may fall together in a confused heap.

Not having a full line of such supports on which to hang the weaving of my thoughts—I simply overturn my Indian basket of chips picked up after "Blazing the Way," they being merely bits of beginnings in the Northwest.

—E. I. Denny

BLAZING THE WAY

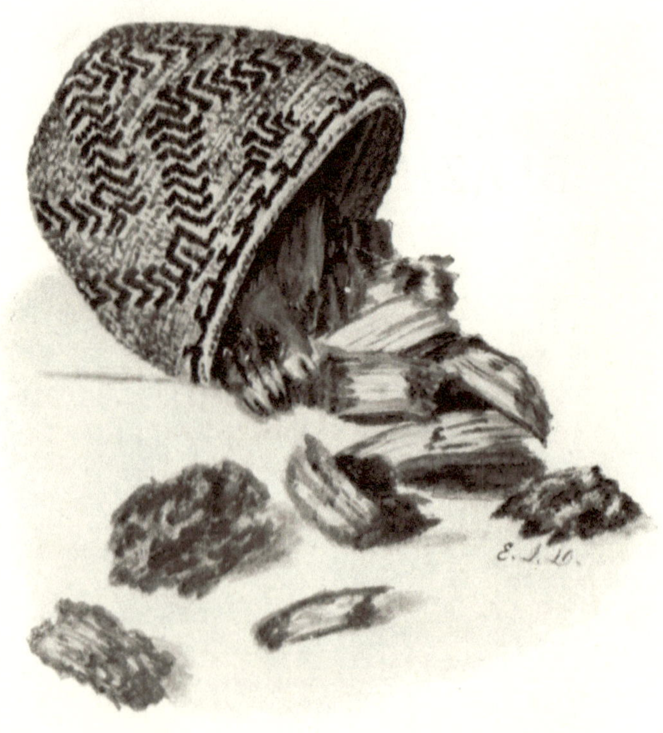

CHIPS PICKED UP AFTER BLAZING THE WAY

PART I

THE GREAT MARCH

CHAPTER I

CROSSING THE PLAINS

With Faith's clear eye we saw afar
In western sky our empire's star,
And strong of heart and brave of soul,
We marched and marched to reach the goal.
Unrolled a scroll, the great, gray plains,
And traced thereon our wagon trains;
Our blazing campfires marked the road
As night succeeding night they glowed.
—Song of the Pioneers

THE NOBLE army of courageous, enduring, persistent, progressive pioneers who from time to time were found threading their way across the illimitable wilderness, forty or fifty years ago, in detached companies, often unknown and unknowing each other, have proved conclusively that an age of marvelous heroism is but recently past.

The knowledge, foresight, faith and force exhibited by many of these daring men and women proclaimed them endowed with the genius of conquerors.

The merely physical aspect of the undertaking is over-powering.

To transport themselves and their effects in slow and toil-some ways, through hundreds of miles of weary wilderness, uninhabited except by foes, over beetling mountain ranges, across swift and dangerous rivers, through waterless deserts, in the shadow of continual dread, required a fortitude and staying power seldom equaled in the history of human effort.

But above and beyond all this, they carried the profound convictions of Christian men and women, of patriots and martyrs. They battled with the forces of Nature and implaca-ble enemies; they found, too, that their moral battles must be openly fought year after year, often in the face of riotous dis-regard of the laws of God and man. Arrived at their journey's end, they planted the youngest scions of the Tree of Liberty; they founded churches and schools, carefully keeping the traditions of civilization, yet in many things finding greater and truer freedom than they had left behind.

The noblest of epics, masterpieces of painting, stupen-dous operas or the grandest spectacular drama could but meagerly or feebly express the characters, experiences and environment of those who crossed the plains for the Pacific slope in the midst of the nineteenth century.

> A mighty nation moving west,
> With all its steely sinews set
> Against the living forests. Hear
> The shouts, the shots of pioneers!
> The rended forests, rolling wheels,
> As if some half-checked army reels,
> Recoils, redoubles, comes again,
> Loud-sounding like a hurricane."
> –Joaquin Miller

It is my intention to speak more especially of one little company who were destined to take a prominent part in the laying of foundations in the State of Washington.

Previous to 1850, glowing accounts of the fertility, mildness, beauty and general desirability of Oregon Territory, which then included Washington, reached the former friends and acquaintances of Farley Pierce, Liberty Wallace, the Rudolphs and others who wrote letters concerning this favored land. Added to the impression made thereby, the perusal of Fremont's travels, the desire for a change of climate from the rigorous one of Illinois, the possession of a pioneering spirit and the resolution was taken, "To the far Pacific Coast we will go;" acting upon it, they took their places in the great movement having for its watchword, "Westward Ho!"

John Denny, a Kentuckian by birth, a pioneer of Indiana and Illinois, whose record as a soldier of 1812, a legislator in company and fraternal relations with Lincoln, Baker, Gates and Trumbull, distinguished him for the most admirable qualities, was the leading spirit; his wife, Sarah Latimer Denny, a Tennessean, thrifty, wise, faithful and far-seeing, who had for many widowed years previous to her marriage to John Denny, wrought out success in making a home and educating her three children in Illinois, was a fit leader of pioneer women.

These, with their grown-up sons and daughters, children and grandchildren, began the great journey across the plains, starting from Cherry Grove, Knox County, Illinois, on April 10th, 1851. Four "prairie schooners," as the canvas-covered wagons were called, three of them drawn by four-horse teams, one with a single span, a few saddle horses and two faithful watchdogs, whose value is well known to those who have traveled the wilds, made up the train.

The names of these brave-hearted ones, ready to dare and endure all, are as follows:

John Denny, Sarah Latimer Denny and their little daughter, Loretta; A. A. Denny, Mary A. Denny and their two children, Catherine and Lenora; C. D. Boren, Mrs. Boren and their daughter, Gertrude; the only unmarried woman, Miss Louisa Boren, sister of Mrs. A. A. Denny and C. D. Boren; C. Crawford and family; four unmarried sons of John Denny, D. T. Denny, James, Samuel and Wiley Denny.

The wrench of parting with friends made a deep and lasting wound; no doubt every old pioneer of the Pacific Coast can recall the anguish of that parting, whose scars the healing years have never effaced.

The route followed by our pioneers was the old emigrant road along the north side of the Platte River, down the Columbia and up the Willamette to Portland, Oregon Territory, which they afterwards left for their ultimate destination, Puget Sound, where they found Nature so bountiful, a climate so moderate and their surroundings so ennobling that I have often heard them say they had no wish to return to dwell in the country from whence they came.

Past the last sign of civilization, the Mormon town of Kanesville, a mile or two east of the Missouri River, the prairie schooners were fairly out at sea. The great Missouri was crossed at Council Bluffs by ferryboat on the 5th of May. The site of the now populous city of Omaha was an untrodden waste. From thence they followed the beaten track of the many who had preceded them to California and Oregon.

Hundreds of wagons had ground their way over the long road before them, and beside this road stretched the narrower beaten track of the ox-drivers.

On the Platte, shortly after crossing the Missouri, a violent thunderstorm with sheets of rain fell upon them at night, blowing down their tents and saturating their belongings, thereby causing much discomfort and inconvenience. Of necessity the following day was spent in drying out the whole equipment.

It served as a robust initiation in roughing it; up to that time they had carefully dressed in white night robes and lay down in neatly made beds, but many a night after this storm were glad to rest in the easiest way possible, when worn by travel and too utterly weary of the long day's heat and dust, with grinding and bumping of wheels, to think of the niceties of dainty living.

For a time spring smiled on all the land; along the Platte the prairies stretched away on either hand, delightfully green and fresh, on the horizon lay fleecy white clouds, islands of vapor in the ethereal azure sea above; but summer came on apace and the landscape became brown and parched.

The second day west of the Missouri our train fell in with a long line of eighteen wagons drawn by horses, and fraternizing with the occupants, joined in one company. This new company elected John Denny as Captain. It did not prove a harmonious combination, however; discord arose, and nowhere does it seem to arise so easily as in camp. There was disagreement about standing guard; fault was found with the Captain and another was elected, but with no better results. Our pioneers found it convenient and far pleasanter to paddle their own canoes, or rather prairie schooners, and so left the contentious ones behind.

Long days of travel followed over the monotonous expanse of prairie, each with scarcely varying incidents, toils and dangers. The stir of starting in the morning, the morning forward movement, the halt for the noonday meal, cooked over a fire of buffalo chips, and the long, weary afternoon of heat and dust whose passing brought the welcome night, marked the journey through the treeless region.

At one of the noonings, the hopes of the party in a gastronomic line were woefully disappointed. A pailful of choice home-dried peaches, cooked with much care, had been set on a wagon tongue to cool and some unlucky movement precipitated the whole luscious, juicy mass into the sand below. It was an occurrence to make the visage lengthen, so far, far distant were the like of them from the hungry travelers.

Fuel was scarce a large part of the way until west of Fort Laramie, the pitch pine in the Black Hills made such fires as delight the hearts of campers. In a stretch of two hundred miles but one tree was seen, a lone elm by the river Platte, which was finally cut down and the limbs used for firewood. When near this tree, the train camped over Sunday, and our party first saw buffaloes, a band of perhaps twenty. D. T. Denny and C. D. Boren of the party went hunting in the hills three miles from the camp but other hunters had been among them and scattered the band, killing only one or two; however they generously divided the meat with the new arrivals. Our two good hunters determined to get one if possible and tried stalking a shaggy-maned beast that was separated from the herd, a half mile from their horses left picketed on the grassy plain. Shots were fired at him without effect and he ran away unhurt, fortunately for himself as well as his pursuers. One of the hunters, D. T. Denny, said it might have been a very serious matter for them to have been charged by a wounded buffalo out on the treeless prairie where a man had nothing to dodge behind but his own shadow.

On the prairie before they reached Fort Laramie a blinding

hailstorm pelted the travelers.

D. T. Denny, who was driving a four-horse team in the teeth of the storm, relates that the poor animals were quite restive, no doubt suffering much from their shelterless condition. They had been well provided for as to food; their drivers carried corn which lasted for two hundred miles. The rich grass of five hundred miles of prairie afforded luxurious living beyond this, and everywhere along the streams where camp was made there was an abundance of fresh herbage to be found.

Many lonely graves were seen, graves of pioneers, with hopes as high, mayhap, as any, but who pitched their silent tents in the wilderness to await the Judgment Day.

A deep solemnity fell upon the living as the train wound along, where on the side of a mountain was a lone grave heaped up with stones to protect it from the ravages of wolves. Tall pines stood around it and grass and flowers adorned it with nature's broidery. Several joined in singing an old song beginning:

> "I came to the place
> Where the white pilgrim lay,
> And pensively stood by his tomb,
> When in a low whisper I heard something say,
> 'How sweetly I sleep here alone.'"

Echoed only by the rustling of the boughs of scattered pines, moving gently in the wind.

As they approached the upheaved mountainous country, lively interest, a keen delight in the novelty of their surroundings, and surprise at unexpected features were aroused in the minds of the travelers.

A thoughtful one has said that the weird beauty of the

Wind River Mountains impressed her deeply, their image has never left her memory and if she were an artist she could faithfully represent them on canvas.

A surprise to the former prairie dwellers was the vast extent of the mountains, their imaginations having projected the sort of mountain range that is quite rare, a single unbroken ridge traversed by climbing up one side and going down the other! But they found this process must be repeated an indefinite number of times and over such roughness as their imaginations had never even suggested.

What grinding, heaving and bumping over huge boulders! What shouting and urging of animals, what weary hours of tortured endurance dragged along! One of them remembers, too, perhaps vaguely, the suffering induced by an attack of the mysterious mountain fever.

The desert also imposed its tax of misery. Only at night could the desert be safely crossed. Starting at four o'clock in the afternoon they traveled all the following night over an arid, desolate region, the Green River desert, thirty miles, a strange journey in the dimness of a summer night with only the star-lamps overhead. In sight of the river, the animals made a rush for the water and ran in to drink, taking the wagons with them.

Often the names of the streams crossed were indicative of their character, suggestive of adventure or descriptive of their surroundings. Thus "Sweetwater" speaks eloquently of the refreshing draughts that slaked the thirst in contrast with the alkaline waters that were bitter; Burnt River flowed past the blackened remains of an ancient forest and Bear River may have been named for the ponderous game secured by a lucky hunter.

By July of 1851 the train reached Old Fort Hall, composed

of a stockade and log houses, situated on the Snake River, whose flood set toward the long-sought Pacific shore.

While camped about a mile from the fort the Superintendent wrote for them directions for camping places where wood and water could be obtained, extending over the whole distance from Fort Hall to the Dalles of the Columbia River. He told James Denny, brother of D. T. Denny, that if they met Indians they must on no account stop at their call, saying that the Indians of that vicinity were renegade Shoshones and horse thieves.

On the morning of the fifth of July an old Indian visited the camp, but no significance was attached to the incident, and all were soon moving quietly along in sight of the Snake River; the road lay on the south side of the river, which is there about two hundred yards wide. An encampment of Indians was observed, on the north side of the river, as they wound along by the American Falls, but no premonition of danger was felt, on the contrary, they were absorbed in the contemplation of the falls and basin below. Dark objects were seen to be moving on the surface of the wide pool and all supposed them to be ducks disporting themselves after the manner of harmless water fowl generally. What was their astonishment to behold them swiftly and simultaneously approach the river bank, spring out of the water and reveal themselves full grown savages!

With guns and garments, but few of the latter probably, on their heads, they swam across and climbed up the bank to the level of the sage brush plain. The leader, attired in a plug hat and long, black overcoat flapping about his sinewy limbs, gun in hand, advanced toward the train calling out, "How-de-do! How-de-do! Stop! Stop!" twice repeating the words. The Captain, Grandfather John Denny, answered "Go back," emphasizing the order by vigorous gestures. Mindful of the friendly caution of the Superintendent at Fort Hall, the train moved on. The gentleman of the plains retired to his band, who dodged back behind the sagebrush and began firing at the train. One bullet threw up the dust under the horse ridden by one of the company. The frightened women and children huddled down as low as possible in the bottoms of the wagons, expecting the shots to penetrate the canvas walls of their moving houses. In the last wagon, in the most exposed position, one of the mothers sat pale and trembling like an aspen leaf; the fate of the young sister and two little daughters in the event of capture, beside the danger of her own immediate death were too dreadful to contemplate. In their extremity one said, "O, why don't they hurry! If I were driving I would lay on the lash!"

When the Indians found that their shots took no effect, they changed their tactics and ran down along the margin of the river under shelter of the bank, to head off the train at a point where it must go down one hill and up another. There were seven men with five rifles and two rifle-pistols, but these would have been of little avail if the teams had been disabled. D. T. Denny drove the forward wagon, having one rifle and the pistols; three of the men were not armed.

All understood the maneuver of the Indians and were anxious to hurry the teams unless it was Captain John Denny, who was an old soldier and may have preferred to fight.

Sarah Denny, his wife, looked out and saw the Indians going down the river; no doubt she urged him to whip up. The order was given and after moments that seemed hours, down the long hill they rushed pell-mell, without lock or brake, the prairie schooners tossing like their namesakes on a stormy sea. What a breathless, panting, nightmare it seemed! If an axle had broken or a linchpin loosened the race would have been lost. But on, madly careening past the canyon where the Indians intended to intercept them, tearing up the opposite hill with desperate energy, expecting every moment to hear the blood-curdling warwhoop, nor did they slacken their speed to the usual pace for the remainder of the day. As night approached, the welcome light of a campfire, that of J. N. Low's company, induced them to stop. This camp was on a level near a bluff; a narrow deep stream flowed by into the Snake River not far away. The cattle were corraled, with the wagons in a circle and a fire of brushwood built in the center.

Around the Denny company's campfire, the women who prepared the evening meal were in momentary fear of receiving a shot from an ambushed foe, lit as they were against the darkness, but happily their fears were not realized. Weary as the drivers were, guards were posted and watched all night. The dogs belonging to the train were doubtless a considerable protection, as they would have given the alarm had the enemy approached.

One of the women went down to the brook the next morning to get water for the camp and saw the tracks of Indian ponies in the dust on the opposite side of the stream. Evidently they had followed the train to that point, but feared to attack the united forces of the two camps.

After this race for life the men stood guard every night; one of them, D. T. Denny, was on duty one-half of every other night and alternately slept on the ground under one of the wagons.

This was done until they reached the Cayuse country. On Burnt River they met thirty warriors, the advance guard of their tribe who were moving, women, children, drags and dogs. The Indians were friendly and cheeringly announced

"Heap sleep now; we are *good* Indians."

The Denny and Low trains were well pleased to join their forces and traveled as one company until they reached their journey's end.

The day after the Indian attack, friendly visits were made and Mrs. J. N. Low recalls that she saw two women of Denny's company frying cakes and doughnuts over the campfire, while two others were well occupied with the youngest of the travelers, who were infants.

There were six men and two women in Low's company and when the two companies joined they felt quite strong and traveled unmolested the remainder of the way.

An exchange of experiences brought out the fact that Low's company had crossed the Missouri the third day of May and had traveled on the south side of the Platte at the same time the Denny company made their way along the north side of the same stream.

At a tributary called Big Blue, as Mrs. Low relates, she observed the clouds rolling up and admonished her husband to whip up or they would not be able to cross for days if they delayed; they crossed, ascended the bluffs where there was a semicircle of trees, loosed the cattle and picketed the horses. By evening the storm reached them with lightning, heavy thunder and great piles of hail. The next morning the water had risen half way up tall trees.

The Indians stole the lead horse of one of the four-horse teams and Mrs. Low rode the other on a man's saddle. Many western equestriennes have learned to be not too particular as to horse, habit or saddle and have proven also the greater safety and convenience of cross-saddle riding.

In the Black Hills while traveling along the crest of a high ridge, where to get out of the road would have been disastrous, the train was met by a band of Indians on ponies, who pressed up to the wagons in a rather embarrassing way, bent apparently upon riding between and separating the teams, but the drivers were too wise to permit this and kept close together, without stopping to parley with them, and after riding alongside for some distance, the designing but baffled redskins withdrew.

The presence of the native inhabitants sometimes proved a convenience; especially was this true of the more peaceable tribes of the far west. On the Umatilla River the travelers were glad to obtain the first fresh vegetable since leaving the cultivated gardens and fields of their old homes months before. One of the women traded a calico apron for green peas, which were regarded as a great treat and much enjoyed.

Farther on, as they neared the Columbia, Captain Low, who was riding ahead of the train, met Indians with salmon, eager to purchase so fine a fish and not wishing to stop the wagon, pulled off an overshirt over his head and exchanged it for the piscatorial prize.

The food that had sustained them on the long march was almost military in its simplicity. Corn meal, flour, rice (a little, as it was not then in common use), beans, bacon and dried fruits were the main dependence. They could spend but little time hunting and fishing. On Bear River "David" and "Louisa" each caught a trout, fine, speckled beauties. "David" and the other hunters of the company also killed sage hens, antelope and buffalo.

After leaving the Missouri River they had no opportunity to buy anything until they reached the Snake River, where they purchased some dried salmon of the Indians.

CHAPTER II

AFTER EIGHTY days travel over one thousand seven hundred sixty-five miles of road these weary pilgrims reached the mighty river of the West, the vast Columbia.

At The Dalles, the road Across the Plains was finished, from thence the great waterways would lead them to their journey's end.

It was there the immigrants first feasted on the delicious river salmon, fresh from the foaming waters. The Indians boiled theirs, making a savory soup, the odor of which would almost have fed a hungry man; the white people cooked goodly pieces in the trusty camp frying pan.

Not then accustomed to such finny monsters, they found a comparison for the huge cuts as like unto sides of pork, and a receptacle for the giant's morsels in a seaworthy washingtub. However, high living will pall unto the taste; one may really tire of an uninterrupted piscatorial banquet, and one of the company, A. A. Denny, declared his intention of introducing some variety in the bill of fare. "Plague take it," he said, "I'm tired of salmon—I'm going to have some chicken."

But alas! the gallinaceous fowl, roaming freely at large, had also feasted frequently on fragments no longer fresh of the overplus of salmon, and its flavor was indescribable, wholly impossible, as the French say. It was "fishy" fish rather than fowl.

At The Dalles the company divided, one party composed of a majority of the men started over the mountains with the wagons and teams; the women and children prepared to descend the river in boats.

In one boat, seated on top of the "plunder" were Mrs. A. A. Denny and two children, Miss Louisa Boren, Mrs. Low and four children and Mrs. Boren and one child. The other boat was loaded in like manner with a great variety of useful and necessary articles, heaped up, on top of which sat several women and children, among whom were Mrs. Sarah Denny, grandmother of the writer, and her little daughter, Loretta.

A long summer day was spent in floating down the great canyon where the majestic Columbia cleaves the Cascade Range in twain. The succeeding night the first boat landed on an island in the river, and the voyagers went ashore to camp. During the night one of the little girls, Gertrude Boren, rolled out of her bed and narrowly escaped falling into the hurrying stream; had she done so she must have certainly been lost, but a kind Providence decreed otherwise. Re-embarking the following day, gliding swiftly on the current, they traversed a considerable distance and the second night approached the Cascades.

Swifter and more turbulent, the rushing flood began to break in more furious foam-wreaths on every jagged rock, impotently striving to stay its onward rush to the limitless ocean.

Sufficient light enabled the observing eye to perceive the writhing surface of the angry waters, but the boatmen were stupified with drink!

All day long they had passed a bottle about which contained a liquid facetiously called "Blue Ruin" and near enough their ruin it proved.

I have penned the following description which met with the approval of one of the principal actors in what so nearly proved a tragedy:

It was midnight on the mighty Columbia. A waning moon cast a glowworm light on the dark, rushing river; all but one of the weary women and tired little children were deeply sunken in sleep. The oars creaked and dipped monotonously; the river sang louder and louder every boat's length. Drunken, bloated faces leered foolishly and idiotically; they admonished each other to "Keep 'er goin'."

The solitary watcher stirred uneasily, looked at the long lines of foam out in midstream and saw how fiercely the white waves contended, and far swifter flew the waters than at any hour before. What was the meaning of it? Hark! that humming, buzzing, hissing, nay, bellowing roar! The blood flew to her brain and made her senses reel; they must be nearing the last landing above the falls, the great Cascades of the Columbia.

But the crew gave no heed.

Suddenly she cried out sharply to her sleeping sister, "Mary! Mary! wake up! we are nearing the falls, I hear them roar."

"What is it, Liza?" she said sleepily.

"O, wake up! we shall all be drowned, the men don't know what they are doing."

The rudely awakened sleepers seemed dazed and did not

make much outcry, but a strong young figure climbed over the mass of baggage and confronting the drunken boatmen, plead, urged and besought them, if they considered their own lives, or their helpless freight of humanity, to make for the shore.

"Oh, men," she pleaded, "don't you hear the falls, they roar louder now. It will soon be too late, I beseech you turn the boat to shore. Look at the rapids beyond us!"

"Thar haint no danger, Miss, leastways not yet; wots all this fuss about anyhow? No danger," answered one who was a little disturbed; the others were almost too much stupified to understand her words and stood staring at the bareheaded, black haired young woman as if she were an apparition and were no more alarmed than if the warning were given as a curious mechanical performance, having no reference to themselves.

Repeating her request with greater earnestness, if possible, a man's voice broke in saying, "I believe she is right, put in men quick, none of us want to be drowned."

Fortunately this penetrated their besotted minds and they put about in time to save the lives of all on board, although they landed some distance below the usual place.

A little farther and they would have been past all human help.

One of the boatmen cheerfully acknowledged the next day that if it "hadn't been fur that purty girl they had a' gone over them falls, shure."

The other boat had a similar experience; it began to leak profusely before they had gone very far and would soon have sunk, had not the crew, who doubtless were sober, made all haste to land.

My grandmother has often related to me how she clasped

her little child to her heart and resigned herself to a fate which seemed inevitable; also of a Mrs. McCarthy, a passenger likewise, becoming greatly excited and alternately swearing and praying until the danger was past. An inconvenient but amusing feature was the soaked condition of the "plunder" and the way the shore and shrubbery thereon were decorated with "hiyu ictas," as the Chinook has it, hung out to dry. Finding it impossible to proceed, this detachment returned and took the mountain road.

A tramway built by F. A. Chenoweth, around the great falls, afforded transportation for the baggage of the narrowly saved first described. There being no accommodations for passengers, the party walked the tramroad; at the terminus they unloaded and stayed all night. No "commodious and elegant" steamer awaited them, but an old brig, bound for Portland, received them and their effects.

Such variety of adventure had but recently crowded upon them that it was almost fearfully they re-embarked. A. A. Denny observed to Captain Low, "Look here, Low, they say women are scarce in Oregon and we had better be careful of ours." Presumably they were, as both survive at the present day.

From a proud ranger of the dashing main, the old brig had come down to be a carrier of salt salmon packed in barrels, and plunder of immigrants; as for the luckless passengers, they accommodated themselves as best they could.

The small children were tied to the mast to keep them from falling overboard, as there were no bulwarks.

Beds were made below on the barrels before mentioned and the travel-worn lay down, but not to rest; the mosquitos were a bloodthirsty throng and the beds were likened unto a corduroy road.

One of the women grumbled a little and an investigation proved that it was, as her husband said, "Nothing but the tea-kettle" wedged in between the barrels.

Another lost a moccasin overboard and having worn out all her shoes on the way, went with one stockinged foot until they turned up the Willamette River, then went ashore to a farmhouse where she was so fortunate as to find the owner of a new pair of shoes which she bought, and was thus able to enter the "city" of Portland in appropriate footgear.

After such vicissitudes, dangers and anxiety, the little company were glad to tarry in the embryo metropolis for a brief season; then, having heard of fairer shores, the restless pioneers moved on.

CHAPTER III

THE SETTLEMENT AT ALKI

MIDWAY BETWEEN Port Townsend and Olympia, in full view looking west from the city of Seattle, is a long tongue of land, washed by the sparkling waves of Puget Sound, called Alki Point. It helps to make Elliott Bay a beautiful land-locked harbor and is regarded with interest as being the site of the first settlement by white people in King County in what was then the Territory of Oregon. *Alki* is an Indian word pronounced with the accent on the first syllable, which is *al* as in altitude; *ki* is spoken as *ky* in silky. Alki means "by and by."

It doth truly fret the soul of the old settler to see it printed and hear it pronounced Al-ki.

The first movement toward its occupancy was on this wise: A small detachment of the advancing column of settlers, D. T. Denny and J. N. Low, left Portland on the Willamette, on the 10th of September, 1851, with two horses carrying provisions and camp outfit.

These men walked to the Columbia River to round up a band of cattle belonging to Low. The cattle were ferried over the river at Vancouver and from thence driven over the old Hudson Bay Company's trail to the mouth of Cowlitz River, a tributary of the Columbia, up the Cowlitz to Warbass Landing and on to Ford's prairie, a wide and rich one, where the band were left to graze on the luxuriant pasturage.

On a steep, rocky trail along the Cowlitz River, Denny was following along not far behind a big, yellow ox that was scrambling up, trying vainly to get a firm foothold, when Low, foreseeing calamity, called to him to "Look out!" Denny swerved a little from the path and at that moment the animal lost its footing and came tumbling past them, rolling over several times until it landed on a lower level, breaking off one of its horns. Here was a narrow escape although not from a wild beast. They could not then stop to secure the animal although it was restored to the flock some time after.

From Ford's prairie, although footsore and weary, they kept on their way until Olympia was reached. It was a long tramp of perhaps two hundred fifty miles, the exact distance could not be ascertained as the trail was very winding.

As described by one of our earliest historians, Olympia then consisted of about a dozen one-story frame cabins, covered with split cedar siding, well ventilated and healthy, and perhaps twice as many Indian huts near the custom house, as Olympia was then the port of entry for Puget Sound.

The last mentioned structure afforded space on the ground floor for a store, with a small room partitioned off for a post-office.

Our two pioneers found here Lee Terry, who had been engaged in loading a sailing vessel with piles. He fell in with the two persistent pedestrians and thus formed a triumvirate of conquerors of a new world. The pioneers tarried not in the embryo city but pushed on farther down the great Inland Sea.

With Captain Fay and several others they embarked in an open boat, the Captain, who owned the boat, intending to purchase salmon of the Indians for the San Francisco market. Fay was an old whaling captain. He afterwards married Mrs. Alexander, a widow of Whidby Island, and lived there until his death.

The little party spent their first night on the untrod shores of Sgwudux, the Indian name of the promontory now occupied by West Seattle, landing on the afternoon of September 25th, 1851, and sleeping that night under the protecting boughs of a giant cedar tree.

On the 26th, Low, Denny and Terry hired two young Indians of Chief Sealth's (Seattle's) *tillicum* (people), who were camped near by, to take them up the Duwampsh River in a canoe. Safely seated, the paddles dipped and away they sped over the dancing waves. The weather was fair, the air clear and a magnificent panorama spread around them. The whole forest-clad encircling shores of Elliott Bay, untouched by fire or ax, the tall evergreens thickly set in a dense mass to the water's edge stood on every hand. The great white dome of Mount Rainier, 14,444 feet high, before them, toward which they traveled; behind them, stretched along the western horizon, Towiat or Olympics, a grand range of snow-capped mountains whose foothills were covered with a continuous forest.

Entering the Duwampsh River and ascending for several miles they reached the farther margin of a prairie where Low and Terry, having landed, set out over an Indian trail through the woods, to look at the country, while Denny followed on the river with the Indians. On and on they went until Denny became anxious and fired off his gun but received neither shot nor shout in answer. The day waned, it was growing dark, and as he returned the narrow deep river took on a melancholy aspect, the great forest was gloomy with unknown fears, and he was alone with strange, wild men whose language was almost unintelligible. Nevertheless, he landed and camped with them at a place known afterward as the Maple Prairie.

Morning of the 27th of September saw them paddling up the river again in search of the other two explorers, whom they met coming down in a canoe. They had kept on the trail until an Indian camp was reached at the junction of Black and Duwampsh Rivers the night before. All returned to Sgwudux, their starting point, to sleep under the cedar tree another night.

On the evening of the 27th a scow appeared and stopped near shore where the water was quite deep. Two women on board conversed with Captain Fay in Chinook, evidently quite proud of their knowledge of the trade jargon of the Northwest. The scow moved on up Elliott Bay, entered Duwampsh River and ascended it to the claim of L. M. Collins, where another settlement sprang into existence.

On the 28th the pioneers moved their camp to Alki Point or Sma-qua-mox as it was named by the Indians.

Captain Fay returned from down the Sound on the forenoon of the 28th. That night, as they sat around the campfire, the pioneers talked of their projected building and the idea of split stuff was advanced, when Captain Fay remarked, "Well, I think a log house is better in an Indian country."

"Why, do you think there is any danger from the Indians?" he was quickly asked.

"Well," he replied, with a sly twinkle in his eye, "It would keep off the stray bullets when they *poo mowich*" (shoot deer).

These hints, coupled with subsequent experiences, awoke the anxiety of D. T. Denny, who soon saw that there were swarms of savages to the northward. Those near by were friendly, but what of those farther away?

One foggy morning, when the distance was veiled in obscurity, the two young white men, Lee and David, were startled to see a big canoe full of wild Indians from away down the Sound thrust right out of the dense fog; they landed and came ashore; the chief was a tall, brawny fellow with a black beard. They were very impudent, crowding on them and trying to get into the little brush tent, but Lee Terry stood in the doorway leaning, or braced rather, against the tree upon which one end of the frail habitation was fastened. The white men succeeded in avoiding trouble but they felt inwardly rather "shaky" and were much relieved when their rude visitors departed. These Indians were Skagits.

The brush shelter referred to was made of boughs laid over a pole placed in the crotch of another pole at one end, the other end being held by a crotch fastened to a tree. In it was placed their scanty outfit and supplies, and there they slept while the cabin was building.

A townsite was located and named "New York," which no doubt killed the place, exotics do not thrive in the Northwest; however, the name was after changed to Alki.

D. T. Denny and Lee Terry were left to take care of the "townsite" while J. N. Low returned with Captain Fay to Olympia and footed it over the trail again to the Columbia. He carried with him a letter to A. A. Denny in Portland, remarkable as the first one penned by D. T. Denny on Puget Sound, also in that upon it and the account given by Low depended the decision of the rest of the party to settle on the shores of the great Inland Sea. The substance of the letter was, "Come as soon as you can; we have found a valley that will accommodate one thousand families," referring to that of the Duwampsh River.

These two, David T. Denny and Lee Terry, proceeded to lay the foundation of the first cabin built on Elliott Bay and also the first in King County. Their only tools were an ax and a hammer. The logs were too heavy for the two white men to handle by themselves, and after they were cut, passing Indians, muscular braves, were called on to assist, which they willingly did, Mr. Denny giving them bread as a reward, the same being an unaccustomed luxury to them.

Several days after the foundation was laid, L. M. Collins and "Nesqually John," an Indian, passed by the camp and rising cabin, driving oxen along the beach, on their way to the claim selected by Collins on the fertile banks of the Duwampsh River.

When D. T. Denny and Lee Terry wrote their names on the first page of our history, they could not fully realize the import of their every act, yet no doubt they were visionary. Sleeping in their little brush tent at night, what dreams may have visited them! Dreams, perhaps, of fleets of white-winged ships with the commerce of many nations, of busy cities, of throngs of people. Probably they set about chopping down the tall fir trees in a cheerful mood, singing and whistling to the astonishment of the pine squirrels and screech owls thus rudely disturbed. Their camp equipage and arrangements were of the simplest and rudest and Mr. Denny relates that Lee Terry would not cook so he did the cooking. He made a "johnny cake" board of willow wood to bake bread upon.

Fish and game were cooked before the camp fire. The only cooking vessel was a tin pail.

One evening Old Duwampsh Curley, whose Indian name was Su-whalth, with several others, visited them and begged

the privilege of camping near by. Permission given, the Indians built a fire and proceeded to roast a fine, fat duck trans-
fixed on a sharp stick, placing a large clam shell underneath
to catch the gravy. When it was cooked to their minds, Curley
offered a choice cut to the white men, who thanked him but
declined to partake, saying that they had eaten their supper.

Old Curley remembered it and in after years often reminded his white friend of the incident, laughing slyly, *He! He!
Boston man halo tikke Siwash muck-a-muck* (white man do
not like Indian's food), knowing perfectly well the reason
they would not accept the proffered dainty.

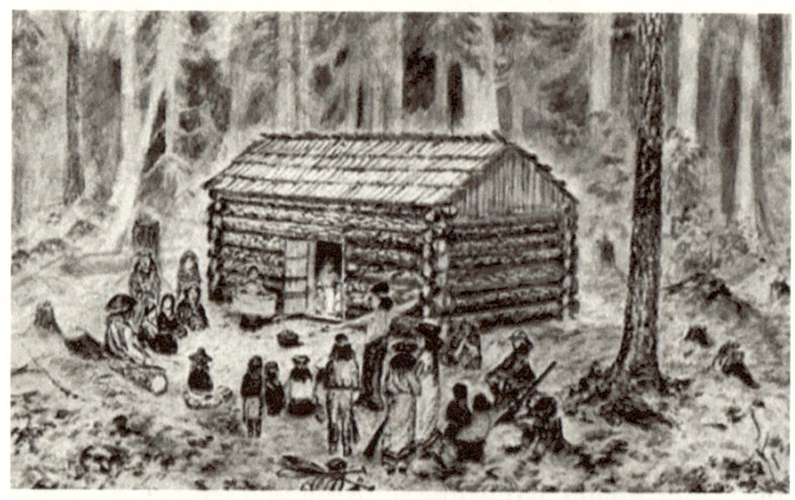

BARGAINING WITH INDIANS AT ALKI, 1851

J. N. Low had returned to Portland and Terry went to
Olympia on the return trip of Collins' scow, leaving David T.
Denny alone with "New York," the unfinished cabin and the
Indians. For three weeks he was the sole occupant and was
ill a part of the time.

Meanwhile, the families left behind had not been idle, but
having made up their minds that the end of their rainbow

rested on Puget Sound, set sail on the schooner *Exact*, with others who intended to settle at various points on the Inland Sea, likewise a party of gold hunters bound for Queen Charlotte's Island.

They were one week getting around Cape Flattery and up the Sound as far as Alki Point. It was a rough introduction to the briny deep, as the route covered the most tempestuous portion of the northwest coast. Well acquainted as they were with prairie schooners, a schooner on the ocean was another kind of craft and they enjoyed (?) their first experience of seasickness crossing the bar of the Columbia. As may be easily imagined, the fittings were not of the most luxurious kind and father, mother and the children gathered socially around a washing tub to pay their respects to Neptune.

The gold miners, untouched by mal de mer, sang jolly songs and played cards to amuse themselves. Their favorite ditty was the round "Three Blind Mice" and they sang also many good old campmeeting songs. Poor fellows! they were taken captive by the Indians of Queen Charlotte's Island and kept in slavery a number of years until Victorians sent an expedition for their rescue, paid their ransom and they were released.

On a dull November day, the thirteenth of the month, this company landed on Alki Point.

There were A. A. Denny, his wife, Mary Boren Denny, and their three little children; Miss Louisa Boren, a younger sister of Mrs. Denny; C. D. Boren and his family; J. N. Low, Mrs. Low and their four children and Wm. N. Bell, Mrs. Sarah Bell and their family.

John and Sarah Denny with their little daughter, Loretta, remained in Oregon for several years and then removed to the Sound.

On that eventful morning the lonely occupant of the

unfinished cabin was startled by an unusual sound, the rattling of an anchor chain, that of the *Exact*. Not feeling well he had the night before made some hot tea, drank it, piled both his own and Lee Terry's blankets over him and slept long and late. Hearing the noise before mentioned he rose hastily, pushed aside the boards leaned up for a door and hurried out and down to the beach to meet his friends who left the schooner in a long boat. It was a gloomy, rainy time and the prospect for comfort was so poor that the women, except the youngest who had no family cares, sat them down on a log on the beach and wept bitter tears of discouragement. Not so with Miss Louisa Boren, whose lively curiosity and love of nature led her to examine everything she saw, the shells and pebbles of the beach, rank shrubbery and rich evergreens that covered the bank, all so new and interesting to the traveler from the far prairie country.

But little time could be spent, however, indulging in the luxury of woe as all were obliged to exert themselves to keep their effects from being carried away by the incoming tide and forgot their sorrow in busily carrying their goods upon the bank; food and shelter must be prepared, and as ever before they met the difficulties courageously.

The roof of the cabin was a little imperfect and one of the pioneer children was rendered quite uncomfortable by the more or less regular drip of the rain upon her and in after years recalled it saying that she had forever after a prejudice against camping out.

David T. Denny inadvertantly let fall the remark that he wished they had not come. A. A. Denny, his brother, came to him, pale with agitation, asking what he meant, and David attempted to allay his fears produced by anxiety for his helpless family, by saying that the cabin was not comfortable in its unfinished state.

The deeper truth was that the Sound country was swarming with Indians. Had the pioneers fully realized the risk they ran, nothing would have induced them to remain; their very unconsciousness afterward proved a safeguard.

The rainy season was fairly under way and suitable shelter was an absolute necessity.

Soon other houses were built of round fir logs and split cedar boards.

The householders brought quite a supply of provisions with them on the *Exact*; among other things a barrel of dried apples, which proved palatable and wholesome. Sea biscuit, known as hard-bread, and potato bread made of mashed potatoes and baked in the oven were oft times substitutes for or adjuncts of the customary loaf.

There was very little game in the vicinity of the settlement and at first they depended on the native hunters and fishermen who brought toothsome wild ducks and venison, fresh fish and clams in abundance.

One of the pioneers relates that some wily rascals betrayed them into eating pieces of game which he afterward was convinced were cut from a cougar. The Indians who brought it called it *mowich* (deer), but the meat was of too light a color for either venison or bear, and the conformation of the leg bones in the pieces resembled *felis* rather than *cervus*.

But the roasts were savory, it was unseemly to make too severe an examination and the food supply was not then so certain as to permit indulgence in an over-nice discrimination.

The inventive genius of the pioneer women found generous exercise in the manufacture of new dishes. The variations were rung on fish, potatoes and clams in a way to pamper epicures. Clams in fry, pie, chowder, soup, stew, boil and bake—even pickled clams were found an agreeable relish. The great variety of food fishes from the kingly salmon to the tiny smelt, with crabs, oysters, etc., and their many modes of preparation, were perpetually tempting to the pioneer appetite.

The question of food was a serious one for the first year, as the resources of this land of plenty were unknown at first, but the pushing pioneer proved a ready and adaptable learner.

Flour, butter, syrup, sugar, tea and coffee were brought at long intervals over great distances by sailing vessels. By the time these articles reached the settlement their value became considerable.

Game, fish and potatoes were staple articles of diet and judging from the stalwart frames of the Indians were safe and substantial.

Trading with the Indians brought about some acquaintance with their leading characteristics.

On one occasion, the youngest of the white women, Louisa Boren, attempted to barter some red flannel for a basket of potatoes.

The basket of *wapatoes* occupied the center of a level spot in front of the cabin, backed by a semicircle of perhaps twenty-five Indians. A tall, bronze tyee (chief) stood up to wa-wa (talk). He wanted so much cloth; stretching out his long arms to their utmost extent, fully two yards.

"No," she said, "I will give you so much," about one yard.

Wake, cultus potlatch (No, that is just giving them away) answered the Indian, who measured several times and insisted that he would not trade for an inch less. Out of patience at last, she disdainfully turned her back and retired inside the cabin behind a mat screen. No amount of coaxing from the savages could induce her to return, and the disappointed spectators filed off, bearing their *hyas mokoke* (very valuable) potatoes with them, no doubt marveling at the firmness of the white *slanna* (woman).

A more successful deal in potatoes was the venture of A. A. Denny and J. N. Low, who traveled from Alki to Fort Nesqually, in a big canoe manned by four Indians and obtained fifty bushels of little, round, red potatoes grown by Indians from seed obtained from the "Sking George" men. The green hides of beeves were spread in the bottom of the canoe and the potatoes piled thereon.

Returning to Alki it was a little rough and the vegetables were well moistened with salt chuck, as were the passengers also, probably, deponent saith not.

It is not difficult for those who have traveled the Sound in all kinds of weather to realize the aptness of the expression of the Chinese cook of a camping party who were moving in a large canoe; when the waves began to rise, he exclaimed in agitation, "Too littlee boat for too muchee big waters." It is well to bear in mind that the "Sound" is a great inland sea. A tenderfoot's description of the water over which he floated, the timorous occupant of a canoe, testifies that it looked to him to be "Two hundred feet deep, as clear as a kitten's eye and as cold as death."

All the different sorts of canoes of which I shall speak in another chapter look "wobbly" and uncertain, yet the Indians make long voyages of hundreds of miles by carefully observing the wind and tide.

A large canoe will easily carry ten persons and one thousand pounds of baggage. One of these commodious travelers, with a load of natives and their *ictas* (baggage) landed on a stormy day at Alki and the occupants spent several hours ashore. While engaged with their meal one of them exclaimed, *Nannitch!* (look) at the same time pointing at the smoke of the campfire curling steadily straight upward. Without another word they tumbled themselves and belongings aboard and paddled off in silent satisfaction.

The ascending column of smoke was their barometer which read "Fair weather, no wind."

The white people, unacquainted with the shores, tides and winds of the great Inland Sea, did well to listen to their Indian canoemen; sometimes their unwillingness to do so exposed them to great danger and even loss of life.

The Indians living on Elliott Bay were chiefly the indigenous tribe of D'wampsh or Duwampsh, changed by white people into "Duwamish."

They gave abundant evidence of possessing human feeling beneath their rough exterior.

One of the white women at Alki, prepared some food for a sick Indian child which finally recovered. The child's father, "Old Alki John," was a very "hard case," but his heart was tender toward his child, and to show his gratitude he brought and offered as a present to the kind white *slanna* (woman) a bright, new tin pail, a very precious thing to the Indian mind. Of course she readily accepted his thanks but persuaded him to keep the pail.

Savages though they were, or so appeared, the Indians of Elliott Bay were correctly described in these words:

> "We found a race, though rude and wild,
> Still tender toward friend or child,
> For dark eyes laughed or shone with tears
> As joy or sorrow filled the years.
> Their black-eyed babes the red men kissed
> And captive brothers sorely missed;

With broken hearts brown mothers wept
When babes away by death were swept."
                    —Song of the Pioneers

But there were amusing as well as pathetic experiences. The Indians were like untaught children in many things. Their curiosity over-came them and their innocent impertinence sometimes required reproof.

In a cabin at Alki one morning, a white woman was frying fish. Warming by the fire stood "Duwampsh Curley;" the odor of the fish was doubtless appetizing; Curley was moved with a wish to partake of it and reached out a dark and doubt-ful-looking hand to pick out a piece. The white woman had a knife in her hand to turn the pieces and raised it to strike the imprudent hand which was quickly and sheepishly withdrawn.

Had he been as haughty and ill-natured as some savages the result might have been disastrous, but he took the reproof meekly and mended his manners instead of retaliating.

Now and then the settlers were spectators in dramas of Indian romance.

"Old Alki John" had a wife whose history became interest-ing. For some unknown reason she ran away from Puyallup to Alki. Her husband followed her, armed with a Hudson Bay musket and a frame of mind that boded no good. While A. A. Denny, D. T. Denny and Alki John were standing together on the bank one day Old John's observing eye caught sight of a strange Indian ascending the bank, carrying his gun muz-zle foremost, a suggestive position not indicative of peace-ful intentions. *Nannitch* (look) he said quietly; the stranger advanced boldly, but Old John's calm manner must have had a soothing effect upon the bloodthirsty savage, as he concluded to *wa-wa* (talk) a little before fighting.

So the gutturals and polysyllables of the native tongue fairly flew about until evidently, as Mr. D. T. Denny relates, some sort of compromise was effected. Not then understanding the language, he could not determine just the nature of the arrangement, but has always thought it was amicably settled by the payment of money by "Old Alki John" to her former husband. This Indian woman was young and fair, literally so, as her skin was very white, she being the whitest squaw ever seen among them; her head was not flattened, she was slender and of good figure. Possibly she had white blood in her veins; her Indian name was "Si-a-ye."

Being left a widow, she was not left to pine alone very long; another claimed her hand and she became Mrs. Yeow-de-pump. When this one joined his brethren in the happy hunting ground, she remained a widow for some time, but is now the wife of the Indian Zacuse, mentioned in another place.

There were women cabin builders. Each married woman was given half the donation claim by patent from the government; improvement on her part of the claim was therefore necessary.

On a fine, fair morning in the early spring of 1852, two women set forth from the settlement at Alki, to cross Elliott Bay in a fishing canoe, with Indians to paddle and a large dog to protect them from possible wild animals in the forest, for in that wild time, bears, cougars and wolves roamed the shores of Puget Sound.

Landed on the opposite shore, the present site of Seattle, they made their way slowly and with difficulty through the dense undergrowth of the heavy forest, there being not so much as a trail, over a long distance. Arrived at the chosen spot, they cut with their own hands some small fir logs and laid the foundation of a cabin. While thus employed the weather underwent a change and on the return was rather threatening. The wind and waves were boisterous, the canine passenger was frightened and uneasy, thus adding to the danger. The water washed into the canoe and the human occupants suffered no little anxiety until they reached the beach at home.

One of the conditions of safe travel in a canoe is a quiet and careful demeanor, the most approved plan being to sit down in the bottom of the craft and *stay there.*

To have a large, heavy animal squirming about, getting up and lying down frequently, must have tried their nerve severely and it must have taken good management to prevent a serious catastrophe. The Bell family were camped at that time on their claim in a rude shelter of Indian boards and mats.

The handful of white men at Alki spent their time and energy in getting out piles for the San Francisco market. At first they had very few appliances for handling the timber. The first vessel to load was the brig Leonesa, which took a cargo of piles, cut, rolled and hauled by hand, as there were no cattle at the settlement.

There were also no roads and Lee Terry went to Puyallup for a yoke of oxen, which he drove down on the beach to Alki. Never were dumb brutes better appreciated than these useful creatures.

But the winter, or rather rainy season, wore away; as spring approached the settlers explored the shores of the Sound far and near and it became apparent that Alki must wait till "by and by," as the eastern shore of Elliott Bay was found more desirable and the pioneers prepared to move again by locating donation claims on a portion of the land now covered by a widespread city, which will bring us to the next chapter, "The Founding of Seattle and Indian War."

The following is a brief recapitulation of the first days on Puget Sound; in these later years we see the rapid and skillful construction of elegant mansions, charming cottages and stately business houses, all in sight of the spot where stood the first little cabin of the pioneer. The builders of this cabin were D. T. Denny, J. N. Low and Lee Terry, assisted by the Indians, the only tools, an ax and a hammer, the place Alki Point, the time, the fall of 1851.

They baked their bread before the fire on a willow board hewed from a piece of a tree which grew near the camp; the only cooking vessel was a tin pail; the salmon they got off the Indians was roasted before the fire on a stick.

The cabin was unfinished when the famous landing was made, November 13th, 1851, because J. N. Low returned to Portland, having been on the Sound but a few days, then Lee Terry boarded Collins' scow on its return trip up Sound leaving D. T. Denny alone for about three weeks, during most of which time he was ill. This was Low's cabin; after the landing of Bell, Boren and A. A. Denny and the others of the party, among whom were Low and C. C. Terry, a roof was put on the unfinished cabin and they next built A. A. Denny's and then two cabins of split cedar for Bell and Boren and their families.

When they moved to the east side of Elliott Bay, Bell's was the first one built. W. N. Bell and D. T. Denny built A. A. Denny's on the east side, as he was sick. D. T. Denny had served an apprenticeship in cabin building, young as he was, nineteen years of age, before he came to Puget Sound.

The first of D. T. Denny's cabins he built himself with the aid of three Indians. There was not a stick or piece of sawed stuff in it.

However, by the August following his marriage, which took place January 23rd, 1853, he bought of H. L. Yesler lumber from his sawmill at about $25.00 per M. to put up a little board house, sixteen by twenty feet near the salt water, between Madison and Marion streets, Seattle.

This little home was my birthplace, the first child of the first white family established at Elliott Bay. Mr. and Mrs. D. T. Denny had been threatened by Indians and their cabin robbed, so thought it best to move into the settlement.

CHAPTER IV

FOUNDING OF SEATTLE AND INDIAN WAR

THE MOST astonishing change wrought in the aspect of nature by the building of a city on Puget Sound is not the city itself but the destruction of the primeval forest. By the removal of the thick timber the country becomes unrecognizable; replaced by thousands of buildings of brick, wood and stone, graded streets, telephone and electric light systems, steam, electric and cable railways and all the paraphernalia of modern civilization, the contrast is very great. The same amount of energy and money expended in a treeless, level country would probably have built a city three times as large as Seattle.

In February, 1852, Bell, Boren and the Dennys located claims on the east side of Elliott Bay. Others followed, but it was not until May, 1853, that C. D. Boren and A. A. Denny filed the first plat of the town, named for the noted chief, "Seattle." The second plat was filed shortly after by D. S. Maynard. Maynard was a physician who did not at first depend on the practice of his profession; perhaps the settlers were too vigorous to require pills, powders and potions, at any rate he proposed to engage in the business of packing salmon.

The settlers at Alki moved over to their claims in the spring of 1852, some of them camping until they could build log cabins.

Finally all were well established and then began the hand to hand conflict for possession of the ground. The mighty forest must yield to fire and the ax; then from the deep bosom of the earth what bounty arose!

The Indians proved efficient helpers, guides and workers in many ways. One of the pioneers had three Indians to help him build his cabin.

To speak more particularly of the original architecture of the country, the cabins, built usually of round logs of the Douglas fir, about six inches in diameter, were picturesque, substantial and well suited to the needs of the pioneer. A great feature of the Seattle cabin was the door made of thick boards hewed out of the timber as there was no sawmill on the bay until H. L. Yesler built the first steam sawmill erected on the Sound. This substantial door was cut across in the middle with a diagonal joint; the lower half was secured by a stout wooden pin, in order that the upper half might be opened and the *wa-wa* (talk) proceed with the native visitor, who might or might not be friendly, while he stood on the outside of the door and looked in with eager curiosity, on the strange ways of the "Bostons."

The style of these log cabins was certainly admirable, adapted as they were to the situation of the settler. They were inexpensive as the material was plentiful and near at hand, and required only energy and muscle to construct them; there were no plumber's, gas or electric light bills coming in every month, no taxes for improvements and a man could build a lean-to or hay-shed without a building permit. The interiors were generally neat, tasteful and home-like, made so by the versatile pioneer women who occupied them.

These primitive habitations were necessarily scattered as it was imperative that they should be placed so as to perfect the titles of the donation claims. Sometimes two settlers were able to live near each other when they held adjoining claims, others were obliged to live several miles away from the main settlement and far from a neighbor, in lonely, unprotected places.

What thoughts of the homes and friends they had left many weary leagues behind, visited these lonely cabin dwellers!

The husband was engaged in clearing, slashing and burning log heaps, cutting timber, hunting for game to supply the larder, or away on some errand to the solitary neighbor's or distant settlement. Often, during the livelong day the wife was alone, occupied with domestic toil, all of which had to be performed by one pair of hands, with only primitive and rude appliances; but there were no incompetent servants to annoy, social obligations were few, fashion was remote and its tyranny unknown, in short, many disagreeable things were lacking. The sense of isolation was intensified by frequently recurring incidents in which the dangers of pioneer life became manifest. The dark, mysterious forest might send forth from its depths at any moment the menace of savage beast or relentless man.

The big, grey, timber wolf still roamed the woods, although it soon disappeared before the oncoming wave of invading settlers. Generally quite shy, they required some unusual attraction to induce them to display their voices.

On a dark winter night in 1853, the lonely cabin of D. T. and Louisa Denny was visited by a pair of these voracious beasts, met to discuss the remains of a cow, belonging to

W. N. Bell, which had stuck fast among some tree roots and died in the edge of the clearing. How they did snarl and howl, making the woods and waters resound with their cries as they greedily devoured the carcass. The pioneer couple who occupied the cabin entered no objection and were very glad of the protection of the solid walls of their primitive domicile. The next day, Mr. Denny, with dog and gun, went out to hunt them but they had departed to some remote region.

On another occasion the young wife lay sick and alone in the cabin above mentioned and a good neighbor, Mrs. Sarah Bell, from her home a mile away, came to see her, bringing some wild pheasant's eggs the men had found while cutting spars. While the women chatted, an Indian came and stood idly looking in over the half-door and his companion lurked in the brush near by.

John Kanem, a brother of the chief, Pat Kanem, afterward told the occupants of the cabin that these Indians had divulged their intention of murdering them in order to rob their dwelling, but abandoned the project, giving as a reason that a *haluimi kloochman* (another or unknown woman) was there and the man was away.

Surely a kind Providence watched over these unprotected ones that they might in after years fulfill their destiny.

During the summer of 1855, before the Indian war, Mr. and Mrs. D. T. Denny were living in a log cabin in the swale, an opening in the midst of a heavy forest, on their donation claim, to which they had moved from their first cabin on Elliott Bay.

Dr. Choush, an Indian medicine man, came along one day in a state of ill-suppressed fury. He had just returned from a Government *potlatch* at the Tulalip agency. In relating how they were cheated he said that the Indians were presented with strips of blankets which had been torn into narrow pieces about six or eight inches wide, and a little bit of thread and a needle or two. The Indians thereupon traded among themselves and pieced the strips together.

He was naturally angry and said menacingly that the white people were few, their doors were thin and the Indians could easily break them in and kill all the "Bostons."

All this could not have been very reassuring to the inmates of the cabin; however they were uniformly kind to the natives and had many friends among them.

Just before the outbreak a troop of Indians visited this cabin and their bearing was so haughty that Mrs. Denny felt very anxious. When they demanded *Klosh mika potlatch wapatoes,* (Give us some potatoes) she hurried out herself to dig them as quickly as possible that they might have no excuse for displeasure, and was much relieved when they took their departure. One Indian remained behind a long time but talked very little. It is supposed that he thought of warning them of the intended attack on the white settlement but was afraid to do so because of the enmity against him that might follow among his own people.

Gov. Stevens had made treaties with the Indians to extinguish their title to the lands of the Territory. Some were dissatisfied and stirred up the others against the white usurpers. This was perfectly natural; almost any American of whatever color resents usurpation.

Time would fail to recount the injuries and indignities heaped upon the Indians by the evil-minded among the whites, who could scarcely have been better than the same class among the natives they sought to displace.

As subsequently appeared, there was a difference of opinion among the natives as to the desirability of white settlements in their domain: Leschi, Coquilton, Owhi, Kitsap, Kamiakin and Kanasket were determined against them, while Sealth (Seattle) and Pat Kanem were peaceable and friendly.

The former, shrewd chieftains, well knew that the white people coveted their good lands.

One night before the war, a passing white man, David T. Denny, heard Indians talking together in one of their "rancherees" or large houses; they were telling how the white men knew that the lands belonging to Tseiyuse and Ohwi, two great Yakima chiefs, were very desirable.

Cupidity, race prejudice and cruelty caused numberless injuries and indignities against the Indians. In spite of all, there were those among them who proved the faithful friends of the white race.

Hu-hu-bate-sute or "Salmon Bay Curley," a tall, hawk-nosed, eagle-eyed Indian with very curly hair, was a staunch friend of the "Bostons."

Thlid Kanem or "Cut-Hand" sent Lake John Che-shi-a-hud to Shilshole to inform this "Curley," who lived there, of the intended attack on Seattle. Curley told Ira W. Utter, a white settler on Shilshole or Salmon Bay, and brought him up to Seattle in his own canoe during the night.

"Duwampsh Curley" or Su-whalth, appears in a very unfavorable light in Bancroft's history. My authority, who speaks the native tongue fluently and was a volunteer in active duty on the day of the battle of Seattle, says it was not Curley who disported himself in the manner therein described. I find this refreshing note pencilled on the margin: "Now this is all a lie about Curley."

Curley rendered valuable assistance on the day of the fight. D. T. Denny saw him go on a mission down the bay at the request of the navy officers, to ascertain the position of the hostiles in the north part of the town.

"Old Mose" or Show-halthlk brought word to Seattle of the approach of the hostile bands in January, 1856.

But I seem to anticipate and hasten to refer again to the daily life of the Founders of Seattle.

Trade here, as at Alki, consisted in cutting piles, spars and timber to load vessels for San Francisco. These ships brought food supplies and merchandise, the latter often consisting of goods, calicoes, blankets, shawls and tinware, suitable for barter with the Indians to whom the settlers still looked for a number of articles of food.

Bread being the staff of life to the white man, the supply of flour was a matter of importance. In the winter of 1852 this commodity became so scarce, from the long delay of ships carrying it, that the price became quite fancy, reaching forty dollars per barrel. Pork likewise became a costly luxury; A. A. Denny relates that he paid ninety dollars for two barrels and when by an untoward fate one of the barrels of the precious meat was lost it was regarded as a positive calamity.

Left on the beach out of reach of high tide, it was supposed to be safe, but during the night it was carried away by the waves that swept the banks under the high wind. At the next low tide which came also at night, the whole settlement turned out and searched the beach, with pitchwood torches, from the head of the Bay to Smith's Cove, but found no trace of the missing barrel of pork.

An extenuating circumstance was the fact that a large salmon might be purchased for a brass button, while red flannel, beads, knives and other *ictas*" (things) were legal tender for potatoes, venison, berries and clams.

Domestic animals were few; I do not know if there was a sheep, pig or cow, and but few chickens, on Elliott Bay at the beginning of the year 1852.

As late as 1859, Charles Prosch relates that he paid one dollar and a half for a dozen eggs and the same price for a pound of butter.

There were no roads, only a few trails through the forest; a common mode of travel was to follow the beach, the traveler having to be especially mindful of the tide as the banks are so abrupt in many places that at high tide the shore is impassable. The Indian canoe was pressed into service whenever possible.

Very gradually ways through the forest were tunneled out and made passable, by cutting the trees and grubbing the larger stumps, but small obstructions were disdained and anything that would escape a wagon-bed was given peaceable possession.

Of the original settlement, J. N. Low and family remained at Alki.

D. T. and Louisa Denny, who were married at the cabin home of A. A. Denny, January 23rd, 1853, moved themselves and few effects in a canoe to their cabin on the front of their donation claim, the habitation standing on the spot for many years occupied by numerous "sweetbrier" bushes, grown from seeds planted by the first bride of Seattle.

Stern realities confronted them; a part of the time they were out of flour and had no bread for days; they bought fish of the Indians, which, together with game from the forest, brought down by the rifle of the pioneer, made existence possible.

And then, too, the pioneer housewife soon became a shrewd searcher for indigenous articles of food. Among these were nettle greens gathered in the woods.

In their season the native berries were very acceptable;

the salmonberry ripening early in June; dewberries and red and black huckleberries were plentiful in July and August.

The first meal partaken of in this cabin consisted of salt meat from a ship's stores and potatoes. They afterward learned to make a whole meal of a medium sized salmon with potatoes, the fragments remaining not worth mention.

The furniture of their cabin was meager, a few chairs from a ship, a bedstead made of fir poles and a ship's stove were the principle articles. One window without glass but closed by a wooden shutter with the open upper half-door served to light it in the daytime, while the glimmer of a dog-fish-oil lamp was the illumination at night.

The stock consisted of a single pair of chickens, a wedding present from D. S. Maynard. The hen set under the door-step and brought out a fine brood of chicks. The rooster soon took charge of them, scratched, called and led them about in the most motherly manner, while the hen, apparently realizing the fact that she was literally a rara avis prepared to bring out another brood.

Mr. and Mrs. D. T. Denny while visiting their friends at Alki on one occasion witnessed a startling scene.

An Indian had come to trade, "Old Alki John," and a mis-understanding appears to have arisen about the price of a sack of flour. The women, seated chatting at one end of the cabin, were chilled with horror to see the white man, his face pale with anger and excitement, raise an ax as if to strike the Indian, who had a large knife, such as many of them wore suspended from the wrist by a cord; the latter, a tall and brawny fellow, regarded him with a threatening look.

Fortunately no blow was struck and the white man gradually lowered the ax and dropped it on the floor. The Indian quietly departed, much to their relief, as a single blow would likely have resulted in a bloody affray and the massacre of all the white people.

At that time there were neither jails, nor courthouse, no churches, but one sawmill, no steamboats, railways or street cars, not even a rod of wagon road in King County, indeed all the conveniences of modern civilization were wanting.

There were famous, historic buildings erected and occupied, other than the cabin homes; the most notable of these was Fort Decatur.

The commodious blockhouse so named after the good sloop-of-war that rescued the town of Seattle from the hostiles, stood on an eminence at the end of Cherry Street overlooking the Bay. At this time there were about three hundred white inhabitants.

The hewn timbers of this fort were cut by D. T. Denny and two others, on the front of the donation claim, and hauled out on the beach ready to load a ship for San Francisco, but ultimately served a very different purpose from the one first intended.

The mutterings of discontent among the Indians portended war and the settlers made haste to prepare a place of refuge. The timbers were dragged up the hill by oxen and many willing hands promptly put them in place; hewn to the line, the joints were close and a good shingle roof covered the building, to which were added two bastions of sawed stuff from Yesler's mill. D. T. Denny remembers the winter was a mild one, and men went about without coats, otherwise "in their shirtsleeves." While they were building the fort, the U. S. Sloop-of-war *Decatur*, sailed up the Bay with a fair breeze, came to anchor almost directly opposite, swung around and fired off the guns, sixteen thirty-two-pounders, making thunderous reverberations far and wide, a sweet sound to the settlers.

Several of the too confident ones laughed and scoffed at the need of a fort while peace seemed secure. One of these doubters was told by Mrs. Louisa Denny that the people laughed at Noah when he built the ark, and it transpired that a party was obliged to bring this objector and his family into the fort from their claim two miles away, after dark of the night before the battle.

A few nights before the attack, a false alarm sent several settlers out in fluttering nightrobes, cold, moonlight and frosty though it was. Mr. Hillory Butler and his wife, Mrs. McConaha and her children calling to the former "Wait for me." It is needless to say that Mr. Butler waited for nobody until he got inside the fort.

The excitement was caused by the shooting of Jack Drew, a deserter from the Decatur. He was instantly killed by a boy of fifteen, alone with his sister whom he thus bravely defended. This was Milton Holgate and the weapon a shotgun, the charge of which took effect in the wanderer's face. As the report rang out through the still night air it created a panic throughout the settlement.

A family living on the eastern outskirts of the village at the foot of a hill were driven in and their house burned. The men had been engaged in tanning leather and had quite a number of hides on hand that must have enriched the flames. The owners had ridiculed the idea that there was danger of an Indian attack and would not assist in building the fort, scoffed at the man-of-war in the harbor and were generally contemptuous of the whole proceeding. However, when fired on by the Indians they fled precipitately to the fort they had scorned. One of them sank down, bareheaded, breathless and panting on a block of wood inside the fort in an exceedingly subdued frame of mind to the great amusement of the soldiery, both Captain and men.

The first decided move of the hostiles was the attack on the White River settlers, burning, killing and destroying as is the wont of a savage foe.

Joe Lake, a somewhat eccentric character, had one of the hairbreadth escapes fall to his share of the terrible times. He was slightly wounded in an attack on the Cox home on White River. Joe was standing in the open door when an Indian not far away from the cabin, seeing him, held his ramrod on the ground for a rest, placed his gun across it and fired at Joe; the bullet penetrated the clothing and just grazed his shoulder. A man inside the cabin reached up for a gun which hung over the door; the Indian saw the movement and guessing its purpose made haste to depart.

The occupants of the Cox residence hurriedly gathered themselves and indispensable effects, and embarking in a canoe, with energetic paddling, aided by the current, sped swiftly down the river into the Bay and safely reached the fort.

Beside the Decatur, a solitary sailing vessel, the Bark *Brontes*, was anchored in the harbor.

Those to engage in the battle were the detachments of men from the Decatur, under Lieutenants Drake, Hughes, Morris and Phelps, ninety-six men and eighteen marines, leaving a small number on board.

A volunteer three months' company of settlers of whom C. C. Hewitt was Captain, Wm. Gilliam, First Lieutenant, D. T. Denny, Corporal and Robert Olliver, Sergeant, aided in the defense.

A number of the settlers had received friendly warning and were expecting the attack, some having made as many as three removals from their claims, each time approaching nearer to the fort.

Mr. and Mrs. D. T. Denny forsook their cabin in the wilderness and spent an anxious night at the home of W. N. Bell, which was a mile or more from the settlement, and the following day moved in to occupy a house near A. A. Denny's, where the Frye block now stands. From thence they moved again to a little frame house near the fort.

Yoke-Yakeman, an Indian who had worked for A. A. Denny and was nicknamed "Denny Jim," played an important part as a spy in a council of the hostiles and gave the warning to Captain Gansevoort of the Decatur of the impending battle.

Mr. and Mrs. Blaine, the pioneer M. E. minister, and his wife, who was the first school teacher of Seattle, went on board the man-of-war on the 22nd of January, 1856, with their infant son, from their home situated where the Boston Block now stands.

On the morning of the 26th, while not yet arisen, she was urging her husband to get a boat so that she might go ashore; he demurred, parleying, with his hand upon the doorknob. Just then they heard the following dialogue:

Mr. H. L. Yesler (who had come aboard in some haste): "Captain, a klootchman says there are lots of Indians back of Tom Pepper's house."

Captain Gansevoort (who was lying in his berth): "John bring me my boots."

H. L. Yesler: "Never mind Captain, just send the lieutenant with the howitzer."

Captain G.: "No sir! Where my men go, I go too John bring me my boots."

And thus the ball opened; a shell was dropped in the neighborhood of "Tom Pepper's house" with the effect to arouse the whole horde of savages, perhaps a thousand, gathered in the woods back of the town.

Unearthly yells of Indians and brisk firing of musketry followed; the battle raged until noon, when there was a lull.

A volume of personal experiences might be written, but I will give here but a few incidents. To a number of the settlers who were about breakfasting, it was a time of breathless terror; they must flee for their lives to the fort. The bullets from unseen foes whistled over their heads and the distance traversed to the fort was the longest journey of their lives. It was remembered afterward that some very amusing things took place in the midst of fright and flight. One man, rising late and not fully attired, donned his wife's red flannel petticoat instead of the bifurcated garment that usually graced his limbs. The "pants" were not handy and the petticoat was put on in a trice.

Louisa Boren Denny, my mother, was alone with her child about two years old, in the little frame house, a short distance from the fort. She was engaged in baking biscuits when hearing the shots and yells of the Indians she looked out to see the marines from the Decatur swarming up out of their boats onto Yesler's wharf and concluded it was best to retire in good order. With provident foresight she snatched the pan from the oven and turned the biscuits into her apron, picked up the child, Emily Inez Denny, with her free hand and hurried out, leaving the premises to their fate. Fortunately her husband, David T. Denny, who had been standing guard, met her in the midst of the flying bullets and assisted her, speedily, into the friendly fort.

A terrible day it was for all those who were called upon to endure the anxiety and suspense that hovered within those walls; perhaps the moment that tried them most was when the report was circulated that all would be burned alive as the Indians would shoot arrows carrying fire on the roof of cedar shingles or heap combustibles against the walls near the ground and thus set fire to the building. To prevent the latter maneuver, the walls were banked with earth all around.

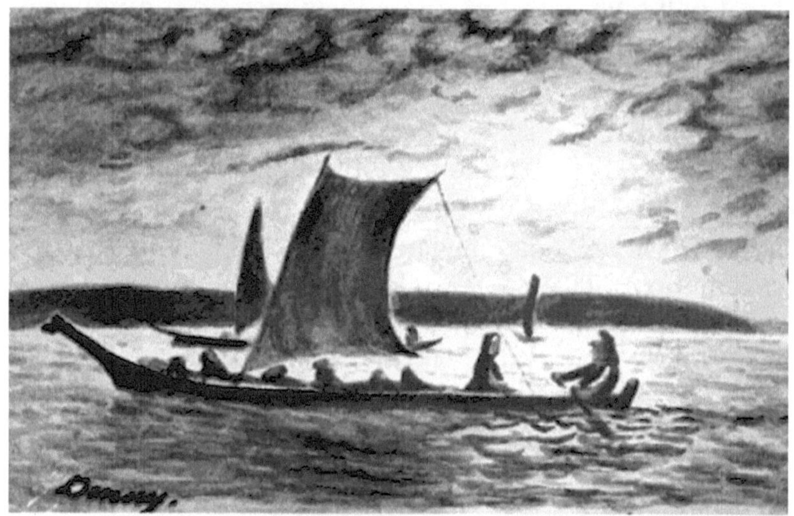

INDIAN CANOES SAILING WITH NORTH WIND

But the Indians kept at a respectful distance, the rifle-balls and shells were not to their taste and it is not their way to fight in the open.

A tragic incident was the death of Milton Holgate. Francis McNatt, a tall man, stood in the door of the fort with one hand up on the frame and Jim Broad beside him; Milton Holgate stood a little back of McNatt, and the bullet from a savage's gun passed either over or under the uplifted arm of McNatt, striking the boy between the eyes.

Quite a number of women and children were taken on board the two ships in the harbor, but my mother remained in the fort.

The battle was again renewed and fiercely fought in the afternoon.

Toward evening the Indians prepared to burn the town, but a brisk dropping of shells from the big guns of the Decatur dispersed them and they departed for cooler regions, burning houses on the outskirts of the settlement as they retreated toward the Duwamish River.

Leschi, the leader, threatened to return in a month with his bands and annihilate the place. In view of other possible attacks, a second block house was built and the forest side of the town barricaded.

Fort Decatur was a two-story building, forty feet square; the upper story was partitioned off into small rooms, where a half dozen or more families lived until it was safe or convenient to return to their distant homes. Each had a stove on which to cook, and water was carried from a well inside the stockade.

There were a number of children thus shut in, who enlivened the grim walls with their shifting shadows, awakened mirth by their playfulness or touched the hearts of their elders by their pathos.

Like a ray of sunlight in a gloomy interior was little Sam Neely, a great pet, a sociable, affectionate little fellow, visiting about from corner to corner, always sure of attention and a kindly welcome. The marines from the man-of-war spoiled him without stint. One of the Sergeants gave his mother a half worn uniform, which she skilfully re-made, gold braid, buttons and all, for little Sam. How proud he was, with everybody calling him the "Little Sergeant"; whenever he approached a loquacious group, some one was sure to say, "Well, Sergeant, what's the news?"

When the day came for the Neely family to move out of the

fort, his mother was very busy and meals uncertain.

He finally appealed to a friend, who had before proven herself capable of sympathy, for something to appease his gnawing hunger, and she promptly gave him a bowl of bread and milk. Down he sat and ate with much relish; as he drained the last drop he observed, "I was just so hungry, I didn't know how hungry I was."

Poor little Sam was drowned in the Duwampsh River the same year, and buried on its banks.

Laura Bell, a little girl of perhaps ten years, during her stay in the fort exhibited the courage and constancy characterizing even the children in those troublous times.

She did a great part of the work for the family, cared for her younger sisters, prepared and carried food to her sick mother who was heard to say with tender gratitude, "Your dear little hands have brought me almost everything I have had." Both have passed into the Beyond; one who remembers Laura well says she was a beautiful, bright, rosy cheeked child, pleasant to look upon.

In unconscious childhood I was carried into Fort Decatur, on the morning of the battle, yet by careful investigation it has been satisfactorily proven that one lasting impression was recorded upon the palimpsest of my immature mind.

A shot was accidentally fired from a gun inside the fort, by which a palefaced, dark haired lady narrowly escaped death. The bullet passed through a loop of her hair, below the ear, just beside the white neck. Her hair was dressed in an old fashioned way, parted in the middle on the forehead and smoothly brushed down over the ears, divided and twisted on each side and the two ropes of hair coiled together at the back of the head. Like a flashlight photograph, her face is imprinted on my memory, nothing before or after for sometime can I claim to recall.

A daughter, the second child of David T. and Louisa Denny, was born in Fort Decatur on the sixteenth of March, 1856, who lived to mature into a gifted and gracious womanhood and passed away from earth in Christian faith and hope on January seventeenth, 1889.

Other children who remained in the fort for varying periods, were those of the Jones, Kirkland, Lewis, McConaha and Boren families.

Of the number of settlers who occupied the fort on the day of the battle, the following are nearly, if not quite all, the families: Wm. N. Bell, Mrs. Bell and several young children; John Buckley and Mrs. Buckley; D. A. Neely and family, one of whom was little Sam Neely spoken of elsewhere; Mr. and Mrs. Hillory Butler, gratefully remembered as the best people in the settlement to visit and help the sick; the Holgates, Mrs. and Miss Holgate, Lemuel Holgate, and Milton Holgate who was killed; Timothy Grow, B. L. Johns and six children, whose mother died on the way to Puget Sound; Joe Lake, the Kirkland family, father and several daughters; Wm. Cox and family and D. T. Denny and family.

During the Indian war, H. L. Yesler took Yoke-Yakeman, or "Denny Jim," the friendly Indian before mentioned, with him across Lake Washington to the hiding place of the Sammumpsh Indians who were aiding the hostiles. Yesler conferred with them and succeeded in persuading the Indians to come out of their retreat and go across the Sound.

While returning, Denny Jim met with an accident which resulted fatally. Intending to shoot some ducks, he drew his shotgun toward him, muzzle first, and discharged it, the load entering his arm, making a flesh wound. Through lack of skill, perhaps, in treating it, he died from the effects, in Curley's house situated on the slope in front of Fort Decatur toward the Bay.

This Indian and the service he rendered should not be forgotten; the same may be appropriately said of the faithful Spokane of whom the following account has been given by eye witnesses:

"At the attack of the Cascades of the Columbia, on the 26th of March, 1856, the white people took refuge in Bradford's store, a log structure near the river. Having burned a number of other buildings, the Indians, Yakimas and Klickitats, attempted to fire the store also; as fast as the shingles were ignited by burning missiles in the hands of the Indians, the first was put out by pouring brine from a pork barrel, with a tin cup, on the incipient blazes, not being able to get any water.

"The occupants, some wounded, suffered for fresh water, having only some ale and whisky. They hoped to get to the river at night, but the Indians illuminated the scene by burning government property and a warehouse.

"James Sinclair, who was shot and instantly killed early in the fight, had brought a Spokane Indian with him. This Indian volunteered to get water for the suffering inmates. A slide used in loading boats was the only chance and he stripped off his clothing, slid down to the river and returned with a bucket of water. This was made to last until the 28th, when, the enemy remaining quiet the Spokane repeated the daring performance of going down the slide and returning with a pailful of water, with great expedition, until he had filled two barrels, a feat deserving more than passing mention."

On Elliott Bay, the cabins of the farther away settlers had gone up in smoke, fired by the hostile Indians. Some were deserted and new ones built far away from the Sound in the depths of the forest. It required great courage to return to their abandoned homes from the security of the fort, yet doubtless the settlers were glad to be at liberty after their enforced confinement. One pioneer woman says it was easy to see *Indians* among the stumps and trees around their cabin after the war.

Many remained in the settlement, others left the country for safer regions, while a few cultivated land under volunteer military guard in order to provide the settlement with vegetables.

The Yesler mill cookhouse, a log structure, was made historical in those days. The hungry soldiers after a night watch were fed there and rushed therefrom to the battle.

While there was no church, hotel, storehouse, courthouse or jail it was all these by turns. No doubt those who were sheltered within its walls, ran the whole gamut of human emotion and experience.

In the *Puget Sound Weekly* of July 30th, 1866, published in Seattle, it was thus described:

"There was nothing about this cook house very peculiar, except the interest with which old memories had invested it. It was simply a dingy-looking hewed log building, about twenty-five feet square, a little more than one story high, with a shed addition in the rear, and to strangers and newcomers was rather an eye-sore and nuisance in the place—standing as it did in the business part of the town, among the more pretentious buildings of modern construction, like a quaint octogenarian, among a band of dandyish sprigs of young America. To old settlers, however, its weather-worn roof and smoke-blackened walls, inside and out, were vastly interesting from long familiarity, and many pleasant and perhaps a few unpleasant recollections were connected with its early history, which we might make subjects of a small volume of great interest, had we time to indite it. Suffice it to say, however, that this old cook house was one among the first buildings erected in Seattle; was built for the use of the saw mill many years since, and though designed especially for a cook house, has been used for almost every conceivable purpose for which a log cabin, in a new and wild country, may be employed.

"For many years the only place for one hundred miles or more along the eastern shores of Puget Sound, where the pioneer settlers could be hospitably entertained by white men and get a square meal, was Yesler's cook house in Seattle, and whether he had money or not, no man ever found the latch string of the cook house drawn in, or went away hungry from the little cabin door; and many an old Puget Sounder remembers the happy hours, jolly nights, strange encounters and wild scenes he has enjoyed around the broad fireplace and hospitable board of Yesler's cook house.

"During the Indian war this building was the general rendezvous of the volunteers engaged in defending the thinly populated country against the depredations of the savages, and was also the resort of the navy officers on the same duty on the Sound. Judge Lander's office was held in one corner of the dining room; the auditor's office, for some time, was kept under the same roof, and, indeed, it may be said to have been used for more purposes than any other building on the Pacific coast. It was the general depository from which law and justice were dispensed throughout a large scope of surrounding country. It has, at different times, served for town hall, courthouse, jail, military headquarters, storehouse, hotel and church; and in the early years of its history served all these purposes at once. It was the place of holding elections, and political parties of all sorts held their meetings in it, and quarreled and made friends again, and ate, drank, laughed, sung, wept, and slept under the same hospitable roof. If there was to be a public gathering of the settlers of any kind and for any purpose, no one ever asked where the place of meeting was to be, for all knew it was to be at the cook house.

"The first sermon, by a Protestant, in King county was preached by the Rev. Mr. Close in the old cook house. The first lawsuit—which was the trial of the mate of the Franklin Adams, for selling ship's stores and appropriating the proceeds—came off, of course, in the old cook house. Justice Maynard presided at this trial, and the accused was discharged from the old cook house with the wholesome advice that in future he should be careful to make a correct return of all his private sales of other people's property.

"Who, then, knowing the full history of this famous old relic of early times, can wonder that it has so long been suffered to stand and moulder, unused, in the midst of the more gaudy surroundings of a later civilization? And who can think it strange, when, at last, its old smoky walls were compelled to yield to the pressure of progression, and be tumbled heedlessly into the street, that the old settler looked sorrowfully upon the vandal destruction, and silently dropped a tear over its leveled ruins. Peace to the ashes of the old cook house."

While the pioneers lingered in the settlement, they enjoyed the luxury of living in houses of sawed lumber. Time has worked out his revenges until what was then disesteemed is much admired now. A substantial and picturesque lodge of logs, furnished with modern contrivances is now regarded as quite desirable, for summer occupation at least.

The struggle of the Indians to regain their domain resulted

in many sanguinary conflicts. The bloody wave of war ran hither and yon until spent and the doom of the passing race was sealed.

Seattle and the whole Puget Sound region were set back ten years in development. Toilsome years they were that stretched before the pioneers. They and their families were obliged to do whatever they could to obtain a livelihood; they were neither ashamed nor afraid of honest work and doubtless enjoyed the reward of a good conscience and vigorous health.

Life held many pleasures and much freedom from modern fret besides. As one of them observed, "We were happy then, in our log cabin homes."

Long after the incidents herein related occurred, one of the survivors of the White River massacre wrote the following letter, which was published in a local paper:

"Burgh Hill, Ohio, Sept. 8.—I notice occasionally a pioneer sketch in the *Post-Intelligencer* relating some incident in the war of 1855-56. I have a vivid recollection of this, being a member of one of the families concerned therein. I remember distinctly the attack upon the fort at Seattle in January, 1856. Though a child, the murdering of my mother and step-father by the Indians a few weeks before made such an impression upon my mind that I was terror-stricken at the thought of another massacre, and the details are indelibly and most vividly fixed in my mind. When I read of the marvelous growth of Seattle I can hardly realize that it is possible. I add my mite to the pioneer history of Seattle and vicinity.

"I was born in Harrison township, Grant county, Wisconsin, November 13, 1848. When I was five months old my father started for the gold diggings in California, but died shortly after reaching that state. In the early part of 1851 my mother married Harvey Jones. In the spring of 1854 we started for Washington territory, overland, reaching our destination on White river in the fall, having been six months and five days in making the trip. Our route lay through Iowa, Nebraska, Wyoming, Idaho, Oregon and Washington territory. To speak in detail of all my recollections of this journey would make this article too lengthy.

"My step-father took up land on White river some twenty miles up the stream from Seattle. At that time there were only five or six families in the settlement, the nearest neighbor to us being about one-fourth mile distant. During the summer of 1855 I went some two and a half miles to school along a path through the dense woods in danger both from wild animals and Indians. Some of the settlers became alarmed at reports of hostile intentions by the Indians upon our settlement and left some two weeks before the outbreak. Among those who thought their fears groundless and remained was our family.

"On Sunday morning, October 28, 1855, while at breakfast we were surprised, and the house surrounded by a band of hostile Indians, who came running from the grass and bushes, whooping and discharging firearms. They seemed to rise from the ground so sudden and stealthy had been the attack. Our family consisted of my step-father (sick at the time), my mother, a half-sister, not quite four years old, a half-brother, not quite two, a hired man, Cooper by name, and myself.

"As soon as the Indians began firing into the house my mother covered us children over with a feather bed in the corner of one of the rooms farthest from the side attacked. In a short time it became evident we were entirely at the mercy of the savages, and after a hurried consultation between my mother and the hired man, he concluded to attempt to escape by flight; accordingly he came into the room where I was, and with an ax pried off the casing of the window and removed the lower sash, and then jumped out, but as was afterward learned he was shot when only a few rods from the house.

"My step-father was shot about the same time inside the house while passing from his room to the one in which my mother was. In a short time there appeared to be a cessation of the firing, and upon looking out from under the bed over us I saw an Indian in the next room carrying something out. Soon we were taken out by them. I did not see my mother. We were placed in the charge of the leader of the band who directed them in their actions. They put bedclothes and other combustible articles under the house and set fire to them, and in this way burned the house. When it was well nigh burned to the ground, we were led away by one of the tribe, who in a short time allowed us to go where we pleased. I first went to the nearest neighbor's, but all was confusion, and no one was about. I then came back to the burned house.

"I found my mother a short distance from the house, or where it had stood, still alive. She warned me to leave speed-ily and soon. I begged to stay with her but she urged me to flee. We made a dinner of some potatoes which had been baked by the fire. I carried my little half-brother and led my half-sister along the path to where I had gone to school during the summer, but there was no one there. I went still further on, but they, too, had gone. I came back to the school house, not knowing what to do. It was getting late. I was tired, as was my sister. My little brother was fretful, and cried to see his mother. I had carried him some three and a half or four miles altogether.

"While trying to quiet them I saw an Indian coming toward us. He had not seen us. I hid the children in the bushes and moved toward him to meet him. I soon had the relief to recognize in him an acquaintance I had often seen while attending school. We knew him as Dave. He told me to bring the children to his wigwam. His squaw was very kind, but my sister and brother were afraid of her. In the night he took us in a canoe down the river to Seattle. I was taken on board the man-of-war, *Decatur*, and they were placed in charge of some one in the fort. An uncle, John Smale, had crossed the plains when we did, but went to California. He was written to about the massacre, and reached us in June, 1856. We went to San Francisco and then to the Isthmus, and from there we went to New York city. From there we were taken to Wisconsin, where my sister and brother remained. I was brought back to Ohio in September, 1856. They both died in October, 1864, of diphtheria, in Wisconsin."

—John I. King, M. D.

CHAPTER V

THE MURDER OF MCCORMICK

THE SHORES of Lake Union, in Seattle, now surrounded by electric and steam railways, sawmills and manufactories, dwellings and public buildings, were clothed with a magnificent, dense, primeval forest, when the adventurous pioneers first looked upon its mirror-like surface. The shadowy depths of the solemn woods held many a dark and tragic secret; contests between enemies in both brute and human forms were doubtless not infrequently hidden there.

Many men came to the far northwest unheralded and unknown to the few already established, and wandering about without guides, unacquainted with the dangers peculiar to the region, were incautious and met a mysterious fate.

For a long time the *Pioneer and Democrat*, of Olympia, Washington, one of the earliest newspapers of the northwest, published an advertisement in its columns inquiring for James Montgomery McCormick, sent to it from Pennsylvania. It is thought to have been one and the same person with the subject of this sketch. Even if it were not, the name will do as well as any other.

One brilliant summer day in July of 1853, a medium sized man, past middle age, was pushing his way through the black raspberry jungle on the east side of Lake Union, gathering handfuls of the luscious fruit that hung in rich purple clusters above his head. A cool bubbling spring, that came from far up the divide toward Lake Washington, tempted him and stooping down he drank of the refreshing stream where it filled a little pool in the shadow of a mossy log. Glancing about him, he marked with a keen delight the loveliness of the vegetation, the plumy ferns, velvet mosses and drooping cedars; how grateful to him must have been the cool north breeze wandering through the forest! No doubt he thought it a pleasant place to rest in before returning to the far away settlement. Upon the mossy log he sat contentedly, marveling at the stillness of the mighty forest.

The thought had scarcely formed itself when he was startled by the dipping of paddles, wild laughter and vociferous imitations of animals and birds. A canoe grated on the beach and after a brief expectant interval, tramping feet along the trail betokened an arrival and a group of young Indians came in sight, one of whom carried a Hudson Bay musket.

Kla-how-ya (How do you do), said the leader, a flathead, with shining skin recently oiled, sinister black brows, and thick black hair cut square and even at the neck.

At first they whistled and muttered, affecting little interest in his appearance, yet all the while were keenly studying him.

The white man had with him a rifle, revolver and camp ax. The young savages examined the gun, lifting it up and sighting at a knot-hole in a distant tree; then the ax, the sharp edge of which they fingered, and the revolver, to their minds yet more fascinating.

They were slightly disdainful as though not caring to own

such articles, thereby allaying any fears he may have had as to their intentions. Being able to converse but little with the natives, the stranger good-naturedly permitted them to examine his weapons and even his clothing came under their scrutiny. His garments were new, and well adapted to frontier life.

When he supposed their curiosity satisfied, he rose to go, when one of the Indians asked him, *Halo chicamum?* (Have you any money?) he incautiously slapped his hip pocket and answered *Hiyu chicamum* (plenty of money), perhaps imagining they did not know its use or value, then started on the trail.

They let him go a little way out of sight and in a few, half-whispered, eager, savage words agreed to follow him, with what purpose did not require a full explanation.

Noiselessly and swiftly they followed on his track. One shot from the musket struck him in the back of the head and he fell forward and they rushed upon him, seized the camp ax and dealt repeated blows; life extinct, they soon stripped him of coat, shirt, and pantaloons, rifled the pockets, finding $200 and a few small trinkets, knife or keys. With the haste of guilt they threw the body still clothed in a suit of undergarments, behind a big log, among the bushes and hurried away with their booty, paddling swiftly far up the lake to their camp.

A dark, cloudy night followed and the Indians huddled around a little fire, ever and anon starting at some sound in the gloomy forest. Already very superstitious, their guilt made them doubly afraid of imaginary foes. On a piece of mat in the center of the group lay the money, revolver, etc., of which they had robbed the unfortunate white man. They intended to divide them by *slahal,* the native game played with *stobsh* and *slanna* (men and women), as they called the round black and white disks with which they gambled. A bunch of shredded cedar bark was brought from the canoe and the game began. All were very skillful and continued for several hours, until at last they counted the clothes to one, all the money to another, and the revolver and trifles to the rest. One of the less fortunate in a very bad humor said "The game was not good, I don't want this little *cultus* (worthless) thing."

"O, you are stupid and don't understand it," they answered tauntingly, thereupon he rolled himself in his blanket and sulked himself to sleep, while the others sat half dreamily planning what they would do with their booty.

Very early they made the portage between Lakes Union and Washington and returned to their homes.

But they did not escape detection.

Only a few days afterward an Indian woman, the wife of Hu-hu-bate-sute or "Salmon Bay Curley," crossed Lake Union to the black raspberry patch to gather the berries. Creeping here and there through the thick undergrowth, she came upon a gruesome sight, the disfigured body of the murdered white man. Scarcely waiting for a horrified *Achada!* she fled incontinently to her canoe and paddled quickly home to tell her husband. Hu-hu-bate-sute went back with her and arrived at the spot, where one log lay across another, hollowed out the earth slightly, rolled in and covered the body near the place where it was discovered.

Suspecting it was the work of some wild, reckless Indians he said nothing about it.

Their ill-gotten gains troubled the perpetrators of the deed, brought them no good fortune and they began to think there was *tamanuse* about them; they gave the revolver away, bestowed the small articles on some unsuspecting *tenas* (children) and gave a part of the money to "Old Steve," whose Indian name was Stemalyu.

The one who criticised the division of the spoils, whispered about among the other Indians dark hints concerning the origin of the suddenly acquired wealth and gradually a feeling arose against those who had the money. Quarreling one day over some trifle, one of them scornfully referred to the other's part of the cruel deed: "You are wicked, you killed a white man," said he. The swarthy face of the accused grew livid with rage and he plunged viciously at the speaker, but turning, eel-like, the accuser slipped away and ran out of sight into the forest. An old Indian followed him and asked "What was that you said?"

"O nothing, just idle talk."

"You had better tell me," said the old man sternly.

After some hesitation he told the story. The old man was deeply grieved and so uneasy that he went all the way to Shilshole (Salmon Bay) to see if his friend Hu-hu-bate-sute knew anything about it and that discreet person astonished him by telling him his share of the story. By degrees it became known to the Indians on both lakes and at the settlement.

Meanwhile the wife of the one accused in the contention, took the money and secretly dropped it into the lake.

One warm September day in the fall of the same year, quite a concourse of Indians were gathered out doors near the big Indian house a little north of D. T. Denny's home in the settlement (Seattle); they were having a great *wa-wa* (talk) about something; he walked over and asked them what it was all about.

"Salmon Bay Curley," who was among them, thereupon told him of the murder and the distribution of the valuables.

Shortly after, W. N. Bell, D. T. Denny, Dr. Maynard, E. A. Clark and one or two others, with Curley as a guide, went out to the lake, found the place and at first thought of removing the body, but that being impossible, Dr. Maynard placed the skull, or rather the fragments of it, in a handkerchief and took the two pairs of spectacles, one gold-rimmed, the other steel-rimmed, which were left by the Indians, and all returned to the settlement to make their report.

Investigation followed and as a result four Indians were arrested. A trial before a Justice Court was held in the old Felker house, which was built by Captain Felker and was the first large frame house of sawed lumber erected on the site of Seattle.

At this trial, Klap-ke-lachi Jim testified positively against two of them and implicated two others. The first two were summarily executed by hanging from a tall sharply leaning stump over which a rope was thrown; it stood where the New England Hotel was afterward built. A young Indian and one called Old Petawow were the others accused.

Petawow was carried into court by two young Indians, having somehow broken his leg. There was not sufficient evidence against him to convict and he was released.

C. D. Boren was sheriff and for lack of a jail, the young Indian accused was locked in a room in his own house.

Not yet satisfied with the work of execution, a mob headed by E. A. Clark determined to hang this Indian also. They therefore obtained the assistance of some sailors with block and tackle from a ship in the harbor, set up a tripod of spars, cut for shipment, over which they put the rope. In order to have the coast clear so they could break the "jail," a man was sent to Boren's house, who pretended that he wished to buy some barrels left in Boren's care by a cooper and stacked on the beach some distance away.

The unsuspecting victim of the ruse accompanied him to

the beach where the man detained him as long as he thought necessary, talking of barrels, brine and pickling salmon, and perhaps not liking to miss the "neck-tie party," at last said, "Maybe we'd better get back, the boys are threatening mischief."

Taking the hint instantly, Boren started on a dead run up the beach in a wild anxiety to save the Indian's life. In sight of the improvised scaffold he beheld the Indian with the noose around his neck, E. A. Clark and D. Livingston near by, a sea captain, who was a mere-on-looker, and the four sailors in line with the rope in their hands, awaiting the order to pull.

The sheriff recovered himself enough to shout, "Drop that rope, you rascals!"

"O string him up, he's nothing but a *Siwash*," said one.

"Dry up! you have no right to hang him, he will be tried at the next term of court," said Boren. The sailors dropped the rope, Boren removed the noose from the neck of the Indian, who was silent, bravely enduring the indignity from the mob. The majesty of the law was recognized and the crowd dispersed.

The Indian was sent to Steilacoom, where he was kept in jail for six months, but when tried there was no additional evidence and he was therefore released. Returning to his people he changed his name, taking that of his father's cousin, and has lived a quiet and peaceable life throughout the years.

Sad indeed seems the fate of this unknown wanderer, but not so much so as that of others who came to the Northwest to waste their lives in riotous living and were themselves responsible for a tragic end of a wicked career, so often sorrowfully witnessed by the sober and steadfast.

Of the participants in this exciting episode, D. T. Denny, C. D. Boren and the Indian, whose life was so promptly and courageously saved by C. D. Boren from an ignominious death, are (in 1892) still living in King County, Washington.

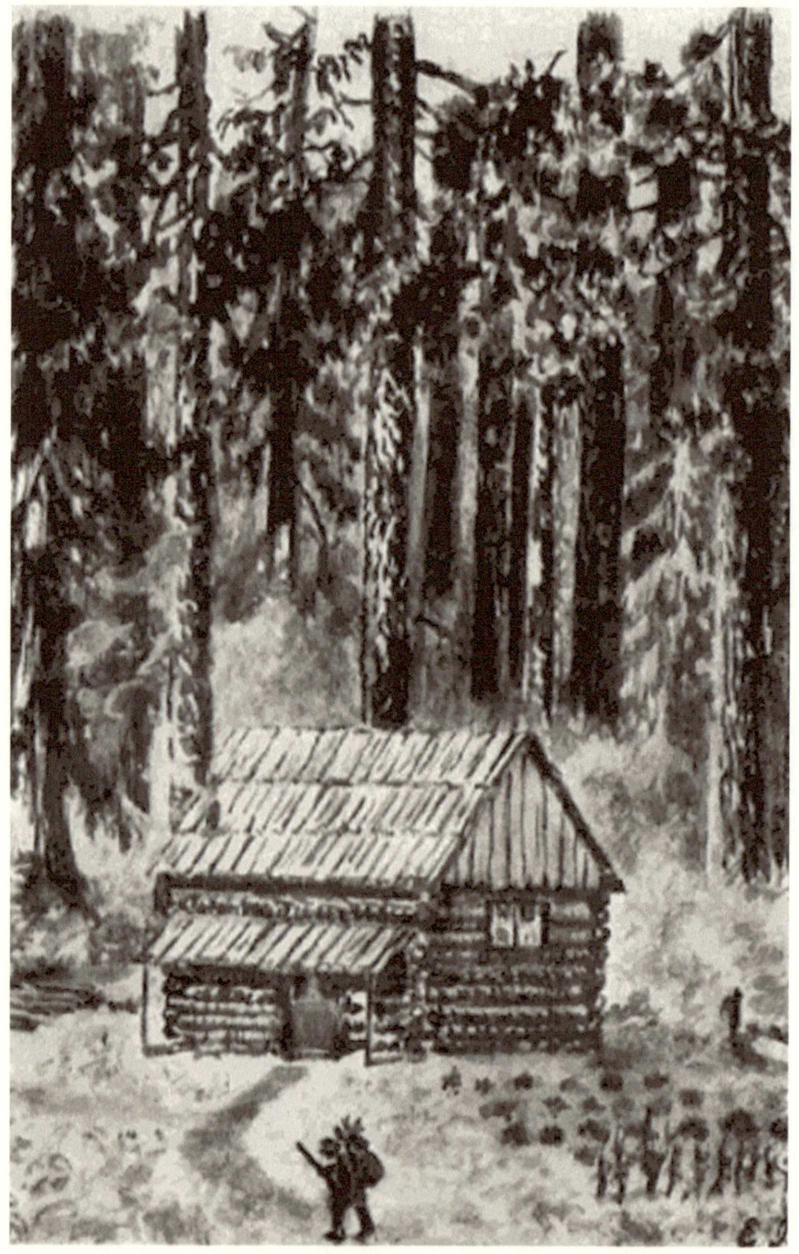

LOG CABIN IN THE SWALE

CHAPTER VI

KILLING COUGARS

IT WAS springtime in an early year of pioneer times. D. T. and Louisa Denny were living in their log cabin in the swale, an opening in the midst of the great forest, about midway between Elliott Bay and Lake Union. Not very far away was their only neighbor, Thomas Mercer, with his family of several young daughters.

On a pleasant morning, balmy with the presage of coming summer, as the two pioneers, David T. Denny and Thomas Mercer, wended, their way to their task of cutting timber, they observed some of the cattle lying down in an open space, and heard the tinkling bell of one of the little band wandering about cropping fresh spring herbage in the edge of the woods. They looked with a feeling of affection at the faithful dumb creatures who were to aid in affording sustenance, as well as a sort of friendly companionship in the lonely wilds.

After a long, sunny day spent in swinging the ax, whistling, singing and chatting, they returned to their cabins as the shadows were deepening in the mighty forest.

In the first cabin there was considerable anxiety manifested by the mistress of the same, revealed in the conversation at the supper table:

"David," said she, "there was something wrong with the cattle today; I heard a calf bawl as if something had caught it and 'Whiteface' came up all muddy and distressed looking."

"Is that so? Did you look to see what it was?"

"I started to go but the baby cried so that I had to come back. A little while before that I thought I heard an Indian halloo and looked out of the door expecting to see him come down to the trail, but I did not see anything at all."

"What could it be? Well, it is so dark now in the woods that I can't see anything; I will have to wait until tomorrow."

Early the next morning, David went up to the place where he had seen the calves the day before, taking "Towser," a large Newfoundland dog with him, also a long western rifle he had brought across the plains.

Not so many rods away from the cabin he found the remnants of a calf upon which some wild beast had feasted the day previous.

There were large tracks all around easily followed, as the ground was soft with spring rains. Towser ran out into the thick timber hard after a wild creature, and David heard something scratch and run up a tree and thought it must be a wild cat.

No white person had ever seen any larger specimen of the feline race in this region.

He stepped up to a big fir log and walked along perhaps fifty feet and looking up a giant cedar tree saw a huge cougar glaring down at him with great, savage yellow eyes, crouching motionless, except for the incessant twitching, to and fro, of the tip of its tail, as a cat does when watching a mouse.

Right before him in so convenient a place as to attract

his attention, stood a large limb which had fallen and stuck into the ground alongside the log he was standing on, so he promptly rested his gun on it, but it sank into the soft earth from the weight of the gun and he quickly drew up, aiming at the chest of the cougar.

The gun missed fire.

Fearing the animal would spring upon him, he walked back along the log about twenty feet, took a pin out of his coat and picked out the tube, poured in fresh powder from his powder horn and put on a fresh cap.

All the time the yellow eyes watched him.

Advancing again, he fired; the bullet struck through its vitals, but away it went bolting up the tree quite a distance. Another bullet was rammed home in the old muzzle loader. The cougar was dying, but still held on by its claws stuck in the bark of the tree, its head resting on a limb. Receiving one more shot in the head it let go and came hurtling down to the ground.

Towser was wild with savage delight and bit his prostrate enemy many times, chewing at the neck until it was a mass of foam, but not once did his sharp teeth penetrate the tough, thick hide.

Hurrying back, David called for Mercer, a genial man always ready to lend a hand, to help him get the beast out to the cabin. The two men found it very heavy, all they could stagger under, even the short distance it had to be carried.

As soon as the killing of the cougar was reported in the settlement, two miles away, everybody turned out to see the monster.

Mrs. Catherine Blaine, the school teacher, who had gone home with the Mercer children, saw the animal and marveled at its size.

Henry L. Yesler and all the mill hands repaired to the spot to view the dead monarch of the forest, none of whom had seen his like before. Large tracks had been seen in various places but were credited to timber wolves. This cougar's forearm measured the same as the leg of a large horse just above the knee joint.

Such an animal, if it jumped down from a considerable height, would carry a man to the ground with such force as to stun him, when he could be clawed and chewed up at the creature's will.

While the curious and admiring crowd were measuring and guessing at the weight of the cougar, Mr. Yesler called at the cabin. He kept looking about while he talked and finally said, "You are quite high-toned here, I see your house is papered," at which all laughed good-naturedly. Not all the cabins were "papered," but this one was made quite neat by means of newspapers pasted on the walls, the finishing touch being a border of nothing more expensive than blue calico.

At last they were all satisfied with their inspection of the first cougar and returned to the settlement.

A moral might be pinned here: if this cougar had not dined so gluttonously on the tender calf, which no doubt made excellent veal, possibly he would not have come to such a sudden and violent end.

Had some skillful taxidermist been at hand to mount this splendid specimen of Felis Concolor, the first killed by a white man in this region, it would now be very highly prized.

Some imagine that the danger of encounters with cougars has been purposely exaggerated by the pioneer hunters to create admiring respect for their own prowess. This is not my opinion, as I believe there is good reason to fear them, especially if they are hungry.

They are large, swift and agile, and have the advantage in the dense forest of the northwest Pacific coast, as they can station themselves in tall trees amid thick foliage and pounce upon deer, cattle and human beings.

Several years after the killing of the first specimen, a cow was caught in the jaw by a cougar, but wrenched herself away in terror and pain and ran home with the whole frightened herd at her heels, into the settlement of Seattle.

The natives have always feared them and would much rather meet a bear than a cougar, as the former will, ordinarily, run away, while the latter is hard to scare and is liable to follow and spring out of the thick undergrowth.

In one instance known to the pioneers first mentioned in this chapter, an Indian woman who was washing at the edge of a stream beat a cougar off her child with a stick, thereby saving its life.

In early days, about 1869 or '70, a Mr. T. Cherry, cradling oats in a field in Squowh Valley, was attacked by a cougar; holding his cradle between him and the hungry beast, he backed toward the fence, the animal following until the fence was reached. A gang of hogs were feeding just outside the enclosure and the cougar leaped the fence, seized one of the hogs and ran off with it.

A saloon-keeper on the Snohomish River, walking along the trail in the adjacent forest one day with his yellow dog, was startled by the sudden accession to their party of a huge and hungry cougar. The man fled precipitately, leaving the dog to his fate. The wild beast fell to and made a meal of the hapless canine, devouring all but the tip of his yellow tail, which his sorrowing master found near the trail the next day.

A lonely pioneer cabin on the Columbia River was enclosed by a high board fence. One sunny day as the two children of the family were playing in the yard, a cougar sprang from a neighboring tree and caught one of the children; the mother ran out and beat off the murderous beast, but the child was dead.

She then walked six or seven miles to a settlement carrying the dead child, while leading the other. What a task! The precious burden, the heavier load of sorrow, the care of the remaining child, the dread of a renewed attack from the cougar and the bodily fatigue incident to such a journey, forming an experience upon which it would be painful to dwell.

Many more such incidents might be given, but I am reminded at this point that they would appropriately appear in another volume.

Since the first settlement there have been killed in King County nearly thirty of these animals.

C. Brownfield, an old settler on Lake Union, killed several with the aid of "Jack," a yellow dog which belonged to D. T. Denny for a time, then to A. A. Denny.

C. D. Boren, with his dog, killed others.

Moses Kirkland brought a dog from Louisiana, a half bloodhound, with which Henry Van Asselt hunted and killed several cougars.

D. T. Denny killed one in the region occupied by the suburb of Seattle known as Ross. It had been dining off mutton secured from Dr. H. A. Smith's flock of sheep. It was half grown and much the color of a deer.

Toward Lake Washington another flock of sheep had been visited by a cougar, and Mr. Wetmore borrowed D. T. Denny's little dog "Watch," who treed the animal, remaining by it all night, but it escaped until a trap was set, when, being more hungry than cautious, it was secured.

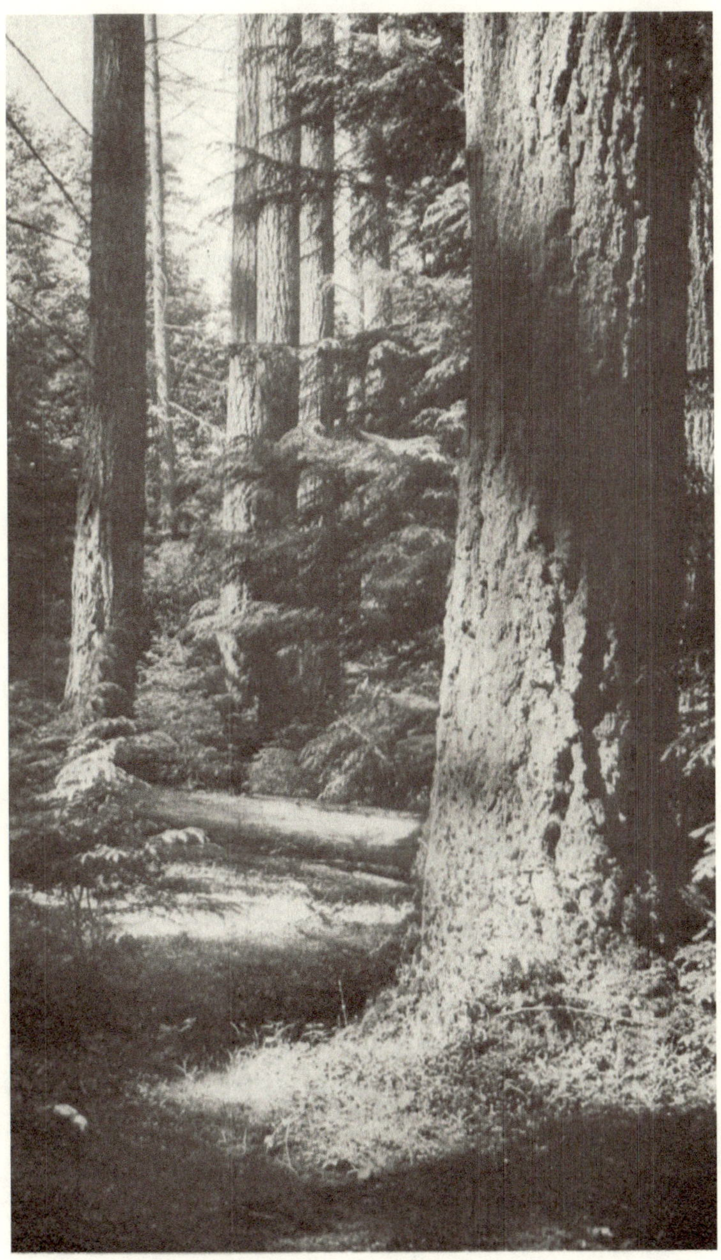

WHERE WE WANDERED LONG AGO

CHAPTER VII

PIONEER CHILD LIFE

THE VERY thought of it makes the blood tingle and the heart leap. No element was wanting for romance or adventure. Indians, bears, panthers, far journeys, in canoes or on horseback, fording rivers, camping and tramping, and all in a virgin wilderness so full of grandeur and loveliness that even very little children were impressed by the appearance thereof. The strangeness and newness of it all was hardly understood by the native white children as they had no means of comparing this region and mode of life with other countries and customs.

Traditions did not trouble us; the Indians were generally friendly, the bears were only black ones and ran away from us as fast as their furry legs would carry them; the panthers did not care to eat us up, we felt assured, while there was plenty of venison to be had by stalking, and on a journey we rode safely, either on the pommel of father's saddle or behind mother's, clinging like small kittens or cockleburs.

Familiarity with the coquettish canoe made us perfectly at home with it, and in later years when the tenderfoot arrived, we were convulsed with inextinguishable laughter at what seemed to us an unreasoning terror of a harmless craft.

Ah! we lived close to dear nature then! Our play-grounds were the brown beaches or the hillsides covered with plumy young fir trees, the alder groves or the slashings where we hacked and chopped with our little hatchets in imitation of our elders or the Father of His Country and namesake of our state. Running on long logs, the prostrate trunks of trees several hundred feet long, and jumping from one to another was found to be an exhilarating pastime.

When the frolicsome Chinook wind came singing across the Sound, the boys flew home built kites of more or less ambitious proportions and the little girls ran down the hills, performing a peculiar skirt dance by taking the gown by the hem on either side and turning the skirt half over the head. Facing the wind it assumed a balloonlike inflation very pleasing to the small performer. It was thought the proper thing to let the hair out of net or braids at the time, as the sensation of air permeating long locks was sufficient excuse for its "weirdness" as I suppose we would have politely termed it had we ever heard the word. Instead we were more likely to be reproved for having such untidy heads and perhaps reminded that we looked as wild as Indians. "As wild as Indians," the poor Indians! How they admired the native white children! Without ceremony they claimed blood brotherhood, saying, "You were born in our *illahee* (country) and are our *tillicum* (people). You eat the same food, will grow up here and belong to us."

Often we were sung to sleep at night by their *tamanuse* singing, as we lived quite near the bank below which many Indians camped, on Elliott Bay.

I never met with the least rudeness or suffered the slightest injury from an Indian except on one occasion. Walking upon the beach one day three white children drew near a group of Indian camps. Almost deserted they were, probably the inhabitants had gone fishing; the only being visible was a boy about ten years of age. Snarling out some bitter words in an unknown tongue, he flung a stone which struck hard a small head, making a slight scalp wound. Such eyes! they fairly glittered with hatred. We hurried home, the victim crying with the pain inflicted, and learned afterward that the boy was none of our *tillicum* but a stranger from the Snohomish tribe. What cruel wrong had he witnessed or suffered to make him so full of bitterness?

The Indian children were usually quite amiable in disposition, and it seemed hard to refuse their friendly advances which it became necessary to do. In their primitive state they seemed perfectly healthy and happy little creatures. They never had the toothache; just think of that, ye small consumers of colored candies! Unknown to them was the creeping horror that white children feel when about to enter the terrible dentist's den. They had their favorite fear, however, the frightful *statalth*, or "stick siwash," that haunted the great forest. As near as we could ascertain, these were the ghosts of a long dead race of savages who had been of gigantic stature and whose ghosts were likewise very tall and dreadful and very fond of chasing people out of the woods on dark nights. Plenty of little white people know what the sensation is, produced by imagining that something is coming after them in the dark.

I have seen a big, brawny, tough looking Indian running as fast as he could go, holding a blazing pitchwood torch over his head while he glanced furtively over his shoulder for the approaching statalth.

Both white and Indian children were afraid of the Northern Indians, especially the Stickeens, who were head-takers.

We were seldom panic stricken; born amid dangers there seemed nothing novel about them and we took our environment as a matter of course. We were taught to be courageous but not foolhardy, which may account for our not getting oftener in trouble.

The boys learned to shoot and shoot well at an early age, first with shot guns, then rifles. Sometimes the girls proved dangerous with firearms in their hands. A sister of the writer learned to shoot off the head of a grouse at long range. A girl schoolmate, when scarcely grown, shot and killed a bear. My brothers and cousin, Wm. R. Boren, were good shots at a tender age and killed numerous bears, deer, grouse, pheasants, ducks, wild pigeon, etc., in and about the district now occupied by the city of Seattle.

The wild flowers and the birds interested us deeply and every spring we joyfully noted the returning bluebirds and robins, the migrating wren and a number of other charming feathered friends. The high banks, not then demolished by grades, were smothered in greenery and hung with banners of bloom every succeeding season.

We clambered up and down the steep places gathering armfuls of lillies (trillium), red currant (ribes sanguineum), Indian-arrow-wood (spiraea), snowy syringa (philadelphus) and blue forgetmenots and the yellow blossoms of the Oregon grape (berberis glumacea and aquifolium), which we munched with satisfaction for the *soursweet*, and the scarlet honeysuckle to bite off the honeyglands for a like purpose.

The salmonberry and blackberry seasons were quite delightful. To plunge into the thick jungle, now traversed by Pike Street, Seattle, was a great treat. There blackberries attained Brobdignagian hugeness, rich and delicious.

On a Saturday, our favorite reward for lessons and work well done, was to be allowed to go down the lovely beach with its wide strip of variegated shingle and bands of brown, ribbed sand, as far as the "three big stones," no farther, as there were bears, panthers and Indians, as hereinbefore stated, inhabiting the regions round about.

One brilliant April day we felt very brave, we were bigger than ever before, five was quite a party, and the flowers were O! so enchanting a little farther on. Two of us climbed the bank to gather the tempting blossoms.

Our little dog, "Watch," a very intelligent animal, took the lead; scarcely had we gained the top and essayed to break the branch of a wild currant, gay with rose colored blossoms, when Watch showed unusual excitement about something, a mysterious something occupying the cavernous depths of an immense hollow log. With his bristles up, rage and terror in every quivering muscle, he was slowly, very slowly, backing toward us.

Although in the woods often, we had never seen him act so before. We took the hint and to our heels, tumbled down the yielding, yellow bank in an exceedingly hasty and unceremonious manner, gathered up our party of thoroughly frightened youngsters and hurried along the sand homeward, at a double quick pace.

Hardly stopping for a backward glance to see if the "something" was coming after us, we reached home, safe but subdued.

Not many days after the young truants were invited down to an Indian camp to see the carcass of a cougar about nine feet long. There it lay, stretched out full length, its hard, white teeth visible beyond the shrunken lips, its huge paws quite helpless and harmless.

It is more than probable that this was the "something" in the great hollow log, as it was killed in the vicinity of the place where our stampede occurred.

Evidently Watch felt his responsibility and did the best he could to divert the enemy while we escaped.

The dense forest hid many an unseen danger in early days and it transpired that I never saw a live cougar in the woods, but even a dead one may produce real old fashioned fright in a spectator.

Having occasion, when attending the University, at the age of twelve, to visit the library of that institution, a strange adventure befell me; the selection of a book absorbed my mind very fully and I was unprepared for a sudden change of thought. Turning from the shelves, a terrible sight met my eyes, a ferocious wild beast, all its fangs exhibited, in the opposite corner of the room. How did each particular hair stand upright and perspiration ooze from every pore! A moment passed and a complete collapse of the illusion left the victim weak and disgusted; it was only the stuffed cougar given to the Faculty to be the nucleus of a great collection.

The young Washingtonians, called "clam-diggers," were usually well fed, what with venison, fish, grouse and berries, game of many kinds, and creatures of the sea, they were really pampered, in the memory of the writer. But it is related by those who experienced the privations incident to the first year or two of white settlement, that the children were sometimes hungry for bread, especially during the first winter at Alki. Fish and potatoes were plentiful, obtained from the Indians, syrup from a vessel in the harbor, but bread was scarce. On one occasion, a little girl of one of the four white families on Elliott Bay, was observed to pick up an old crust and carry it around in her pocket. When asked what she intended to do with that crust, with childish simplicity she replied, "Save it to eat with syrup at dinner." Not able to resist its delicious flavor she kept nibbling away at the crust until scarcely a crumb remained; its dessicated surface had no opportunity to be masked with treacle.

To look back upon our pioneer menu is quite tantalizing.

The fish, of many excellent kinds, from the "salt-chuck," brought fresh and flapping to our doors, in native baskets by Indian fishermen, cooked in many appetizing ways; clams of all sizes from the huge bivalves weighing three-quarters of a pound a piece to the tiny white soup clam; sustain me, O my muse, if I attempt to describe their excellence. Every conceivable preparation, soup, stew, baked, pie, fry or chowder was tried with the happiest results. The Puget Sound oyster, not the stale, globe-trotting oyster of however aristocratic antecedents, the enjoyment in eating of which is chiefly as a reminiscence, but the fresh western oyster, was much esteemed.

The crab, too, figured prominently on the bill of fare, dropped alive in boiling water and served in scarlet, *a la naturel*.

A pioneer family gathered about the table enjoying a feast of the stalk-eyed crustaceans, were treated to a little diversion in this wise. The room was small, used for both kitchen and diningroom, as the house boasted of but two or three rooms, consequently space was economized.

A fine basket of crabs traded from an Indian were put in a tin pan and set under the table; several were cooked, the rest left alive. As one of the children was proceeding with the dismemberment necessary to extract the delicate meat, as if to seek its fellows, the crab slipped from her grasp and slid beneath the table. Stooping down she hastily seized her crab, as she supposed, but to her utter astonishment it seemed to have come to life, it *was* alive, kicking and snapping. In a moment the table was in an uproar of crab catching and wild laughter. The mother of the astonished child declares that to this day she cannot help laughing whenever she thinks of the crab that came to life.

It was to this home that John and Sarah Denny, and their little daughter, Loretta, came to visit their son, daughter and the grandchildren, in the winter of 1857-8.

Grandmother was tall and straight, dressed in a plain, dark gown, black silk apron and lace cap; her hair, coal black, slightly gray on the temples; her eyes dark, soft and gentle. She brought a little treat of Oregon apples from their farm in the Waldo Hills, to the children, who thought them the most wonderful fruit they had ever seen, more desirable than the golden apples of Hesperides.

We were to return with them, joyful news! What visions of bliss arose before us! new places to see and all the nice things and good times we children could have at grandfather's farm.

When the day came, in the long, dark canoe, manned by a crew of Indians, we embarked for Olympia, the head of navigation, bidding "good-bye" to our friends, few but precious, who watched us from the bank, among whom were an old man and his little daughter.

A few days before he had been sick and one of the party sent him a steaming cup of ginger and milk which, although simple, had proved efficacious; ere we reached our home again he showed his gratitude in a substantial manner, as will be seen farther on.

At one beautiful resting place, the canoe slid up against a strip of shingle covered with delicate shells; we were delighted to be allowed to walk about, after sitting curled up in the bottom of the canoe for a long time, to gather crab, pecten and periwinkle shells, even extending our ramble to a lovely grove of dark young evergreens, standing in a grassy meadow.

The first night of the journey was spent in Steilacoom. It was March of 1858 and it was chilly traveling on the big salt water. We were cold and hungry but the keeper of the one hotel in the place had retired and refused to be aroused, so we turned to the only store, where the proprietor received us kindly, brought out new blankets to cover us while we camped on the floor, gave us bread and a hot oyster stew, the best his place afforded. His generous hospitality was never forgotten by the grateful recipients who often spoke of it in after years.

I saw there a "witches' scene" of an old Indian woman boiling devilfish or octopus in a kettle over a campfire, splendidly lit against the gloom of night, and all reflected in the water.

At the break of day we paddled away over the remainder of the salt-chuck, as the Indians call the sea, until Stetchas was reached. Stetchas is "bear's place," the Indian name for the site of Olympia.

From thence the mail stage awaited us to Cowlitz Landing. The trip over this stretch of country was not exactly like a triumphal progress. The six-horse team plunged and floundered, while the wagon sank up to the hub in black mud; the language of the driver has not been recorded.

At the first stop out from Olympia, the Tilley's, famous in the first annals, entertained us. At a bountiful and appetizing meal, one of the articles, boiled eggs, were not cooked to suit Grandfather John Denny. With amusing bluntness he sent the chicken out to be killed before he ate it, complaining that the eggs were not hard enough. Mrs. Tilly made two or three efforts and finally set the dish down beside him saying, "There, if that isn't hard enough you don't deserve to have any."

The long rough ride ended at Warbass' Landing on the Cowlitz River, a tributary of the Columbia, and another canoe trip, this time on a swift and treacherous stream, was safely made to Monticello, a mere little settlement. A tiny steamboat, almost microscopic on the wide water, carried us across the great Columbia with its sparkling waves, and up the winding Willamette to Portland, Oregon.

From thence the journey progressed to the falls below Oregon City.

At the portage, we walked along a narrow plank walk built up on the side of the river bank which rose in a high round-ed hill. Its noble outline stood dark with giant firs against a blue spring sky; the rushing, silvery flood of the Willamette swept below us past a bank fringed with wild currants just coming into bloom.

At the end of the walk there stood a house which repre-sented itself as a resting place for weary travelers. We spent the night there but Alas! for rest; the occupants were conviv-ial and "drowned the shamrock" all night long; as no doubt they felt obliged to do for wasn't it "St. Patrick's Day in the mornin'?"

Most likely we three, the juveniles, slumbered peaceful-ly until aroused to learn that we were about to start "sure enough" for grandfather's farm in the Waldo Hills.

At length the log cabin home was reached and our interest deepened in everything about. So many flowers to gather as they came in lively processional, blue violets under the

oaks, blue-flags all along the valley; such great, golden buttercups, larkspurs, and many a wildling we scarcely called
by any name.

All the affairs of the house and garden, field and pasture
seemed by us especially gotten up, for our amusement and
we found endless entertainment therein.

If a cheese was made or churning done we were sure to be
"hanging around" for a green curd or paring, a taste of sweet
butter or a chance to lift the dasher of the old fashioned
churn. The milking time was enticing, too, and we trotted
down to the milking pen with our little tin cups for a drink of
fresh, warm milk from the fat, lowing kine, which fed all day
on rich grasses and waited at the edge of the flower decked
valley for the milkers with their pails.

As summer advanced our joys increased, for there were
wild strawberries and such luscious ones! no berries in after
years tasted half so good.

Some artist has portrayed a group of children on a sunny
slope among the hills, busy with the scarlet fruit and called
it "The Strawberry of Memory"; such was the strawberry of
that summer.

One brilliant June day when all the landscape was steeped
in sunshine we went some distance from home to gather a
large supply. It is needless to say that we, the juvenile con-
tingent, improved the opportunity well; and when we sat at
table the following day and grandfather helped us to generous pieces of strawberry "cobbler" and grandmother poured
over them rich, sweet cream, our satisfaction was complete.
It is likely that if we had heard of the boy who wished for a
neck as long as a giraffe so that he could taste the good things
all the way down, we would have echoed the sentiment.

Mentioning the giraffe, of the animal also we probably had

no knowledge as books were few and menageries, none at all.

No lack was felt, however, as the wild animals were numerous and interesting. The birds, rabbits and squirrels were friendly and fearless then; the birds were especially loved and it was pleasing to translate their notes into endearments for ourselves.

But the rolling suns brought round the day when we must return to our native heath on Puget Sound. Right sorry were the two little "clam-diggers" to leave the little companion of delightful days, and grandparents. With a rush of tears and calling "good-bye! good-bye!" as long as we could see or hear we rode away in a wagon, beginning the long journey, full of variety, back to the settlement on Elliott Bay.

Ourselves, and wagon and team purchased in the "web-foot" country, were carried down the Willamette and across the sweeping Columbia on a steamer to Monticello. There the wagon was loaded into a canoe to ascend the Cowlitz River, and we mounted the horses for a long day's ride, one of the children on the pommel of father's saddle, the other perched behind on mother's steed.

The forest was so dense through which we rode for a long distance that the light of noonday became a feeble twilight, the way was a mere trail, the salal bushes on either side so tall that they brushed the feet of the little riders. The tedium of succeeding miles of this weird wilderness was beguiled by the stories, gentle warnings and encouragement from my mother.

The cicadas sang as if it were evening, the dark woods looked a little fearful and I was advised to "Hold on tight and keep awake, there are bears in these woods."

The trail led us to the first crossing of the Cowlitz River, where father hallooed long and loud for help to ferry us over, from a lonely house on the opposite shore, but only echo and silence returned. The deep, dark stream, sombre forest and deserted house made an eerie impression on the children.

The little party boarded the ferryboat and swimming the horses, alongside crossed without delay.

The next afternoon saw us nearing the crossing of the Cowlitz again at Warbass Landing.

The path crossed a pretty open space covered with ripe yellow grass and set around with giant trees, just before it vanished in the hurrying stream.

Father rode on and crossed, quite easily, the uneven bed of the swift river, with its gravelly islands and deep pools.

When it came our turn, our patient beast plunged in and courageously advanced to near the middle of the stream, wavered and stood still and seemed about to go down with the current. How distinctly the green, rapid water, gravelly shoals and distant bank with its anxious onlookers is photographed on my memory's page!

Only for a moment did the brave animal falter and then sturdily worked her way to the shore. Mr. Warbass, with white face and trembling voice, said "I thought you were gone, sure." His coat was off and he had been on the point of plunging in to save us from drowning, if possible. Willing hands helped us down and into the hospitable home, where we were glad to rest after such a severe trial. A sleepless night followed for my mother, who suffered from the reaction common to such experience, although not panic stricken at the time of danger.

It was here I received my first remembered lesson in *meum et tuum*. While playing under the fruit trees around the house I spied a peach lying on the ground, round, red and fair to see. I took it in to my mother who asked where I got it, if I had asked for it, etc. I replied I had found it outdoors.

"Well, it isn't yours, go and give it to the lady and never pick up anything without asking for it."

A lesson that was heeded, and one much needed by children in these days when individual rights are so little regarded.

The muddy wagon road between this point and Olympia over which the teams had struggled in the springtime was now dry and the wagon was put together with hope of a fairly comfortable trip. It was discovered in so doing that the tongue of the vehicle had been left at Monticello. Not to be delayed, father repaired to the woods and cut a forked ash stick and made it do duty for the missing portion.

At Olympia we were entertained by Mr. and Mrs. Dickinson with whom we tarried as we went to Oregon.

My mother preferred her steed to the steamer plying on the Sound; that same trip the selfsame craft blew up.

On horseback again, we followed the trail from Olympia to the Duwampsh River, over hills and hollows, out on the prairie or in the dark forest, at night putting up at the house of a hospitable settler. From thence we were told that it was only one day's travel but the trail stretched out amazingly. Night, and a stormy one, overtook the hapless travelers.

The thunder crashed, the lightning flamed, sheets of rain came down, but there was no escape.

A halt was called at an open space in a grove of tall cedar trees, a fire made and the horses hitched under the trees.

The two children slept snugly under a fir bark shed made of slabs of bark leaned up against a large log. Father and mother sat by the fire under a cedar whose branches gave a partial shelter. Some time in the night I was awakened by my mother lying down beside me, then slept calmly on.

The next morning everything was dripping wet and we

hastened on to the Duwampsh crossing where lived the old man who stood on the bank at Seattle when we started.

What a comfort it was to the cold, wet, hungry, weary quartette to be invited into a dry warm place! and then the dinner, just prepared for company he had been expecting; a bountiful supply of garden vegetables, beets, cabbage, potatoes, a great dish of beans and hot coffee. These seemed veritable luxuries and we partook of them with a hearty relish.

A messenger was sent to Seattle to apprise our friends of our return, two of them came to meet us at the mouth of the Duwampsh River and brought us down the bay in a canoe to the landing near the old laurel (Madrona) tree that leaned over the bank in front of our home.

The first Fourth of July celebration in which I participated took place in the old M. E. Church on Second Street, Seattle, in 1861.

Early in the morning of that eventful day there was hurrying to and fro in the Dennys' cottage, on Seneca Street, embowered in flowers which even luxuriant as they were we did not deem sufficient. The nimble eldest of the children was sent to a flower-loving neighbor's for blossoms of patriotic hues, for each of the small Americans was to carry a banner inscribed with a strong motto and wreathed with red, white and blue flowers. Large letters, cut from the titles of newspapers spelled out the legends on squares of white cotton, "Freedom for All," "Slavery for none," "United we stand, divided we fall," each surrounded with a heavy wreath of beautiful flowers.

Arrived at the church, we found ourselves a little late, the orator was just rounding the first of his eloquent periods; the audience, principally men, turned to view the disturbers as they sturdily marched up the aisle to a front seat, and seeing the patriotic family with their expressive emblems, broke out in a hearty round of applause. Although very young we felt the spirit of the occasion.

The first commencement exercises at the University took place in 1863. It was a great event, an audience of about nine hundred or more, including many visitors from all parts of the Sound, Victoria, B. C., and Portland, Oregon, gathered in the hall of the old University, then quite new.

I was then nine years of age and had been trained to recite "Barbara Frietchie," it "goes without the saying" that it was received with acclaim, as feeling ran high and the hearts of the people burned within them for the things that were transpiring in the South.

Still better were they pleased and much affected by the singing of "Who Will Care for Mother Now," by Annie May Adams, a lovely young girl of fifteen, with a pure, sympathetic, soprano voice and a touching simplicity of style.

How warm beat the hearts of the people on this far off shore, as at the seat of war, and even the children shouted, sang and wept in sympathy with those who shed their life-blood for their country.

The singing of "Red, White and Blue" by the children created great enthusiasm; war tableaux such as "The Soldier's Farewell," "Who Goes There?" "In Camp," were well presented and received with enthusiastic applause, and whatever apology might have been made for the status of the school, there was none to be made for its patriotism.

Our teachers were Unionists without exception and we were taught many such things; "Rally Round the Flag" was a favorite and up went every right hand and stamped hard every little foot as we sang "Down With the Traitor and Up With the Stars" with perhaps more energy than music.

The children of my family, with those of A. A. Denny's, sometimes held "Union Meetings;" at these were speeches made that were very intense, as we thought, from the top of a stump or barrel, each mounting in turn to declaim against slavery and the Confederacy, to pronounce sentence of execution upon Jeff. Davis, Captain Semmes, et al. in a way to have made those worthies uneasy in their sleep. Every book, picture, story, indeed, every printed page concerning the war was eagerly scanned and I remember sitting by, through long talks of Grandfather John Denny with my father, to which I listened intently.

We finally burned Semmes in effigy to express our opinion of him and named the only poor, sour apple in our orchard for the Confederate president.

For a time there were two war vessels in the harbor, the *Saranac* and *Suwanee*, afterwards wrecked in Seymour Narrows. The Suwanee was overturned and sunk by the shifting of her heavy guns, but was finally raised. Both had fine bands that discoursed sweet music every evening. We stood on the bank to listen, delighted to recognize our favorites, national airs and war songs, from "Just Before the Battle, Mother" to "Star Spangled Banner."

Other beautiful music, from operas, perhaps, we enjoyed without comprehending, although we did understand the stirring strains with which we were so familiar.

In those days the itinerant M. E. ministers were often the guests of my parents and many were the good natured jokes concerning the fatalities among the yellow-legged chickens.

On one occasion a small daughter of the family, whose discretion had not developed with her hospitality, rushed excitedly into the sitting room where the minister was being entertained and said, "Mother, which chicken shall I catch?"

to the great amusement of all.

One of the reverend gentlemen declared that whenever he put in an appearance, the finest and fattest of the flock immediately lay down upon their backs with their feet in the air, as they knew some of them would have to appear on the festal board.

Like children everywhere we lavished our young affections on pets of many kinds. Among these were a family of kittens, one at least of which was considered superfluous. An Indian woman, who came to trade clams for potatoes, was given the little *pish-pish*, as she called it, with which she seemed much pleased, carrying it away wrapped in her shawl.

Her camp was a mile away on the shore of Elliott Bay, from whence it returned through the thick woods, on the following day. Soon after she came to our door to exhibit numerous scratches on her hands and arms made by the *mesachie pish-pish* (bad cat), as she now considered it. My mother healed her wounds by giving her some *supalel* (bread) esteemed a luxury by the Indians, they seldom having it unless they bought a little flour and made ash-cake.

Now this same ash-cake deserves to rank with the southern cornpone or the western Johnny cake. Its flavor is sweet and nut-like, quite unlike that of bread baked in an ordinary oven.

The first Christmas tree was set up in our own house. It was not then a common American custom; we usually called out "Christmas Gift," affecting to claim a present after the Southern "Christmas Gif" of the darkies. One early Christmas, father brought in a young Douglas fir tree and mother hung various little gifts on its branches, among them, bright red Lady apples and sticks of candy; that was our very first Christmas tree. A few years afterward the whole village

joined in loading a large tree with beautiful and costly articles, as times were good, fully one thousand dollars' worth
was hung upon and heaped around it.

When the fourth time our family returned to the donation
claim, now a part of the city of Seattle, we found a veritable
paradise of flowers, field and forest.

The claim reached from Lake Union to Elliott Bay, about a
mile and a half; a portion of it was rich meadow land covered
with luxuriant grass and bordered with flowering shrubs, the
fringe on the hem of the mighty evergreen forest covering
the remainder.

Hundreds of birds of many kinds built their nests here and
daily throughout the summer chanted their hymns of praise.
Robins and wrens, song-sparrows and snow birds, thrushes
and larks vied with each other in joyful song.

The western meadow larks wandered into this great valley,
adding their rich flute-like voices to the feathered chorus.

Woodpeckers, yellow hammers and sap-suckers, beat their
brave tattoo on the dead tree trunks and owls uttered their
cries from the thick branches at night. Riding to church one
Sunday morning we beheld seven little owls sitting in a row
on the dead limb of a tall fir tree, about fourteen feet from
the ground. Winking and blinking they sat, silently staring
as we passed by.

Rare birds peculiar to the western coast, the rufous-backed
hummingbird, like a living coal of fire, and the bush-titmouse
which builds a curious hanging nest, also visited this natural park.

The road we children traveled from this place led through
heavy forest and the year of the drouth (1868) a great fire
raged; we lost but little time on this account; it had not
ceased before we ran past the tall firs and cedars flaming

far above our heads.

Returning from church one day, when about half way home, a huge fir tree fell just behind us, and a half mile farther on we turned down a branch road at the very moment that a tree fell across the main road usually traveled.

The game was not then all destroyed; water fowl were numerous on the lakes and bays and the boys of the family often went shooting.

Rather late in the afternoon of a November day, the two smaller boys, taking a shot gun with them, repaired to Lake Union, borrowed a little fishing canoe of old Tsetseguis, the Indian who lived at the landing, and went to look at some muskrat traps they had set.

It was growing quite dark when they thought of returning. For some reason they decided to change places in the canoe, a very "ticklish" thing to do. When one attempted to pass the other, over went the little cockle-shell and both were struggling in the water. The elder managed to thrust one arm through the strap of the hunting bag worn by the younger and grasped him by the hair, said hair being a luxuriant mass of long, golden brown curls. Able to swim a little he kept them afloat although he could not keep the younger one's head above water. His cries for help reached the ears of a young man, Charles Nollop, who was preparing to cook a beefsteak for his supper—he threw the frying pan one way while the steak went the other, and rushed, coatless and hatless, to the rescue with another man, Joe Raber, in a boat.

An older brother of the two lads, John B. Denny, was just emerging from the north door of the big barn with two pails of milk; hearing, as he thought, the words "I'm drowning," rather faintly from the lake, he dropped the pails uncere-moniously and ran down to the shore swiftly, found only an old shovel-nosed canoe and no paddle, seized a picket and paddled across the little bay to where the water appeared agitated; there he found the boys struggling in the water, or rather one of them, the other was already unconscious. Arriving at the same time in their boat Charley Nollop and Joe Raber helped to pull them out of the water. The long golden curls of the younger were entangled in the crossed cords of the shot pouch and powder flask worn by the older one, who was about to sink for the last time, as he was exhausted and had let go of the younger, who was submerged.

Their mother reached the shore as the unconscious one was stretched upon the ground and raised his arms and felt for the heart which was beating feebly.

The swimmer walked up the hill to the house; the younger, still unconscious, was carried, face downward, into a room where a large fire was burning in an open fireplace, and laid down before it on a rug. Restoratives were quickly applied and upon partial recovery he was warmly tucked in bed. A few feverish days followed, yet both escaped without serious injury.

Mrs. Tsetseguis was much grieved and repeated over and over, "I told the Oleman not to lend that little canoe to the boys, and he said, 'O it's all right, they know how to manage a canoe.'"

Tsetseguis was also much distressed and showed genuine sympathy, following the rescued into the house to see if they were really safe.

The games we played in early days were often the time-honored ones taught us by our parents, and again were inventions of our own. During the Rebellion we drilled as soldiers or played "black man;" by the latter we wrought excitement to the highest pitch, whether we chased the black man, or returning the favor, he chased us.

The teeter-board was available when the neighbor's children came; the wonder is that no bones were broken by our method.

The longest, strongest, Douglas fir board that could be found, was placed across a large log, a huge stone rested in the middle and the children, boys and girls, little and big, crowded on the board almost filling it; then we carefully "waggled" it up and down, watching the stone in breathless and ecstatic silence until weary of it.

Our bravado consisted in climbing up the steepest banks on the bay, or walking long logs across ravines or on steep inclines.

The surroundings were so peculiar that old games took on new charms when played on Puget Sound. Hide-and-seek in a dense jungle of young Douglas firs was most delightful; the great fir and cedar trees, logs and stumps, afforded ample cover for any number of players, from the sharp eyes of the one who had been counted "out" with one of the old rhymes.

The shadow of danger always lurked about the undetermined boundary of our play-grounds, wild animals and wild men might be not far beyond.

We feared the drunken white man more than the sober Indian, with much greater reason. Even the drunken Indian never molested us, but usually ran "amuck" among the inhabitants of the beach.

Neither superstitious nor timid we seldom experienced a panic.

The nearest Indian graveyard was on a hill at the foot of Spring Street, Seattle. It sloped directly down to the beach; the bodies were placed in shallow graves to the very brow and down over the face of the sandy bluff. All this hill was dug down when the town advanced.

The children's' graves were especially pathetic, with their rude shelters, to keep off the rain of the long winter months, and upright poles bearing bits of bright colored cloth, tin pails and baskets.

Over these poor graves no costly monuments stood, only the winds sang wild songs there, the sea-gulls flitted over, the fair, wild flowers bloomed and the dark-eyed Indian mothers tarried sometimes, human as others in their sorrow.

But the light-hearted Indian girls wandered past, hand in hand, singing as they went, pausing to turn bright friendly eyes upon me as they answered the white child's question, *"Ka mika klatawa?"* (Where are you going?)

"*O, kopa yawa*" (O, over yonder), nodding toward the winding road that stretched along the green bank before them. Without a care or sorrow, living a healthy, free, untrammeled life, they looked the impersonation of native contentment.

The social instinct of the pioneers found expression in various ways.

A merry party of pioneer young people, invited to spend the evening at a neighbor's, were promised the luxury of a candy-pull. The first batch was put on to boil and the assembled youngsters engaged in old fashioned games to while away the time. Unfortunately for their hopes the molasses burned and they were obliged to throw it away. There was a reserve in the jug, however, and the precious remainder was set over the fire and the games went on again. Determined to succeed, the hostess stirred, while an equally anxious and careful guest held the light, a small fish-oil lamp. The lamp had a leak and was set on a tin plate; in her eagerness to light the bubbling saccharine substance and to watch the stirring-down, she leaned over a little too far and over went the lamp directly into the molasses.

What consternation fell upon them! The very thought of the fish-oil was nauseating, and that was all the molasses. There was no candy-pulling, there being no grocery just around the corner where a fresh supply might be obtained, indeed molasses and syrup were very scarce articles, brought from a great distance.

The guests departed, doubtless realizing that the "best laid plans ... gang aft agley."

The climate of Puget Sound is one so mild that snow seldom falls and ice rarely forms as thick as windowglass, consequently travel, traffic and amusement are scarcely modified during the winter, or more correctly, the rainy season. Unless it rained more energetically than usual, the children went on with their games as in summer.

The long northern twilight of the summertime and equally long evenings in winter had each their special charm.

The pictures of winter scenes in eastern magazines and books looked strange and unfamiliar to us, but as one saucy girl said to a tenderfoot from a blizzard-swept state, "We see more and deeper snow everyday than you ever saw in your life."

"How is that?" said he.

"On Mount Rainier," she answered, laughing.

Even so, this magnificent mountain, together with many lesser peaks, wears perpetual robes of snow in sight of green and blooming shores.

When it came to decorating for Christmas, well, we had a decided advantage as the evergreens stood thick about us, millions of them. Busy fingers made lavish use of rich garlands of cedar to festoon whole buildings; handsome Douglas firs, reaching from floor to ceiling, loaded with gay presents and blazing with tapers, made the little "clam-diggers'" eyes glisten and their mouths water. In the garden the flowers bloomed often in December and January, as many as twenty-six varieties at once.

One New Year's day I walked down the garden path and plucked a fine, red rosebud to decorate the New Year's cake.

The pussy-willows began the floral procession of wildlings in January and the trilliums and currants were not far behind unless a "cold snap" came on in February and the flowers *dozed on*, for they never seem to *sleep* very profoundly here. By the middle of February there was, occasionally, a general display of bloom, but more frequently it began about the first of March, the seasons varying considerably.

The following poem tells of favorite flowers gathered in the olden time "i' the spring o' the year!"

In the summertime we had work as well as play, out of doors. The garden surrounding our cottage in 1863, overflowed with fruits, vegetables and flowers. Nimble young fingers were made useful in helping to tend them. Weeding beds of spring onions and lettuce, sticking peas and beans, or hoeing potatoes, were considered excellent exercise for young muscles; no need of physical *culchuah* in the school had dawned upon us, as periods of work and rest, study and play, followed each other in healthful succession.

Having a surplus of good things, the children often went about the village with fresh vegetables and flowers, more often the latter, generous bouquets of fragrant and spicy roses and carnations, sweet peas and nasturtiums, to sell. Two little daughters in pretty, light print dresses and white hats were flower girls who were treated like little queens.

There was no disdain of work to earn a living in those days; every respectable person did something useful.

For recreation, we went with father in the wagon over the "bumpy" road when he went to haul wood, or perhaps a long way on the county road to the meadow, begging to get off to gather flowers whenever we saw them peeping from their green bowers.

Driving along through the great forest which stood an almost solid green wall on either hand, we called "O father, stop! stop; here is the lady-slipper place."

"Well, be quick, I can't wait long."

Dropping down to the ground, we ran as fast as our feet could carry us to gather the lovely, fragrant orchid, Calypso Borealis, from its mossy bed.

When the ferns were fully grown, eight or ten feet high, the little girls broke down as many as they could drag, and ran along the road, great ladies, with long green trains!

We found the way to the opening in the woods, where in the midst thereof, grandfather sat making cedar shingles with a drawing knife. Huge trees lay on the ground, piles of bolts had been cut and the heap of shingles, clear and straight of the very best quality, grew apace.

Very tall and grand the firs and cedars stood all around, like stately pillars with a dome of blue sky above; the birds sang in the underbrush and the brown butterflies floated by.

Among all the beautiful things, there was one to rivet the eye and attention; a dark green fir tree, perhaps thirty feet high, around whose trunk and branches a wild honeysuckle vine had twined itself from the ground to the topmost twig.

It had the appearance of a giant candelabrum, with the orange-scarlet blossoms that tipped the boughs like jets of flame.

Many a merry picnic we had in blackberry time, taking our lunch with us and spending the day; sometimes in an

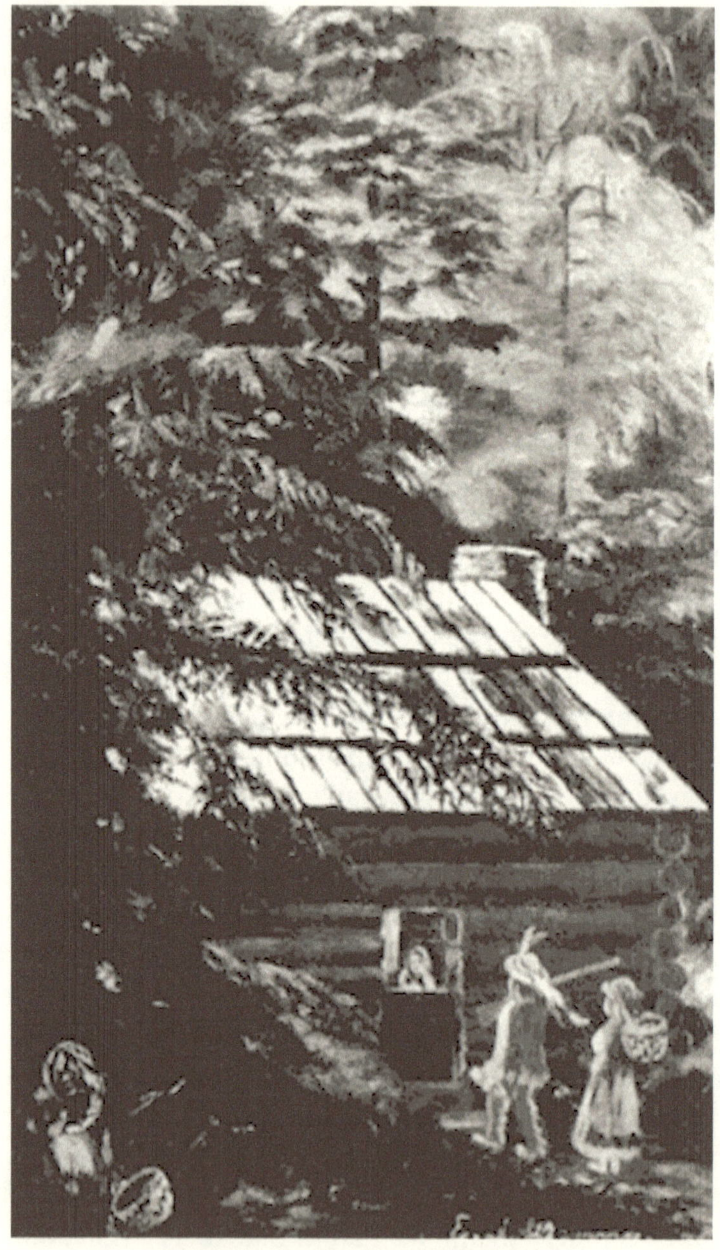

A VISIT FROM OUR TILLICUM

Indian canoe we paddled off several miles, to Smith's Cove or some other likely place.

It was necessary to watch the tide at the Cove or the shore could not be reached across the mudflat.

Once ashore how happy we were; clambering about over the hills, gathering the ripe fruit, now and then turning about to gaze at the snowy sentinel in the southern sky, grand old Mount Rainier.

How wide the sparkling waters of the bay! the sky so pure and clear, the north wind so cool and refreshing. The plumy boughs stirred gently overhead and shed for us the balsamic odors, the flowers waved a welcome at our feet.

In the winter there was seldom any "frost on the rills" or "snow on the hills," but when it did come the children made haste to get all the possible fun out of the unusual pastime of coasting. Mothers were glad when the Chinook wind came and ate up the snow and brought back the ordinary conditions, as the children were frequently sick during a cold spell.

Now the tenderfoot, as the newcomer is called in the west, is apt to be mistaken about the Chinook wind; there is a wet south wind and a dry south wind on Puget Sound. The Chinook, as the "natives" have known it, is a dry wind, clears the sky, and melts and dries up the snow at once. Wet south wind, carrying heavy rain often follows after snow, and slush reigns for a few days. Perhaps this is a distinction without much difference.

Storms rarely occur, I remember but two violent ones in which the gentle south wind seemed to forget its nature and became a raging gale.

The first occurred when I was a small child. The wind had been blowing for some time, gradually increasing in the evening, and as night advanced becoming heavier every hour.

Large stones were taken up from the high bank on the bay and piled on the roof with limbs broken from tough fir trees. Thousands of giant trees fell crashing and groaning to the ground, like a continuous cannonade; the noise was terrific and we feared for our lives.

At midnight, not daring to leave the house, and yet fearing that it might be overthrown, we knelt and commended ourselves to Him who rules the storm.

About one o'clock the storm abated and calmly and safely we lay down to sleep.

The morning broke still and clear, but many a proud monarch of the forest lay prone upon the ground.

Electric storms were very infrequent; if there came a few claps of thunder the children exclaimed, "O mother, hear the thunder storm!"

"Well, children, that isn't much of a thunder storm; you just ought to hear the thunder in Illinois, and the lighting was a continual blaze."

Our mother complained that we were scarcely enough afraid of snakes; as there are no deadly reptiles on Puget Sound, we thrust our hands into the densest foliage or searched the thick grass without dread of a lurking enemy.

The common garter snake, a short, thick snake, whose track across the dusty roads I have seen, a long lead-colored snake and a small brown one, comprise the list known to us.

Walking along a narrow trail one summer day, singing as I went, the song was abruptly broken, I sprang to one side with remarkable agility, a long, wiggling thing "swished" through the grass in an opposite direction. Calling for help, I armed myself with a club, and with my support, boldly advanced to seek out the serpent. When discovered we belabored it so earnestly that its head was well-nigh severed from its body.

It was about five feet long, the largest I had even seen, whether poisonous or not is beyond my knowledge.

There are but two spiders known to be dangerous, a white one and a small black "crab" spider. A little girl acquaintance was bitten by one of these, it was supposed, though not positively known; the bite was on the upper arm and produced such serious effects that a large piece of flesh had to be removed by the surgeon's knife and amputation was narrowly escaped.

A mysterious creature inhabiting Lake Union sometimes poisoned the young bathers. One of my younger brothers was bitten on the knee, and a lameness ensued, which continued for several months. There was only a small puncture visible with a moderate swelling, which finally passed away.

The general immunity from danger extends to the vegetable world, but very few plants are unsafe to handle, chief among them being the Panax horridum or "devil's club."

So the happy pioneer children roamed the forest fearlessly and sat on the vines and moss under the great trees, often making bonnets of the shining salal leaves pinned together with rose thorns or tiny twigs, making whistles of alder, which gave forth sweet and pleasant sounds if successfully made; or in the garden making dolls of hollyhocks, mallows and morning glories.

CHAPTER VIII

MARCHING EXPERIENCES OF ESTHER CHAMBERS

THE FOLLOWING thrilling account, written by herself and first published in the *Weekly Ledger* of Tacoma, Washington, of June 3, 1892, is to be highly commended for its clear and forcible style:

"My father, William Packwood, left Missouri in the spring of 1844 with my mother and four children in an ox team to cross the plains to Oregon.

"My mother's health was very poor when we started. She had to be helped in and out of the wagon, but the change by traveling improved her health so much that she gained a little every day, and in the course of a month or six weeks she was able to get up in the morning and cook breakfast, while my father attended his team and did other chores. I had one sister older than myself, and I was only six years old. My little sister and baby brother, who learned to walk by rolling the water keg as we camped nights and mornings, were of no help to my sick mother.

"The company in which we started was Captain Gilliam's and we traveled quite a way when we joined Captain Ford's company, making upward of sixty wagons in all.

"Our company was so large that the Indians did not molest us, although we, after letting our stock feed until late in the evening, had formed a large corral of the wagons, in which we drove the cattle and horses, and stood guard at night, as the Indians had troubled small companies by driving off their stock, but they were not at all hostile to us.

"We came to a river and camped. The next morning we were visited by Indians, who seemed to want to see us children, so we were terribly afraid of the Indians, and, as father drove in the river to cross, the oxen got frightened at the Indians and tipped the wagon over, and father jumped and held the wagon until help came. We thought the Indians would catch us, so we jumped to the lower part of the box, where there was about six inches of water. The swim and fright I will never forget—the Indian fright, of course.

"I was quite small but I do remember the beautiful scenery. We could see antelope, deer, rabbits, sage hens and coyotes, etc., and in the camp we children had a general good time. All joined at night in the plays. One night Mr. Jenkins' boys told me to ask their father for his sheath knife to cut some sticks with. When using it on the first stick, I cut my lefthand forefinger nail and all off, except a small portion of the top of my finger, and the scar is still visible.

"On another evening we children were having a nice time, when a boy by the name of Stephen, who had been in the habit of hugging around the children's shoulders and biting them, hugged me and bit a piece almost out of my shoulder. This was the first time I remember seeing my father's wrath rise on the plains, as he was a very even-tempered man. He said to the offending boy, 'If you do that again, I shall surely whip you.'

"A few days later we came to a stream that was deep but narrow. Mr. Stephens, this boy's father, was leading a cow by a rope tied around his waist and around the cow's head for the purpose of teaching the rest of the cattle to swim. The current being very swift, washed the cow down the stream, dragging the man. The women and children were all crying at a great rate, when one of the party went to Mrs. Stephens, saying, 'Mr. Stephens is drowning.' 'Well,' she replied, 'there is plenty of more men where he came from.' Mr. Stephens, his cow and all lodged safely on a drift. They got him out safely, but he did not try to swim a stream with a cow tied to his waist again.

"We could see the plains covered with buffalo as we traveled along, just like the cattle of our plains are here.

"One day a band of buffalo came running toward us, and one jumped between the wheel cattle and the wheels of the wagon, and we came very near having a general stampede of the cattle; so when the teamsters got their teams quieted down, the men, gathering their guns, ran and killed three of the buffalo, and all of the company were furnished with dried beef, which was fine for camping.

"We came to a place where there was a boiling spring that would cook eggs, and a short distance from this was a cold, clear spring, and a short distance from this was a heap of what looked like ashes, and when we crossed it the cattle's' feet burned until they bawled. Another great sight I remember of seeing was an oil spring.

"Then we reached the Blue Mountains. Snow fell as we traveled through them.

"We then came down in the Grande Ronde valley, and it seemed as if we had reached a paradise. It was a beautiful valley. Here Indians came to trade us dried salmon, la camas cakes and dried crickette cakes. We traded for some salmon and the la camas cakes, but the crickette cakes we did not hanker after.

"A man in one train thought he would fool an Indian chief, so he told the Indian he would swap his girl sixteen years old, for a couple of horses. The bargain was made and he took the horses, and the Indian hung around until near night. When the captain of the company found out that the Indian was waiting for his girl to go with him, the captain told the man that we might all be killed through him, and made him give up the horses to the chief. The Indian chief was real mad as he took the horses away.

"We went on down to The Dalles, where we stopped a few days. There was a mission at The Dalles where two missionaries lived, Brewer and Waller. We emigrants traded some of our poor, tired cattle off to them for some of their fat beef, and some coarse flour chopped on a hand mill, like what we call chop-feed nowadays.

"Then we had to make a portage around the falls, and the women and children walked. I don't remember the distance, but we walked until late at night, and waded in the mud knee-deep, and my mother stumped her toe and fell against a log or she might have gone down into the river. We little tots fell down in the mud until you'd have thought we were pigs.

"The men drove around the falls another way, and got out of provisions.

"My father, seeing a boat from the high bluffs, going down to the river hailed it, and when he came down to the boat he found us. He said he had gotten so hungry that he killed a crow and ate it, and thought it tasted splendid. He took provisions to the cattle drivers and we came on down the river to Fort Vancouver. It rained on us for a week and our bedclothes were drenched through and through, so at night we would open our bed of wet clothes and cuddle in them as though we were in a palace car, and all kept well and were not sick a day in all of our six months' journey crossing the plains. My mother gained and grew fleshy and strong.

"Next we arrived in what is now the city of Portland, which then consisted of a log cabin and a few shanties. We stayed there a few days to dry our bedding.

"Then we moved out to the Tualatin Plains, where we wintered in a barn, with three other families, each family having a corner of the barn, with fire in the center and a hole in the roof for the smoke to go out. My father went to work for a man by the name of Baxton, as all my father was worth in money, I think, was twenty-five cents, or something like that. He arrived with a cow, calf and three oxen, and had to support his family by mauling rails in the rain, to earn the wheat, peas and potatoes we ate, as that was all we could get, as bread was out of the question. Shortly after father had gone to work my little brother had a rising on his cheek. It made him so sick that mother wanted us little tots to go to the place where my father was working. It being dark, we got out of our way and went to a man, who had an Indian woman, by the name of Williams. In the plains there are swales that fill up with water when the heavy rains come, and they are knee deep. I fell in one of these, but we got to Mr. Williams all right. But when we found our neighbor we began crying, so Mr. Williams persuaded us to come in and he would go and get father, which he did, and father came home with us to our barn house. My little brother got better, and my father returned to his work again.

"Among the settlers on the Tualatin Plains were Mr. Lackriss, Mr. Burton, Mr. Williams and General McCarver, who had settled on farms before we came, and many a time did we go to their farms for greens and turnips, which were something new and a great treat to us.

"Often the Indians used to frighten us with their war dances, as we called them, as we did not know the nature of Indians, so, as General McCarver was used to them, we often asked him if the Indians were having a war dance for the purpose of hostility. He told us, that was the way they doctored their sick.

"General McCarver settled in Tacoma when the townsite was first laid out and is well known. He died in Tacoma, leaving a family.

"After we moved out to the Tualatin Plains, many a night when father was away we lay awake listening to the dogs barking, thinking the Indians were coming to kill us, and when father came home I felt safe and slept happily.

"In the spring of 1845 my father took a nice place in West Yamhill, about two miles from the Willamette River and we had some settlers around, but our advantage for a school was poor, as we were too far from settlers to have a school, so my education, what little I have, was gotten by punching the cedar fire and studying at night, but, however, we were a happy family, hoping to accumulate a competency in our new home.

"One dog, myself and elder sister and brother were carrying water from our spring, which was a hundred yards or more from our house, when a number of Indians came along. We were afraid of them and all hid. I hid by the trail, when an old Indian, seeing me, yelled out, *'Adeda!'* and I began to laugh, but my sister was terribly frightened and yelled at me to hide, so they found all of us, but they were friendly to us, only a wretched lot to steal, as they stole the only cow we had brought through, leaving the calf with us without milk.

"My father was quite a hunter, and deer were plenty, and once in a while he would get one, so we did get along without milk. During the first year we could not get bread, as there were no mills or places to buy flour. A Canadian put up a small chop mill and chopped wheat something like feed is chopped now.

"My father being a jack-of-all-trades, set to work and put up a turning lathe and went to making chairs, and my mother and her little tots took the straw from the sheaves and braided and made hats. We sold the chairs and hats and helped ourselves along in every way we could and did pretty well.

"One day, while my father's lathe was running, some one yelled 'Stop!' A large black bear was walking through the yard. The men gave him a grand chase, but bruin got away from them.

"My father remained on this place until the spring of 1847, when he and a number of other families decided to move to Puget Sound. During that winter they dug two large canoes, lashed them together as a raft or flatboat to move on, and sold out their places, bought enough provisions to last that summer, and loading up with their wagons, families and provisions, started for Puget Sound.

"Coming up the Cowlitz River was a hard trip, as the men had to tow the raft over rapids and wade. The weather was very bad. Arriving at what was called the Cowlitz Landing we stayed a few days and moved out to the Catholic priest's place (Mr. Langlay's) where the women and children remained while the men went back to Oregon for our stock. They had to drive up the Cowlitz River by a trail, and swim the rivers. My father said it was a hard trip.

"On arriving at Puget Sound we found a good many settlers. Among them, now living that I know of, was Jesse Ferguson, on Bush Prairie. We stayed near Mr. Ferguson's place until my father, McAllister and Shager, who lives in Olympia, took them to places in the Nisqually bottoms. My father's place then, is now owned by Isaac Hawk.

"Mr. McAllister was killed in the Indian war of 1855-6, leaving a family of a number of children, of whom one is Mrs. Grace Hawk. The three families living in the bottom were often frightened by the saucy Indians telling us to leave, as the King George men told them to make us go, so on one occasion there came about 300 Indians in canoes. They were painted and had knives, and said they wanted to kill a chief that lived by us by the name of Quinasapam. When he saw the warriors coming he came into our house for protection, and all of the Indians who could do so came in after him. Mr. Shager and father gave them tobacco to smoke. So they smoked and let the chief go and took their departure. If there were ever glad faces on this earth and free hearts, ours were at that time.

"My father and Mr. McAllister took a job of bursting up old steamboat boilers for Dr. Tolmie for groceries and clothing, and between their improving their farms they worked at this. While they were away the Indians' dogs were plenty, and, like wolves, they ran after everything, including our only milch cow, and she died, so there was another great loss to us, but after father got through with the old boilers, he took another job of making butter firkins for Dr. Tolmie and shingles also. This was a great help to the new settlers. The Hudson Bay Company was very kind to settlers.

"In 1849 the gold fever began to rage and my father took the fever. I was standing before the fire, listening to my mother tell about it, when my dress caught fire, and my mother and Mrs. Shager got the fire extinguished, when I found my hair was off on one side of my head and my dress missing. I felt in luck to save my life.

"In the spring of 1850 all arrangements were made for the California gold mines and we started by land in an ox team. We went back through Oregon and met our company in Yamhill, where we had lived. They joined our company of about thirty wagons. Portions of our journey were real pleasant, but the rest was terribly rough. In one canyon we crossed a stream seventy-five times in one day, and it was the most unpleasant part of our journey.

"After two months' travel we arrived in Sacramento City, Cal., and found it tolerably warm for us, not being used to a warm climate.

"Father stayed in California nearly two years. Our fortune was not a large one. We returned by sea to Washington and made our home in the Nisqually Bottom.

"On April 30, 1854, I was married to a man named G. W. T. Allen and lived with him on Whidby Island seven years, during which time four children were born. We finally agreed to disagree. Only one of our children by my first husband is living. She is Mrs. L. L. Andrews of Tacoma, Washington. He is in the banking business. On July 7, 1863, I was married to my present husband, McLain Chambers. We have lived in Washington ever since. We have had nine children. Our oldest, a son, I. M. Chambers, lives on a farm near Roy, Wash. Others are married and live at Roy, Yelm and Stampede. We have two little boys at home. Have lost three within the last three years. We live a mile and a half southeast of Roy, Wash.

"I have lived here through all the hostilities of the war. Dr. Tolmie sent wagons to haul us to the fort for safety. My present husband was a volunteer and came through with a company of scouts, very hungry. They were so hungry that when they saw my mother take a pan of biscuits from the stove, one of them saying, 'Excuse me, but we are almost starved,' grabbed the biscuits from the pan, eating like a hungry dog.

"I suppose you have heard of the murder of Col. I. N. Ebey of Whidby Island? He was beheaded by the Northern or Fort Simpson Indians and his family and George Corliss and his wife made their escape from the house by climbing out of the windows, leaving even their clothes and bushwhacking it until morning. I was on Whidby Island about seven miles from where he was killed, that same night, alone with my little girl, now Mrs. Andrews. When one of our neighbors called at the gate and said, 'Colonel Ebey was beheaded last night,' I said 'Captain Barrington, it cannot be, as I have been staying here so close by alone without being disturbed.' Shortly after the Indians came armed, and one of them came up to me, shaking a large knife in his hand saying, '*Iskum mika tenas* and *klatawa copa stick* or we will kill you.' I said to him, 'I don't understand; come and go to the field where my husband and an Indian boy are,' but they refused to go and left me soon. I started for the field with my child, and the further I went the more scared I got until when I reached my husband, I cried like a child. He ran to the house and sent a message to the agent on the reservation, but they skipped out of his reach, and never bothered me again, but I truly suffered as though I were sick, although I stayed alone with a boy eight or nine years old."

A BOY OF SEVEN WHO CAME TO

SHOW HIS FATHER THE WAY

In the same columns with the preceding sketch appeared R. A. Bundy's story of his juvenile adventures:

"I will try to give an account of my trip crossing the plains in the pioneer days. You need not expect a flowery story, as you will observe before I get through. The chances for an education in those days were quite different from what they are today. Here goes with my story, anyway:

"My father left his old home in the State of Illinois in the month of April in the year 1865. As I was a lad not seven years of age until the 27th of the month, of course I was obliged to go along to show the old man the way.

"We were all ready to start, and a large number of others that were going in the same train had gathered at our place. There were also numerous relatives present to bid us good-bye, and warn us of the big undertaking we were about to embark in, and tell of the dangers we would encounter. But a lad of my age always thinks it is a great thing to go along with a covered wagon, especially if 'pap' is driving. I crawled right in and did not apprehend anything dangerous or wearisome about a short trip like that. I will have to omit dates and camping places, as I was too young to pay any attention to such things; and you may swear that I was always around close. Everything went along smoothly with me for a short time. Riding in a covered wagon was a picnic, but my father's team was composed of both horses and cattle, and the oxen soon became tenderfooted and had to be turned loose and driven behind the wagons.

"About this time A. L. McCauley, whose account of the trip has appeared in the 'Ledger,' fell in with the train. He thought himself a brave man and as he had had a 'right smart' experience in traveling, especially since the war broke out, and was used to going in the lead and had selected a great many safe camping places for himself during that time, the men thought he would be a good man to hide from the Indians, so he was elected captain. He went ahead and showed my old man the way. I being now relieved of this responsibility, stayed behind the train and drove the tenderfooted oxen. When McCauley found a camping place I always brought up the rear.

"That was not quite so much of a picnic as some of us old-timers have nowadays at Shilo. I found out after driving oxen a few days, that I was going 'with' the old man.

"For a week or two my job was not as bad as some who have never tried it might imagine. But six months of travel behind the wagons barefooted, over sagebrush, sand toads, hot sand and gravel, rattlesnakes, prickly pears, etc., made me sometimes wish I had gone back home when the old dog did, or that 'pap' had sold me at the sale with the other property. In spite of my disagreeable situation, however, I kept trudging alone, bound to stay with the crowd. I thought my lot was a rough one when I saw other boys older than myself riding and occasionally walking just for pleasure. I could not see where the fun came in, and thought that if the opportunity was offered I could stand it to ride all the time. I thought I had the disadvantage until the Indians got all the stock.

"I remember one night that our famous captain said he had found us a good, safe camping place. The next morning the people were all right but the horses and cattle were all gone. For a while it looked like the whole train would have to walk. I did not care so much for myself but I thought it would be hard on those that were not used to it.

"During the day the men got a part of the horses back, and I was feeling pretty good, thinking the rest would get to ride, but along in the afternoon my joyful mood was suddenly changed. All the men, excepting a few on the sick list, were out after the stock, when the captain and some other men came running into camp as fast as their horses could carry them. The captain got off his horse, apparently almost scared to death. He told the women that they would never see their men again; that the Indians were coming from every direction. That was in the Wood River country, and it made me feel pretty bad after walking so far. We were all frightened, and some boys and myself found a hiding place in a wagon. We got under a feather bed and waited, expecting every minute that the Indians would come. They did not come so we came out and found that the captain was feeling rather weak and had laid down to have a rest. Shortly after we came out, one of the men came in leading an Indian pony. It was then learned that the captain and some of the men with him had been running from some of the men belonging to the train, thinking they were Indians. They found all their horses but two and captured two Indian ponies. The next day we journeyed on and I felt more like walking, knowing that the others could ride. We did not meet with any other difficulty that seriously attracted my attention.

"We arrived on the Touchet at Waitsburg in October or November, and don't you forget it, I had spent many a hot, tiresome day, having walked all the way across the plains."

CHAPTER IX

AN OLYMPIA WOMAN'S TRIP ACROSS THE PLAINS IN 1851

M RS. C. J. CROSBY of Olympia, Washington, contributes this narrative of her personal experience, to the literature of the Northwest:

"It was in the early spring of '51 that my father took the emigrant fever to come West, to what was then termed Oregon Territory, and get some of Uncle Sam's land which was donated to any one who had the perseverance and courage to travel six long weary months, through a wild, savage country with storms and floods as well as the terrible heat and dust of summer to contend against. Our home was in Covington, Indiana, and my father, Jacob Smith, with his wife and five children, myself being the eldest, started from there the 24th day of March for a town called Council Bluffs on the Missouri River, where all the emigrants bought their supplies for their long journey in the old time prairie schooner. Our train was composed of twenty-four wagons and a good number of people. A captain was selected, whose duty it was to ride ahead of the train and find good camping place for the day or night, where there was plenty of wood, water and grass.

"The first part of our journey we encountered terrible floods, little streams would suddenly become raging torrents and we were obliged to cross them in hastily-constructed boats; two incidents I distinctly remember.

"We had traveled all day and in the evening came to a stream called the Elk Horn, where we had some trouble and only part of the train crossed that night—we were among the number; well, we got something to eat as best we could, and being very tired all went to bed as early as possible; the river was a half mile from where we camped, but in the night it overflowed and the morning found our wagons up to the hubs in water, our cooking utensils floating off on the water, except those that had gone to the bottom, and all the cattle had gone off to find dry ground, and for a while things in general looked very discouraging. However, the men started out at daylight in search of the stray cattle, soon found them and hitched them to the wagons and started for another camping place, and to wait until we were joined by those who were left behind the night before. We all rejoiced to leave that river as soon as possible, but not many days expired before we came to another river which was worse than the first one—it was exceedingly high and very swift, but by hard work and perseverance they got all the wagons across the river without any accident, with the exception of my father's, which was the last to cross. They got about half way over when the provision wagon slid off the boat and down the river it went. Well, I can hardly imagine how any one could understand our feelings unless they had experienced such a calamity; to see all the provisions we had in the world floating away before our eyes and not any habitation within many hundred miles of us; for a while we did indeed feel as though the end had come this time sure. We could not retrace our footsteps, or go forward without provisions; each one in the train had only enough for their own consumption and dare not divide with their best friend; however, while they were debating what was best to do, our wagon had landed on a sandbar and the men waded out and pulled it ashore. It is needless for me to say there was great rejoicing in the camp that day; of course, nearly everything in the wagon was wet, but while in camp they were dried out. Fortunately the flour was sealed up in tin cans; the corn meal became sour before it got dry, but it had to be used just the same. In a few days we were in our usual spirits, but wondering what new trials awaited us, and it came all too soon; the poor cattle all got poisoned from drinking alkali water; at first they did not know what to do for them, but finally someone suggested giving them fat bacon, which brought them out all right in a day or two. Then their feet became very sore from constant traveling and thorns from the cactus points, and we would be obliged to remain in camp several days for them to recruit.

"As we proceeded farther on our way we began to fear the Indians, and occasionally met strolling bands of them all decked out with bows and arrows, their faces hideous with paint and long feathers sticking in their top-knots, they looked very fierce and savage; they made us understand we could not travel through their country unless we paid them. So the men gave them some tobacco, beads and other trinkets, but would not give them any ammunition; they went away angry and acted as though they would give us trouble.

"Some of the men stood guard every night to protect the camp as well as the horses and cattle, as they would drive them off in the night and frequently kill them.

"Thus we traveled from day to day, ever anxious and on the lookout for a surprise from some ambush by the wayside, they were so treacherous, but kind Providence protected us and we escaped the fate of the unfortunate emigrants who preceded us.

"Fortunately there was but little sickness in our train and only one death, that of my little brother; he was ill about two weeks and we never knew the cause of his death. At first it seemed an impossibility to go away and leave him alone by the wayside, and what could we do without a coffin and not any boards to make one? A trunk was thought of and the little darling was laid away in that. The grave had to be very deep so the wild animals could not dig up the body, and the Indians would plunder the graves, too, so it was made level with the ground. We felt it a terrible affliction; it seemed indeed the climax of all we had endured. It was with sad hearts we once again resumed our toilsome journey.

"We saw the bones of many people by the wayside, bleaching in the sun, and it was ever a constant reminder of the dear little one that was left in the wilderness. However, I must not dwell too long over this dark side of the picture, as there was much to brighten and cheer us many times; there were many strange, beautiful things which were a great source of delight and wonder, especially the boiling springs, the water so hot it would cook anything, and within a short distance springs of ice water, and others that made a noise every few minutes like the puffing of a steamer. Then there were rocks that resembled unique old castles, as they came into view in the distance. All alone in the prairie was one great rock called Independence Rock; it was a mile around it, half a mile wide and quite high in some places; there were hundreds of emigrants' names and dates carved on the side of the rock as high as they could reach. It reminded one of a huge monument. I wonder if old Father Time has effaced all the names yet?

"In the distance we saw great herds of buffalo and deer; the graceful, swift-footed antelope was indeed a sight to behold, and we never grew tired of the lovely strange flowers we found along the road.

"The young folks, as well as the old, had their fun and jokes, and in the evening all would gather 'round the campfire, telling stories and relating the trials and experiences each one had encountered during the day, or meditating what the next day would bring forth of weal or woe. Thus the months and days passed by, and our long journey came to an end when we reached the Dalles on the Columbia River, where we embarked on the small steamer that traveled down the river and landed passengers and freight at a small place called the Cascades. At this place there was a portage of a half mile; then we traveled on another steamer and landed in Portland the last day of October, the year 1851, remained there during the winter and in the spring of 1852 came to Puget Sound with a number of others who were anxious for some of Uncle Sam's land.

"Olympia, a very small village, was the only town on the Sound except Fort Steilacoom, where a few soldiers were stationed. We spent a short time in Olympia before going to Whidby Island, where my father settled on his claim, and we lived there five years, when we received a patent from the government, but before our home was completed he had the misfortune to break his arm, and, not being properly set, he was a cripple the remainder of his life."

In 1852 there were a couple of log houses at Alki Point, occupied by Mr. Denny and others; they called the "town" New York. We went ashore from the schooner and visited them.

To the above properly may be added an account published in a Seattle paper:

"Mrs. C. J. Crosby, of Olympia, gives the following interesting sketch of her early days on Whidby Island:

"As I am an old settler and termed a moss-back by those who have come later, I feel urged to relate a few facts pertaining to my early life on Whidby Island in the days of 1852. My father, Jacob Smith, with his wife and five children, crossed the plains the year of 1851. We started from Covington, Indiana, on the 24th day of March and arrived in Portland, Oregon, the last day of October.

"We remained there during the winter, coming to Olympia the spring of 1852, where we spent a short time before going down to the island. My father settled on a claim near Pen's Cove, and almost opposite what is now called Coupeville. We lived there five years, when he sold his claim to Capt. Swift for three thousand five hundred dollars and we returned to Olympia.

"The year '52 we found several families living on the island; also many bachelors who had settled on claims. I have heard my mother say she never saw the face of a white woman for nine months. My third sister was the second white child born on the island. I remember once we did not have any flour or bread for six weeks or more. We lived on potatoes, salmon and clams. Finally a vessel came in the Sound bringing some, but the price per barrel was forty-five dollars and it was musty and sour. Mother mixed potatoes with the flour so that we could eat it at all, and also to make it last a long time.

"There is also another incident impressed on my memory that I never can forget. One morning an Indian came to the house with some fish oil to sell, that and tallow candles being the only kind of light we had in those days. She paid him all he asked for the oil, besides giving him a present, but he wanted more. He got very angry and said he would shoot her. She told him to shoot and took up the fire shovel to him. Meantime she told my brother to go to a neighbor's house, about half a mile distant, but before the men arrived the Indian cleared out. However, had it not been for the kindness of the Indians we would have suffered more than we did."

From other published accounts I have culled the following:

"Peter Smith crossed the plains in 1852 and settled near Portland. When it was known the Indians would make trouble, Mr. Smith, being warned by a friendly Indian, took his family to Fort Steilacoom and joined the 'Home Guard,' but shortly afterward joined a company of militia and saw real war for three months.

"Just before the hostilities in 1855, two Indians visited his house. One of them was a magnificent specimen of physical manhood and chief of his tribe. They wanted something to eat. Now several settlers had been killed by Indians after gaining access to their houses, but, nothing daunted, Mrs. Smith went to work and prepared a very fine dinner, and Mr. S. made them sandwiches for their game bag, putting on an extra allowance of sugar, and appeared to be as bold as a lion. He also accepted an invitation to visit their camp, which he did in their company, and formed a lasting friendship.

"The mince, fruit and doughnuts did their good work.

"During the war Mr. Smith had his neck merely bruised by a bullet. On his return home he found the Indians had been there before him and stolen his hogs and horses and destroyed his grain, a loss of eleven hundred dollars, for which he has never received any pay."

CHAPTER X

CAPT. HENRY ROEDER ON THE TRAIL

APT. ROEDER came by steamer to Portland and thence made his way to Olympia overland from the mouth of the Cowlitz River. This was in the winter of 1852. The story of this journey is best told in the words of the veteran pioneer himself, who has narrated his first experiences in the then Territory of Oregon as follows:

"In company with R. V. Peabody, I traveled overland from the mouth of the Cowlitz, through the mud to Olympia. We started early in December from Portland. It took us four days to walk from the Cowlitz River to Olympia, and it was as hard traveling as I have ever seen. Old residents will remember what was known as Sanders' Bottom. It was mud almost to your waist. We stopped one night with an old settler, whose name I cannot now recall, but whom we all called in those days 'Old Hardbread.' On the Skookumchuck we found lodging with Judge Ford, and on arriving at Olympia we put up with Mr. Sylvester, whose name is well known to all the old residents on the Sound. I remember that at Olympia we got our first taste of the Puget Sound clam, and mighty glad we were, too, to get a chance to eat some of them.

"From Olympia to Seattle we traveled by Indian canoe. I remember distinctly rounding Alki Point and entering the harbor of Elliott Bay. I saw what was, perhaps, the first house that was built, where now stands the magnificent city of Seattle. This was a cabin that was being erected on a narrow strip of land jutting out into the bay, which is now right in the heart of Seattle. Dr. Maynard was the builder. It was situated adjoining the lot at Commercial and Main Streets, occupied by the old Arlington just before the fire of 1889. The waters of the Sound lapped the shores of the narrow peninsula upon which it was built, but since then the waters have been driven back by the filling of earth, sawdust and rock, which was put on both sides of the little neck of land.

"After a few days' stay here, Peabody and I journeyed by Indian canoe to Whatcom. We carried our canoe overland to Hood Canal. On the second day out we encountered a terrible storm and put into shelter with a settler on the shore of the canal. His name was O'Haver, and he lived with an Indian wife. We had white turnips and dried salmon for breakfast and dried salmon and white turnips for dinner. This bill of fare was repeated in this fashion for three days, and I want to tell you that we were glad when the weather moderated and we were enabled to proceed.

"We were told that we could procure something in the edible line at Port Townsend, but were disappointed. The best we could obtain at the stores was some hard bread, in which the worms had propagated in luxuriant fashion. This food was not so particularly appetizing, as you may imagine. A settler kindly took pity on us and shared his slender stock of food. Thence we journeyed to Whatcom, where I have resided nearly ever since."

Capt. Roeder told also before he had finished his recital of an acquaintance he had formed in California with the noted Spanish murderer and bandit, Joaquin, and his tribe of cut-throats and robbers. Joaquin's raids and his long career in crime among the mining camps of the early days of California are part of the history of that state. Capt. Roeder was traveling horseback on one occasion between Marysville and Rush Creek. This was in 1851. The night before he left Marysville the sheriff and a posse had attempted to capture Joaquin and his band. The authorities had offered a reward of $10,000 for Joaquin and $5,000 for his men, dead or alive. The sheriff went out from Marysville with a cigar in his mouth and his sombrero on the side of his head, as if he were attending a picnic. It was his own funeral, however, instead of a picnic, for his body was picked out of a fence corner, riddled with bullets.

"I was going at a leisurely gait over the mountain road or bridle path that led from Marysville to Rush Creek," said Capt. Roeder. "Suddenly, after a bend in the road, I found myself in the midst of a band of men mounted on bronchos. They were dark-skinned and of Spanish blood. Immediately I recognized Joaquin and 'Three-Fingered Jack,' his first lieutenant. My heart thumped vigorously, and I thought that it was all up with me. I managed somehow to control myself and did not evince any of the excitement I felt or give the outlaws any sign that I knew or suspected who they were.

"One of the riders, after saluting me in Spanish, asked me where I was from and whither I was traveling. I told them freely and frankly, as if the occurrence were an everyday transaction. Learning that I had just come from Marysville, the seat of their last outrage, they inquired the news. I told them the truth—that the camp was in a state of great excitement, due to the late visit of the outlaw, Joaquin, and his band; that the sheriff had been murdered and three or four miners and others in the vicinity had been murdered and robbed. It was Joaquin's pleasant practice to lariat a man, rob him and cut his throat, leaving the body by the roadside. They asked me which way Joaquin had gone and I told them that he was seen last traveling towards Arizona. As a matter of fact, the outlaw and his band were then traveling in a direction exactly opposite from that which I had given.

"My replies apparently pleased them. 'Three-Fingered Jack' proposed a drink, after asking me which way I traveled. I said, 'I would have proposed the compliment long ago had I any in my canteen,' whereat Jack drew his own bottle and offered me a drink.

"You may imagine my feelings then. I knew that if they believed I had recognized them they would give me poison or kill me with a knife. I took the canteen and drank from it. You may imagine my joy when I saw Jack lift the bottle to his lips and drain it. Then I knew that I had deceived them. We exchanged adieus in Spanish, and that is the last I saw of Joaquin and his associate murderers.

PART II

MEN, WOMEN AND ADVENTURES

CHAPTER I

SONG OF THE PIONEERS

WITH FAITH'S clear eye we saw afar
In western sky our empire's star
And strong of heart and brave of soul,
We marched and marched to reach the goal.
Unrolled a scroll, the great gray plains,
And traced thereon our wagon trains,
Our blazing campfires marked the road
As each succeeding night they glowed.

Gaunt hunger, drouth, fierce heat and cold
Beset us as in days of old
Great dragons sought to swallow down
Adventurous heroes of renown.
There menaced us our tawny foes,
Where any bank or hillock rose;
A cloud of dust or shadows' naught
Seemed ever with some danger fraught.

Weird mountain ranges crossed our path
And frowned on us in seeming wrath;
Their beetling crags and icy brows
Well might a hundred fears arouse.
Impetuous rivers swirled and boiled,
As though from mischief ever foiled.
At length in safety all were crossed,
Though roughly were our "schooners" tossed.

135

With joy we saw fair Puget Sound,
White, glistening peaks set all around.
At Alki Point our feet we stayed,
(The women wept, the children played).
On Chamber's prairie, Whidby's isle,
Duwamish river, mile on mile
Away from these, on lake or bay
The lonely settlers blazed the way
For civilization's march and sway.

The mountains, forests, bays and streams,
Their grandeur wove into our dreams;
Our thoughts grew great and undismayed,
We toiled and sang or waiting, prayed.
As suns arose and then went down
We gazed on Rainier's snowy crown.
God's battle-tents gleamed in the west,
So pure they called our thoughts above
To heaven's joy and peace and love.

We found a race tho' rude and wild,
Still tender toward friend or child,
For dark eyes laughed or shone with tears
As joy or sorrow filled the years;
Their black-eyed babes the red men kissed
And captive brothers sorely missed.
With broken hearts, brown mothers wept
When babes away by death were swept.

Chief Sealth stood the white man's friend,
With insight keen he saw the end
Of struggles vain against a foe
Whose coming forced their overthrow.
For pity oft he freed the slaves,
To reasoning cool he called his braves;
But bitter wrongs the pale-face wrought—
Revenge and hatred on us brought.

***

With life the woods and waters teemed,
A boundless store we never dreamed,

Of berries, deer and grouse and fish,
Sufficient for a gourmand's wish.
Our dusky neighbors friendly-wise
Brought down the game before our eyes;
They wiled the glittering finny tribe,
Well pleased to trade with many a jibe.

We lit the forests far and wide
With pitchwood torches, true and tried,
We traveled far in frail canoes,
Cayuses rode, wore Indian shoes,
And clothes of skin, and ate clam stews,
Clam frys and chowder; baked or fried
The clam was then the settler's pride; "
Clam-diggers" then, none dared deride.

***

A sound arose our hearts to thrill,
From whirring saws in Yesler's mill;
The village crept upon the hill.
On many hills our city's spread,
As fair a queen as one that wed
The Adriatic, so 'tis said.
Our tasks so hard are well nigh done—
Today our hearts will beat as one!

Each one may look now to the west
For end of days declared the best,
Since sunset here is sunrise there,
Our heavenly home is far more fair.
As up the slope of coming years
Time pushes on the pioneers,
With peace may e'er our feet be shod
And press at last the mount of God.

—E. I. Denny
Seattle, June, 1893

CHAPTER II

BIOGRAPHICAL NOTES AND SKETCHES—JOHN DENNY

A S ELSEWHERE indicated, only a few of the leading characters will be followed in their careers. Of these, John Denny is fittingly placed first.

John Denny was born of pioneer parents near Lexington, Kentucky, May 4th, 1793. In 1813 he was a volunteer in Col. Richard M. Johnson's regiment of mounted riflemen, and served through the war, participated in the celebrated battle of the Thames in Canada, where Tecumseh was killed and the British army under Proctor surrendered. Disaster fell upon him, the results of which followed him throughout his life. The morning gun stampeded the horses in camp while the soldiers were still asleep, and they ran over John Denny where he lay asleep in a tent, wounding his knee so that the synovial fluid ran out and also broke three of his ribs. In 1823 he removed to Putnam County, Indiana, then an unknown wilderness, locating six miles east of Greencastle, where he resided for the succeeding twelve years. He is remembered as a leading man of energy and public spirit.

In 1835 he removed to Illinois and settled in Knox County,

138

then near the frontier of civilization, where he lived for the next succeeding sixteen years, during which time he represented his county in both branches of the state legislature, serving with Lincoln, Douglas, Baker, Yates, Washburn and Trumbull, with all of whom he formed warm personal friendships, which lasted through life, despite political differences.

In 1851, at an age when most men think they have outlived their usefulness and seek the repose demanded by their failing physical strength, accompanied by his children and grandchildren, he braved the toils and perils of an overland journey to this then remote wilderness upon the extreme borders of civilization and settled upon a farm in Marion County, Oregon, while his sons, Arthur A. and David T., took claims on Elliott Bay and were among the founders of Seattle, where they command universal respect for their intelligence, integrity and public spirit, Arthur having represented the territory as delegate in congress and served several terms in the Territorial Legislature.

David has held many responsible public positions, including Probate Judge and Regent of the University, and is respected by all as a clear-headed and scrupulously honest man and most estimable citizen.

John Denny remained in Oregon about six years, but held no official position there, for the reason that he was an uncompromising Whig and Oregon was overwhelmingly Democratic, including among the leaders of the Democratic party George H. Williams, Judge Deady, Gov. Gibbs and much of the best intellect of the state.

He, however, entered warmly into the political discussions of the times, and many incidents are remembered and many anecdotes told of the astonishment and discomfiture of some of the most pretentious public speakers when meeting the unpretending pioneer farmer in public discussion. He was a natural orator and had improved his gift by practice and extensive reading.

Few professional men were better posted in current history and governmental philosophy or could make a better use of their knowledge in addressing a popular audience.

In 1859 he removed to Seattle, and from that time on to the day of his death was a recognized leader in every enterprise calculated to promote the prosperity of the town or advance its educational and social interests. No public measure, no public meeting to consider public enterprise, was a success in which he was not a central figure, not as an assumed director, but as an earnest co-operator, who enthused others by his own undaunted spirit of enterprise, and when past eighty years of age his voice was heard stirring up the energies of the people, and by his example, no less than his precepts, he shamed the listless and selfish younger men into activity and public spirit.

When any special legislative aid was desired for this section, John Denny was certain to be selected to obtain it; by his efforts mainly the Territorial University was located at this place.

He passed his long and active life almost wholly upon the frontiers of civilization, not from any aversion to the refinements and restraints of social life, for few men possessed higher social qualities or had in any greater degree the nicer instincts of a gentleman—he held a patent of nobility under the signet of the Almighty, and his intercourse with others was ever marked by a courtesy which betokened not only self-respect but a due regard for the rights and opinions of others. He was impelled by as noble ambition as ever sought the conquest of empire or the achievement of personal glory—the subduing of the unoccupied portions of his country to the uses of man, with the patriotic purpose of extending his country's glory and augmenting its resources.

His first care in every settlement was to establish and promote education, religion and morality as the only true foundation of social as well as individual prosperity, and with all his courage and manly strength he rarely, if ever, was drawn into a lawsuit.

John Denny was of that noble race of men, now nearly extinct, who formed the vanguard of Western civilization and were the founders of empire. Their day is over, their vocation ended, because the limit of their enterprise has been reached. Among the compeers of the same stock were Dick Johnson, Harrison, Lincoln, Harden and others famous in the history of the country, who only excelled him in historic note by biding their opportunities in waiting to reap the fruits of the harvest which they had planted. He was the peer of the best in all the elements of manhood, of heart and brain. In all circumstances and surroundings he was a recognized leader of men, and would have been so honored and so commanded that leading place in public history had he waited for the development of the social institutions which he helped to plant in the Western states, now the seat of empire. All who entered his presence were instinctively impressed by his manhood. Yet no man was less pretentious or more unostentatious in his intercourse with others.

He reverenced his manhood, and felt himself here among men his brethren under the eye of a common Father.

He felt that he was bound to work for all like a brother and like a son.

So he was brave, so he was true, so his integrity was unsullied, so not a stain dims his memory; so he rebuked vice and detested meanness and hated with a cordial hate all false-hood, all dishonesty and all trickery; so he was the chivalrous champion of the innocent and oppressed; so he was gentle and merciful, because he was working among a vast family as a brother "recognizing the Great Father, Who sits over all, Who is forever Truth and forever Love."

Such words as these were said of him at the time of his death, when the impressions of his personality were fresh in the minds of the people.

He entered into rest July 28th, 1875.

It is within my recollection that the keen criticisms and droll anecdotes of John Denny were often repeated by his hearers. The power with which he swayed an audience was something wonderful to behold; the burning enthusiasm which his oratory kindled, inciting to action, the waves of convulsive laughter his wit evoked were abundant evidence of his influence.

In repartee, he excelled. At one time when A. A. Denny was a member of the Territorial Legislature, John Denny was on his way to the capital to interview him, doubtless concerning some important measure; he received the hospitality of a settler who was a stranger to him and moreover very curious with regard to the traveler's identity and occupation. At last this questioning brought forth the remarkable statement that he, John Denny, had a son in the lunatic ass-ylum in Olympia whom he intended visiting.

The questioner delightedly related it afterward, laughing heartily at the compliment paid to the Legislature.

In a published sketch a personal friend says: "He was so full of humor that it was impossible to conceal it, and his very presence became a mirth-provoking contagion absolutely irresistible in its effects.

"Let him come when he would, everybody was ready to drop everything else to listen to a story from Uncle John.

"He went home to the States during the war, via the Isthmus of Panama. On the trip down from San Francisco the steamer ran on a rock and stuck fast. Of course, there was a great fright and excitement, many crying out 'We shall all be drowned,' 'Lord save us!' etc. Amid it all Uncle John coolly took in the chances of the situation, and when a little quiet had been restored so he could be heard by all in the cabin, he said: 'Well, I reckon there was a fair bargain between me and the steamship company to carry me down to Panama, and they've got their cash for it, and now if they let me drown out here in this ornery corner, where I can't have a decent funeral, I'll sue 'em for damages, and bust the consarned old company all to flinders.'

"This had the effect to divert the passengers, and helped to prevent a panic, and not a life was lost.

"In early life he had been a Whig and in Illinois had fought many a hard battle with the common enemy. He had represented his district repeatedly in the legislature of that state, and he used to tell with pride, and a good deal of satisfaction, how one day a handful of the Whigs, Old Abe and himself among the number, broke a quorum of the house by jumping from a second-story window, thereby preventing the passage of a bill which was obnoxious to the Whigs.

"The Democrats had been watching their opportunity, and having secured a quorum with but few of the Whigs in the house, locked the doors and proposed to put their measure through. But the Whigs nipped the little game in the manner related."

After Lincoln had become President and John Denny had crossed the Plains and pioneered it in Oregon and Washington

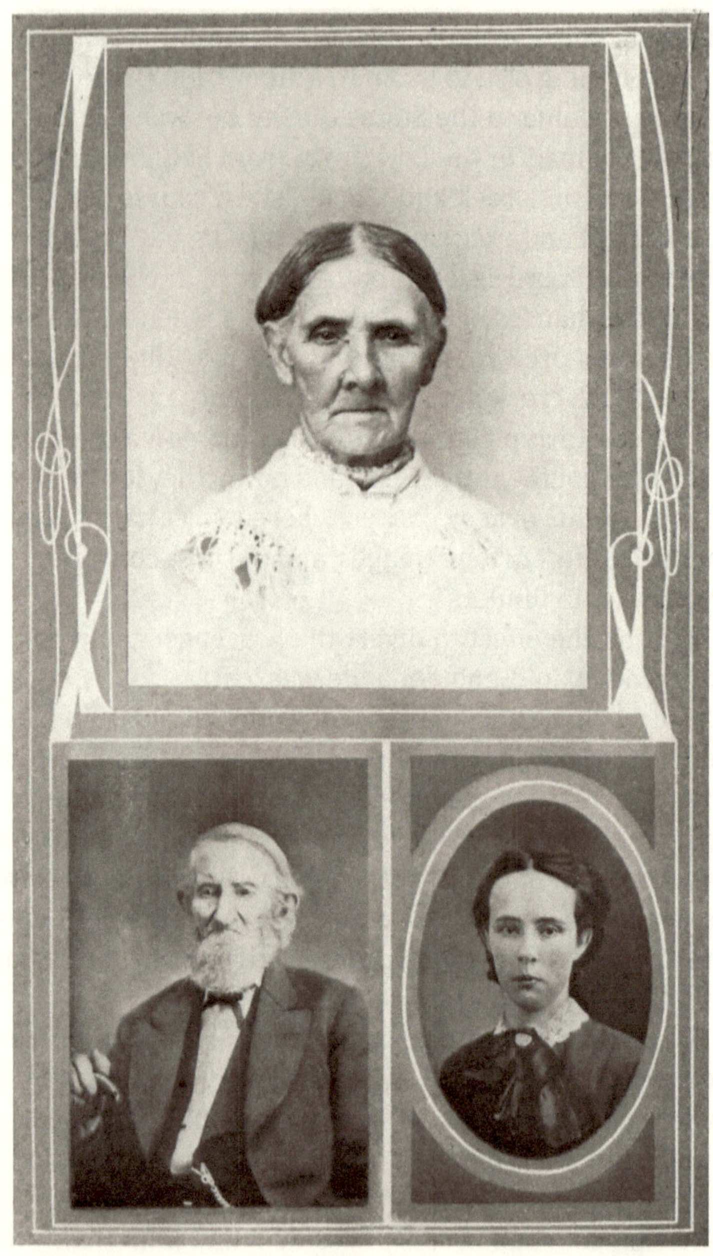

SARAH DENNY, JOHN DENNY, S. LORETTA DENNY

Territories, the latter visited the national capital on important business.

While there Mr. Denny attended a presidential reception and tested his old friend's memory in this way: Forbidding his name to be announced, he advanced in the line and gave his hand to President Lincoln, then essayed to pass on. Lincoln tightened his grasp and said, "No you don't, John Denny; you come around back here and we'll have a talk after a while."

On the stump he was perfectly at home, never coming off second best. His ready wit and tactics were sure to stand him in hand at the needed moment.

In one of the early campaigns of Washington Territory, which was a triangular combat waged by Republicans, Democrats and "Bolters," John Denny, who was then a Republican, became one of the third party. At a political meeting which was held in Seattle, at which I was present, a young man recently from the East and quite dandyish, a Republican and a lawyer, made quite a high-sounding speech; after he sat down John Denny advanced to speak.

He began very coolly to point out how they had been deceived by the rascally Republican representative in his previous term of office, and suddenly pointing his long, lean forefinger directly at the preceding speaker, his voice gathering great force and intensity, he electrified the audience by saying, "And no little huckleberry lawyer can blind us to the facts in the case."

The audience roared, the "huckleberry lawyer's" face was scarlet and his curly locks fairly bristled with embarrassment. The hearers were captivated and listened approvingly to a round scoring of the opponents of the "bolters."

He was a fearless advocate of temperance, or prohibition rather, of woman suffragists when they were weak, few and scoffed at, an abolitionist and a determined enemy of tobacco. I have seen him take his namesake among the grandchildren between his aged knees and say, "Don't ever eat tobacco, John; your grandfather wishes he had never touched it." His oft-repeated advice was heeded by this grandson, who never uses it in any form.

He was tall, slender, with snow-white hair and a speaking countenance full of the most glowing intelligence.

When the news came to the little village of Seattle that he had returned from Washington City, where he had been laboring to secure an appropriation for the Territorial University, two of his little grandchildren ran up the hill to meet him; he took off his high silk hat, his silvery hair shining in the fair sunlight and smiled a greeting, as they grasped either hand and fairly led him to their home.

A beautiful tribute from the friend before quoted closes this brief and inadequate sketch:

"He sleeps out yonder midway between the lakes (Washington and Union), where the shadows of the Cascades in the early morning fall upon the rounded mound of earth that marks his resting place, and the shadows of the Olympics in the early evening rest lovingly and caressingly on the same spot; there, where the song birds of the forest and the wild flowers and gentle zephyrs, laden with the perfume of the fir and cedar, pay a constant tribute to departed goodness and true worth."

SARAH LATIMER DENNY

The subject of this sketch was a Tennessean of an ancestry notable for staying qualities, religious steadfastness and solid character, as well as gracious and kindly bearing.

On her father's side she traced descent from the martyr,

Hugh Latimer, and although none of the name have been called to die at the stake in the latter days, Washington Latimer, nephew of Sarah Latimer Denny, was truly a martyr to principle, dying in Andersonville prison during the Rebellion.

The prevailing sentiment of the family was patriotic and strongly in favor of the abolition movement.

One of the granddaughters pleasurably recalls the vision of Joseph Latimer, father of Sarah, sitting in his dooryard, under the boughs of a great Balm of Gilead tree, reading his Bible.

Left to be the helper of her mother when very young, by the marriage of her elder sister, she quickly became a competent manager in household affairs, sensible of her responsibilities, being of a grave and quiet disposition.

She soon married a young Baptist minister, Richard Freeman Boren, whose conversion and call to the ministry were clear and decided. His first sermon was preached in the sitting room of a private house, where were assembled, among others, a number of his gay and pleasure-loving companions, whom he fearlessly exhorted to a holy life.

His hands were busy with his trade of cabinetmaking a part of the time, for the support of his family, although he rode from place to place to preach.

A few years of earnest Christian work, devoted affection and service to his family and he passed away to his reward, leaving the young widow with three little children, the youngest but eighteen months old.

In her old age she often reverted to their brief, happy life together, testifying that he never spoke a cross word to her.

She told of his premonition of death and her own remarkable dream immediately preceding that event.

While yet in apparently perfect health he disposed of all his tools, saying that he would not need them any more.

One night, toward morning, she dreamed that she saw a horse saddled and bridled at the gate and some one said to her that she must mount and ride to see her husband, who was very sick; she obeyed, in her dream, riding over a strange road, crossing a swollen stream at one point.

At daylight she awoke; a horse with side-saddle on was waiting and a messenger called her to go to her husband, as he was dangerously ill at a distant house. Exactly as in her dream she was conducted, she traversed the road and crossed the swollen stream to reach the place where he lay, stricken with a fatal malady.

After his death she returned to her father's house, but the family migrated from Tennessee to Illinois, spent their first winter in Sangamon County, afterward settling in Knox County.

There the brave young pioneer took up her abode in a log cabin on a piece of land which she purchased with the proceeds of her own hard toil.

The cabin was built without nails, of either oak or black walnut logs, it is not now known, with oak clapboards, braces and weight-poles and puncheon floor. There was one window without glass, a stick and clay mortar chimney, and a large, cheerful fireplace where the backlogs and fore-sticks held pyramids of dancing, ruddy flames, and the good cooking was done in the good old way.

By industry and thrift everything was turned to account. The ground was made to yield wheat, corn and flax; the last was taken through the whole process of manufacture into bed and table linen on the spot. Sheep were raised, the wool sheared, carded, spun, dyed and woven, all by hand, by this indefatigable worker, just as did many others of her time.

They made almost every article of clothing they wore,

besides cloth for sale.

Great, soft, warm feather beds comforted them in the cold Illinois winters, the contents of which were plucked from the home flock of geese.

As soon as the children were old enough, they assisted in planting corn and other crops.

The domestic supplies were almost entirely of home production and manufacture. Soap for washing owed its existence to the ash-hopper and scrap-kettle, and the soap-boiling was an important and necessary process. The modern housewife would consider herself much afflicted if she had to do such work.

And the sugar-making, which had its pleasant side, the sugar camp and its merry tenants.

About half a mile from the cabin stood the sugar maple grove to which this energetic provider went to tap the trees, collect the sap and finally boil the same until the "sugaring off." A considerable event it was, with which they began the busy season.

One of the daughters of Sarah Latimer Denny remembers that when a little child she went with her mother to the sugar camp where they spent the night. Resting on a bed of leaves, she listened to her mother as she sang an old camp meeting hymn, "Wrestling Jacob," while she toiled, mending the fire and stirring the sap, all night long under dim stars sprinkled in the naked branches overhead.

Other memories of childish satisfaction hold visions of the early breakfast when "Uncle John" came to see his widowed sister, who, with affectionate hospitality, set the "Johnny-cake" to bake on a board before the fire, made chocolate, fried the chicken and served them with snowy biscuits and translucent preserves.

For the huge fireplace, huge lengths of logs, for the back-logs, were cut, which required three persons to roll in place.

Cracking walnuts on the generous hearth helped to beguile the long winter evenings. A master might have beheld a worthy subject in the merry children and their mother thus occupied.

If other light were needed than the ruddy gleams the fire gave, it was furnished by a lard lamp hung by a chain and staple in the wall, or one of a pallid company of dipped candles.

Sometimes there were unwelcome visitors bent on helping themselves to the best the farm afforded; one day a wolf chased a chicken up into the chimney corner of the Boren cabin, to the consternation of the small children. Wolves also attacked the sheep alongside the cabin at the very moment when one of the family was trying to catch some lambs; such savage boldness brought hearty and justifiable screams from the young shepherdess thus engaged.

The products of the garden attached to this cabin are remembered as wonderful in richness and variety; the melons, squashes, pumpkins, etc., the fragrant garden herbs, the dill and caraway seeds for the famous seedcakes carried in grandmothers' pockets or "reticules." In addition to these, the wild fruits and game; haws, persimmons, grapes, plums, deer and wild turkey; the medicinal herbs, bone-set and blood-root; the nut trees heavily laden in autumn, all ministered to the comfort and health of the pioneers.

The mistress was known for her generous hospitality then, and throughout her life. In visiting and treating the sick she distanced educated practitioners in success. Never a violent partisan, she was yet a steadfast friend. One daughter has said that she never knew any one who came so near loving her neighbor as herself. Just, reasonable, kind, ever ready with sympathetic and wholesome advice, it was applicably said of her, "She openeth her mouth with wisdom and in her tongue is the law of kindness."

As the years went by the children were sent to school, the youngest becoming a teacher.

Toilsome years they were, but doubtless full of rich reward.

Afterward, while yet in the prime of life, she married John Denny, a Kentuckian and pioneer of Indiana, Illinois and finally of Oregon and Washington.

With this new alliance new fields of effort and usefulness opened before her. The unusual occurrence of a widowed mother and her two daughters marrying a widower and his two sons made this new tie exceeding strong. With them, as before stated, she crossed the plains and "pioneered it" in Oregon among the Waldo Hills, from whence she moved to Seattle on Puget Sound with her husband and little daughter, Loretta Denny, in 1859.

The shadow of pioneer days was scarcely receding, the place was a little straggling village and much remained of beginnings. As before in all other places, her busy hands found much to do; many a pair of warm stockings and mittens from her swift needles found their way into the possession of the numerous grand and great-grandchildren. In peaceful latter days she sat in a cozy corner with knitting basket at hand, her Bible in easy reach.

Her mind was clear and vigorous and she enjoyed reading and conversing upon topics old and new.

Her cottage home with its blooming plants, of which "Grandmother's calla," with its frequent, huge, snowy spathes, was much admired, outside the graceful laburnum tree and sweet-scented roses, was a place that became a Mecca to the tired feet and weary hearts of her kins-folk and acquaintances.

With devoted, filial affection her youngest daughter, S. Loretta Denny, remained with her until she entered into rest, February 10th, 1888.

CHAPTER III

DAVID THOMAS DENNY

DAVID THOMAS Denny was the first of the name to set foot upon the shores of Puget Sound. Born in Putnam County, Indiana, March 17th, 1832, he was nineteen years of age when he crossed the plains with his father's company in 1851. He is a descendant of an ancient family, English and Scotch, who moved to Ireland and thence to America, settling in Berk's County, Pa. His father was John Denny, a notable man in his time, a soldier of 1812, and a volunteer under William Henry Harrison.

The long, rough and toilsome journey across the plains was a schooling for the subsequent trials of pioneer life. Young as he was, he stood in the very forefront, the outmost skirmish line of his advancing detachment of the great army moving West. The anxious watch, the roughest toil, the reconnaissance fell to his lot. He drove a four-horse team, stood guard at night, alternately sleeping on the ground, under the wagon, hunted for game to aid in their sustenance, and, briefly, served his company in many ways with the energy and faithfulness which characterized his subsequent career.

With his party he reached Portland in August, 1851; from thence, with J. N. Low, he made his way to Olympia on Puget Sound, where he arrived footsore and weary, they having traveled on foot the Hudson Bay Company's trail from the Columbia River. From Olympia, with Low, Lee Terry, Captain Fay and others, he journeyed in an open boat to Duwampsh Head, which has suffered many changes of name, where they camped, sleeping under the boughs of a great cedar tree the first night, September 25th, 1851.

The next day Denny, Terry and Low made use of the skill and knowledge of the native inhabitants by hiring two young Indians to take them up the Duwampsh River in their canoe. He was left to spend the following night with the two Indians, as his companions had wandered so far away that they could not return, but remained at an Indian camp farther up the river. On the 28th they were reunited and returned to their first camp, from which they removed the same day to Alki Point.

A cabin was commenced and after a time, Low and Terry returned to Portland, leaving David Thomas Denny, nineteen years of age, the only white person on Elliott Bay. There were then swarms of Indians on the Sound.

For three weeks he held this outpost of civilization, a part of the time being far from well. So impressed was he with the defenselessness of the situation that he expressed himself as "sorry" when his friends landed from the schooner *Exact* at Alki Point on the 13th of November, 1851. No doubt realizing that an irretrievable step had been taken, he tried to reassure them by explaining that "the cabin was unfinished and that they would not be comfortable." Many incidents of his early experience are recorded in this volume elsewhere.

He was married on the 23rd of January, 1853, to Miss Louisa

Boren, one of the most intelligent, courageous and devoted of pioneer women. They were the first white couple married in Seattle. He was an explorer of the eastern side of Elliott Bay, but was detained at home in the cabin by lameness occasioned by a cut on his foot, when A. A. Denny, W. N. Bell and C. D. Boren took their claims, so had fourth choice.

For this reason his claim awaited the growth of the town of Seattle many years, but finally became very valuable.

It was early discovered by the settlers that he was a conscientious man; so well established was this fact that he was known by the sobriquet of "Honest Dave."

Like all the other pioneers, he turned his hand to any useful thing that was available, cutting and hewing timber for export, clearing a farm, hauling wood, tending cattle, anything honorable; being an advocate of total abstinence and prohibition, *he never kept a saloon.*

He has done all in his power to discountenance the sale and use of intoxicants, the baleful effects of which were manifest among both whites and Indians.

Every movement in the early days seems to have been fraught with danger. D. T. Denny traveled in a canoe with two Indians from the Seattle settlement in July, 1852, to Bush's Prairie, back of Olympia, to purchase cattle for A. A. Denny, carrying two hundred dollars in gold for that purpose. He risked his life in so doing, as he afterward learned that the Indians thought of killing him and taking the money, but for some unknown reason decided not to do the deed.

He was a volunteer during the Indian war of 1855-6, in Company C, and with his company was not far distant when Lieut. Slaughter was killed, with several others. Those who survived the attack were rescued by this company.

On the morning of the battle of Seattle, he was standing

guard near Fort Decatur; the most thrilling moment of the day to him was probably that in which he helped his wife and child into the fort as they fled from the Indians.

Although obliged to fight the Indians in self-defense in their warlike moods, yet he was ever their true friend and esteemed by them as such. He learned to speak the native tongue fluently, in such manner as to be able to converse with all the neighboring tribes, and unnumbered times, through years of disappointment, sorrow and trouble, they sought his advice and sympathy.

For a quarter of a century the hand-to-hand struggle went on by the pioneer and his family, to conquer the wilds, win a subsistence and obtain education.

By thrift and enterprise they attained independence, and as they went along helped to lay the foundations of many institutions and enterprises of which the commonwealth is now justly proud.

David Thomas Denny possessed the gifts and abilities of a typical pioneer; a good shot, his trusty rifle provided welcome articles of food; he could make, mend and invent useful and necessary things for pioneer work; it was a day, in fact, when "Adam delved" and "Eve" did likewise, and no man was too fine a "gentleman" to do any sort of work that was required.

Having the confidence of the community, he was called upon to fill many positions of trust; he was a member of the first Board of Trustees of Seattle, Treasurer of King County, Regent of the Territorial University, Probate Judge, School Director, etc., etc.

Although a Republican and an abolitionist, he did not consider every Democrat a traitor, and thereby incurred the enmity of some. Party feeling ran high.

At that time (during the Rebellion) there stood on Pioneer Place in Seattle a very tall flagstaff. Upon the death of a prominent Democrat it was proposed to half-mast the flag on this staff, but during the night the halyards were cut, it was supposed by a woman, at the instigation of her husband and others, but the friends of the deceased hired "Billie" Fife, a well-known cartoonist and painter, to climb to the top and rig a new rope, a fine sailor feat, for which he received twenty dollars.

The first organizer of Good Templar Lodges was entertained at Mr. Denny's house, and he, with several of the family, became charter members of the first organization on October 4th, 1866. He was the first chaplain of the first lodge of I. O. G. T. organized in Seattle.

In after years the subject of this sketch became prominent in the Prohibition movement; it was suggested to him at one time that he permit his name to be used as Prohibition candidate for Governor of the State of Washington, but the suggestion was never carried out. He would have considered it an honor to be defeated in a good cause.

He also became a warm advocate of equal suffrage, and at both New York and Omaha M. E. general conferences he heartily favored the admission of women lay delegates, and much regretted the adverse decision by those in authority.

The old pioneers were and are generally broad, liberal and progressive in their ideas and principles; they found room and opportunity to think and act with more freedom than in the older centers of civilization, consequently along every line they are in the forefront of modern thought.

For its commercial development, Seattle owes much to David Thomas Denny, and others like him, in perhaps a lesser degree. In the days of small beginnings, he recognized the

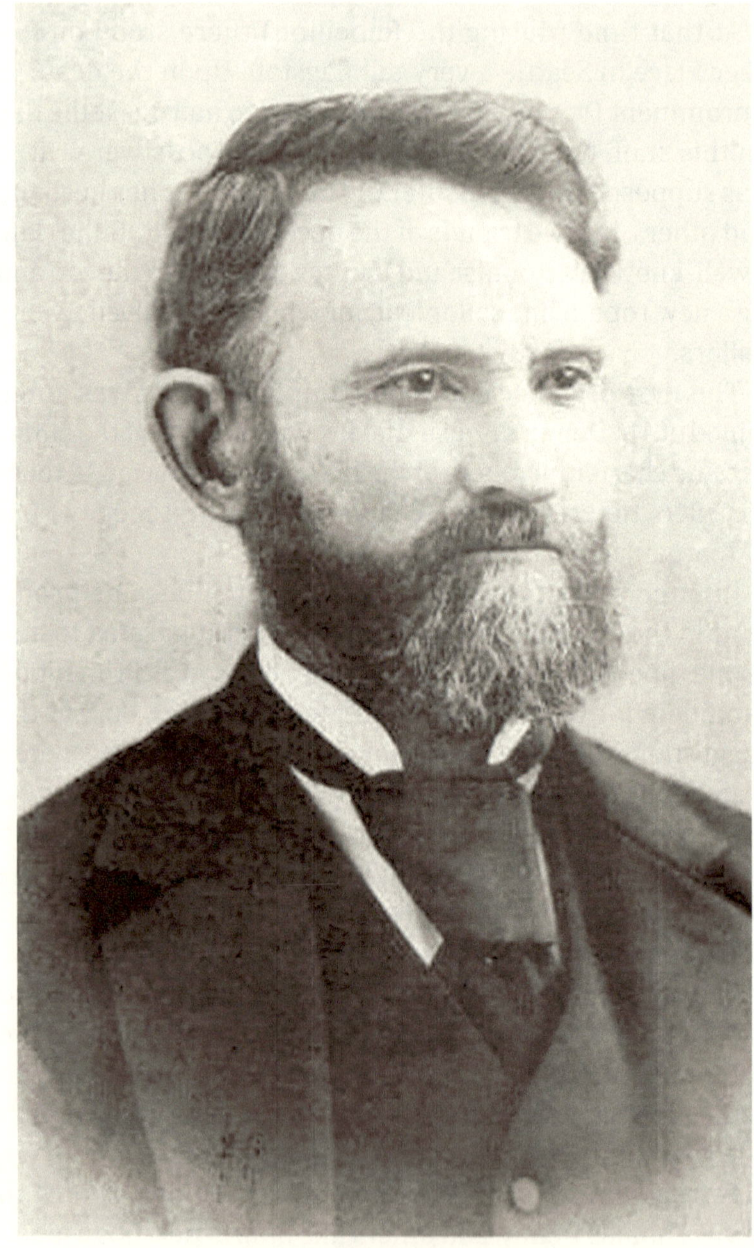

DAVID THOMAS DENNY

possibilities of development in the little town so fortunately located. His hard-earned wealth, energy and talents have been freely given to make the city of the present as well as that which it will be.

D. T. Denny made a valuable gift to the city of Seattle in a plot of land in the heart of the best residence portion of the city. Many years ago it was used as a cemetery, but was afterward vacated and is now a park. He landed on the site of Seattle with twenty-five cents in his pocket. His acquirement of wealth after years of honest work was estimated at three million.

Not only his property, money, thought and energy have gone into the building up of Seattle, but hundreds of people, newly arrived, have occupied his time in asking information and advice in regard to their settling in the West.

He was president of the first street railway company of Seattle, and afterward spent thousands of dollars on a large portion of the system of cable and electric roads of which the citizens of Seattle are wont to boast, unknowing, careless or forgetting that what is their daily convenience impoverished those who built, equipped and operated them. He and his company owned and operated for a time the Consolidated Electric road to North Seattle, Cedar Street and Green Lake; the cable road to Queen Anne Hill, and built and equipped the "Third Street and Suburban" electric road to the University and Ravenna Park.

The building and furnishing of a large sawmill with the most approved modern machinery, the establishing of an electric light plant, furnishing a water supply to a part of the city, and in many other enterprises he was actively engaged.

For many years he paid into the public treasury thousands of dollars for taxes on his unimproved, unproductive real estate, a considerable portion of which was unjustly required and exacted, as it was impossible to have sold the property at its assessed valuation. As one old settler said, he paid "robber taxes."

When, in the great financial panic that swept over the country in 1893, he obtained a loan of the city treasurer and mortgaged to secure it real estate worth at least three times the sum borrowed, the mob cried out against him and sent out his name as one who had robbed the city, forsooth!

This was not the only occasion when the canaille expressed their disapproval.

Previous to, and during the anti-Chinese riot in Seattle, which occurred on Sunday, February 7th, 1886, he received a considerable amount of offensive attention. In the dark district of Seattle, there gathered one day a forerunner of the greater mob which created so much disturbance, howling that they would burn him out. "We'll burn his barn," they yelled, their provocation being that he employed Chinese house servants and rented ground to Mongolian gardeners. The writer remembers that it was a fine garden, in an excellent state of cultivation. No doubt many of the agitators themselves had partaken of the products thereof many times, it being one of the chief sources of supply of the city.

The threats were so loud and bitter against the friends of the Chinese that it was felt necessary to post a guard at his residence. The eldest son was in Oregon, attending the law school of the University; the next one, D. Thos. Denny, Jr., not yet of age, served in the militia during the riot; the third and youngest remained at home ready to help defend the same. The outlook was dark, but after some serious remarks concerning the condition of things, Mr. Denny went up stairs and brought down his Winchester rifle, stood it in a near corner and calmly resumed his reading. As he had dealt with savages before, he stood his ground. At a notorious trial of white men for unprovoked murder of Chinese, it was brought out that "Mr. David Denny, he 'fliend' (friend) of Chinese, Injun and Nigger."

During the time that his great business called for the employment of a large force of men, he was uniformly kind to them, paying the highest market price for their labor. Some were faithful and honest, some were not; instead of its being a case of "greedy millionaire," it was a case of just the opposite thing, as it was well known that he was robbed time and again by dishonest employes.

When urged to close down his mill, as it was running behind, he said "I can't do it, it will throw a hundred men out of employment and their families will suffer." So he borrowed money, paying a ruinous rate of interest, and kept on, hoping that business would improve; it did not and the mill finally went under. A good many employes who received the highest wages for the shortest hours, struck for more, and others were full of rage when the end came and there were only a few dollars due on their wages.

Neither was he a "heartless landlord," the heartlessness was on the other side, as numbers of persons sneaked off without paying their rent, and many built houses, the lumber in which was never paid for.

According to their code it was not *stealing* to rob a person supposed to be wealthy.

The common remark was, "Old Denny can stand it, he's got lots of money."

The anarchist-communistic element displayed their strength and venom in many ways in those days. They heaped abuse on those, who unfortunately for themselves, employed men, and bit the hand that fed them.

Their cry was "Death to Capitalists!" They declared their intention at one time of hanging the leading business men of Seattle, breaking the vaults of the bank open, burning the records and dividing lands and money among themselves. But the reign of martial law at the culmination of their heroic efforts in the Anti-Chinese riot, brought them to their senses, the history of which period may be told in another chapter.

From early youth, David Thomas Denny was a faithful member of the M. E. Church, serving often in official capacity and rendering valuable assistance, with voice, hand and pocketbook. Twice he was sent as lay delegate to the General Conference, a notable body of representative men, of which he was a member in 1888 and again in 1892.

The conference of 1888 met in New York City and held its sessions at the Metropolitan Opera House. His family accompanied him, crossing the continent by the Canadian Pacific R. R. by way of Montreal to New York.

In the latter place, they met their first great sorrow, in the death, after a brief illness, of the beloved youngest daughter, the return and her burial in her native land by the sundown seas. Soon followed other days of sadness and trial; in less than a year, the second daughter, born in Fort Decatur, passed away, and others of the family, hovered on the brink of the grave, but happily were restored.

Loss of fortune followed loss of friends as time went on, but these storms passed and calm returned. He went steadfastly on, confident of the rest that awaits the people of God.

At the age of sixty-seven he was wide awake, alert and capable of enduring hardships, no doubt partly owing to a temperate life. In late years he interested himself in mining and was hopeful of his own and his friends' future, and that of the state he helped to found.

While sojourning in the Cascade Mountains in 1891, David T. Denny wrote the following:

"Ptarmigan Park: On Sept. 25th, 1851, just forty years ago, Leander Terry, an older brother of C. C. Terry, John N. Low and I, landed on what has since been known as Freeport Point, now West Seattle. We found Chief Sealth with his tribe stopping on the beach and fishing for salmon—a quiet, dignified man was Sealth.

"We camped on the Point and slept under a large cedar tree, and the next morning hired a couple of young Indians to take us up the Duwampsh River; stayed one night at the place which was afterward taken for a claim by E. B. Maple, then returned and camped one night at our former place on the Point; then on the morning of the 28th of September went around to Alki Point and put down the foundation of the first cabin started in what is now King County. Looking out over Elliott Bay at that time the site where Seattle now stands, was an unbroken forest with no mark made by the hand of man except a little log fort made by the Indians, standing near the corner of Commercial and Mill Streets.

"Since that day we have had our Indian war, the Crimean war has been fought, the war between Prussia and Austria, that between France and Prussia, the great Southern Rebellion and many smaller wars.

"Then to think of the wonderful achievements in the use of electricity and the end is not yet.

"I should like to live another forty years just to see the growth of the Sound country, if nothing else. I fully believe it is destined to be the most densely populated and wealthiest of the United States. One thing that leads me to this conclusion is the evidence of a large aboriginal population which subsisted on the natural productions of the land and water. Reasoning by comparison, what a vast multitude can be supported by an intelligent use of the varied resources of the country and the world to draw from besides."

And again he wrote:

"Ptarmigan Park, Sept. 28th, 1891: Just forty years ago yesterday, J. N. Low, Lee Terry and myself laid the foundation of the first cabin started in what is now King County, Washington, then Thurston County, Oregon Territory.

"Vast have been the changes since that day.

"Looking back it does not seem so very long ago and yet children born since that have grown to maturity, married, and reared families.

"Many of those who came to Elliott Bay are long since gone to their last home. Lee Terry has been dead thirty-five years, Capt. Robert Fay, twenty or more years, and J. N. Low over two years, in fact most of the early settlers have passed away: John Buckley and wife, Jacob Maple, S. A. Maple, Wm. N. Bell and wife, C. C. Terry and wife, A. Terry, L. M. Collins and wife, Mrs. Kate Butler, E. Hanford, Mother Holgate, John Holgate and many others. If they could return to Seattle now they would not know the place, and yet had it not been for various hindrances, the Indian war, the opposition of the N. P. R. R. and the great fire, Seattle would be much larger than it now is, the country would be much more developed and we would have a larger rural population.

"However, from this time forward, I fully believe the process of development will move steadily on, especially do I believe that we are just commencing the development of the mineral resources of the country. Undoubtedly there has been more prospecting for the precious metals during 1891 than ever before all put together.

"In the Silver Creek region there has been, probably, six hundred claims taken and from all accounts the outlook is very favorable. Also from Cle Elum and Swauk we have glowing accounts.

"In the Ptarmigan Park district about fifty claims have been taken, a large amount of development work done and some very fine samples of ore taken out."

(Signed) D. T. Denny

In the *Seattle Daily Times* of September 25th, 1901:

JUST FIFTY YEARS AGO TODAY

On September 25, 1851, Mr. D. T. Denny, Now Living in This City, Was Greeted on the Shores of Elliott Bay by Chief Seattle.

Fifty years ago today, the first white settlers set foot in King County.

Fifty years ago today, a little band of pioneers rounded Alki Point and grounded their boat at West Seattle. Chief Seattle stalked majestically down the beach and greeted them in his characteristic way. During the ensuing week they were guests of a Western sachem, the king of Puget Sound waters, and never were white men more royally entertained.

At that time Chief Seattle was at the height of his popularity. With a band of five hundred braves behind him, he stood in a position to command the respect of all wandering tribes and of the first few white men, whose heart-hungering and restlessness had driven them from the civilization of the East, across the plains of the Middle West, to the shores of the Pacific.

As Mr. Denny is essentially the premier of this country, it would not be out of order to give a glimpse of his early history. He is the true type of pioneer. Although he is somewhat bent with age, and his hair is white with the snows of many winters, nevertheless, he still shows signs of that ruggedness that was with him in the early Western days of his youth. Not only is he a pioneer, but he came from a family of pioneers. Years and years ago his ancestors crossed the Atlantic and landed on the Atlantic coast. Not satisfied with the prevailing conditions there, they began to push westward, settling in what is now Pennsylvania. As the country became opened up and settled, this Denny family of hardy pioneers again turned their faces to the westward sun, and this time Indiana made them a home, and still later Illinois.

THE START WESTWARD

It was in the latter state that Mr. D. T. Denny and his brother first began to hear stories of the Willamette valley. Wonderful tales were being carried across the plains of the fertility of the land around the Columbia River and the spirit of restlessness that had been characteristic of their ancestors began to tell upon them, and after reading all they could find of this practically unknown wilderness, they bade farewell to their Illinois friends, and started off across the plains.

The start was made on the 10th day of April, 1851, from Knox County, Illinois. D. T. Denny was accompanied by his older brother A. A. Denny, and family. They drove two four-horse teams, and a two-horse wagon, and ten days after the start had been made they crossed the Missouri River. The fourth of July, 1851, found them at Fort Hall on Snake River, Montana, an old Hudson Bay trading station. On the 11th day of August, they reached The Dalles, Oregon, and there, after a brief consultation, they decided to separate.

Mr. A. A. Denny here shipped the wagons and his family down the river on some small vessel they were fortunate enough to find there, while Mr. D. T. Denny took the horses and pushed over the Cascade Mountains. He followed what was then known as the old Barlow road and reached Portland on the 17th day of August.

They decided to stay in Portland for a few days, until they could learn more about the country than they then knew, and it was in that city that the subject of this sketch worked his first day for money. He helped Thomas Carter unload a brig that had reached port from Boston, receiving the sum of three dollars for his labors, and it was the "biggest three dollars he ever earned in his life," so he said.

While at Portland they began to hear stories of Puget Sound, and after a brief consultation, the Denny brothers and Mr. John N. Low, who had also made the journey across the plains, decided to investigate the country that now lies around the Queen City of the West.

OFF FOR ELLIOTT BAY

As A. A. Denny had his family to look after, it was decided that Mr. Low and D. T. Denny would make the trip, and as a consequence, on the 10th day of September they ferried Low's stock across the river to what was then Fort Vancouver. From there they followed the Hudson Bay trail to the Cowlitz River, and up the Cowlitz to Ford's Prairie. Leaving their stock there for a short time, they pushed on to Olympia, now the capital of the state.

When they reached Olympia they found Capt. R. C. Fay and George M. Martin on the point of leaving down Sound to fish for salmon, and Messrs. Low, Denny and Terry arranged to come as far as the Duwamish River with them. The start was made. There was no fluttering of flags nor booming of cannon such as marked the departure of Columbus when he left for a new country, and in fact this little band of men, in an open boat, little dreamed that they would ultimately land within a stone's throw of what was destined to become one of the greatest cities in the West.

Fifty years ago today they camped with Chief Seattle on the promontory across the bay. They slept that night under the protecting branches of a cedar tree, and on the morning of the 26th they hired two of Seattle's braves to paddle them up the river in a dugout canoe. They spent that day in looking over the river bottoms, where are now situated the towns of Maple Prairie and Van Asselt. There were no settlements there then, and nothing but giant pines and firs greeted their gaze for miles. It was a wonderful sight to these hardy Eastern men, and as they wished to know something more of the country, Messrs. Low and Terry decided to leave the canoe and depart on a short tour of exploration. One, two and three hours passed and they failed to put in an appearance. In vain did Mr. Denny fire his gun, and yell himself hoarse, but he was compelled to spend the night in the wilderness with the two Indians.

DECIDED TO LOCATE

The next day, however, or to be explicit, on the 27th of September, he was gratified at the appearance of his friends on the river bank. They had become lost the night before, and falling in with a band of Indians, had spent the night with them. Having seen enough of the country to become convinced that it was the place for them, they returned to what is now West Seattle for the night. After the sun had disappeared behind the Olympics, they heard a scow passing the point, which afterwards they found contained L. M. Collins and family, who had pushed on up the river and settled on the banks of the Duwamish.

On the morning of the 28th they decided to take up claims back of Alki point, and on that day started to lay the foundation of the first cabin in King county. Having decided to settle on Elliott bay, Mr. Low determined to return to Portland for his family, whereupon Mr. Denny wrote the following letter to his brother and sent it with him:

"We have examined the valley of the Duwamish river and find it a fine country. There is plenty of room for one thousand settlers. Come on at once."

By the time Mr. Low had reached Portland, William Bell and C. D. Boren had also become interested in the Puget Sound district, and therefore Messrs. Low, Denny, Bell and Boren, with their families, hired a schooner to take them down the Columbia, up on the outside, in through the Strait, and up the Sound to Alki, reaching the latter point on the 13th of November, 1851.

In speaking of those early pioneer days, Mr. Denny said:

"We built up quite a settlement over on Alki, and the Indians of course came and settled around us. No, we were not molested to any great extent. I remember that on one night, our women folks missed a lot of clothing they had hung out to dry, and I at once went to their big chief and told him what had happened. In a very short time not only were the missing articles returned to us, but a lot that we didn't know were gone."

WHISKY CAUSED TROUBLE

"In those early days, in all my experience with Indians, I have always found them peaceable enough as long as they left whisky alone. Of course we had trouble with them, but it was always due to the introduction of the white man's firewater, which has been more than a curse to the red man.

"When we reached here, the Indians were more advanced than one would have naturally supposed. We were able to buy berries, fish and game of them, and potatoes also. Great fine tubers they were too, much better than any we had ever been able to raise back in Illinois. In fact I don't know what we would have done during the first two winters had it not been for the Indians.

"But talk about game," he continued, a glow coming to his face as the old scenes were brought up to him, "why, I have seen the waters of Elliott Bay fairly black with ducks. Deer and bear were plentiful then and this was a perfect paradise for the man with a rod or gun. Never, I am sure, was there a country in which it was so easy to live as it was in the Puget Sound district fifty years ago."

"In coming across the plains, Mr. Denny, were you attacked by Indians, or have any adventures out of the ordinary?" was asked.

"Well," said he meditatively, "we did have one little brush that might have ended with the loss of all our lives. It was just after leaving Fort Hall, in Montana. We had come up to what I think was called the American Falls. While quite a distance away we noticed the water just below the falls was black, with what we supposed were ducks, but as we drew nearer we saw they were Indians swimming across with one hand and holding their guns high in the air with the other. We turned off slightly and started down the trail at a rattling rate. We had not gone far when a big chief stepped up on the bank. He was dressed mainly in a tall plug hat and a gun, and he shouted, 'How do, how do, stop, stop!' Well, we didn't, and after repeating his question he dropped behind the sage brush and opened fire.

"My brother lay in my wagon sick with mountain fever, and that, of course, materially reduced our fighting force. Had they succeeded in shooting down one of our horses, it would, of course, have been the end of us, but fortunately they did not and we at last escaped them. No, no one was wounded, but it was the worst scrape I ever had with the Indians, and I hope I will never have to go through a similar experience again. It isn't pleasant to be shot at, even by an Indian."

RECOGNIZED THE SPOT

"In 1892," said Mr. Denny, "I went East over the Great Northern. I was thinking of my first experience in Montana when I reached that state, when all of a sudden we rounded a curve and passed below the falls. I knew them in a minute, and instantly those old scenes and trying times came back to me in a way that was altogether too realistic for comfort. No, I have not been back since.

"Mr. Prosch, Mr. Ward and myself," continued this old pioneer, "had intended to take our families over to Alki today and hold a sort of a picnic in honor of what happened fifty years ago, but of course my sickness has prevented us from doing so. I don't suppose we will be here to celebrate the event at the end of another fifty years, and I should have liked to have gone today. Instead, I suppose I shall sit here and think of what I saw and heard at Alki Point just fifty years ago. I can live it over again, in memories at least.

"Now, young man," concluded Mr. Denny, not unkindly, "please get the names of those early pioneers and the dates right. A Seattle paper published a bit of this history a few days ago, and they got everything all mixed up. This is the story, and should be written right, because if it isn't, the story becomes valueless. I dislike very much to have the stories and events of those early days misstated and misrepresented."

In 1899, Mr. Denny had the arduous task of personally superintending the improvement of the old Snoqualmie road around the shore of Lake Kichelas and on for miles through the mountains, building and repairing bridges, making corduroy, blasting out rocks, changing the route at times; after much patient effort and endurance of discomfort and hardship, he left it much improved, for which many a weary way-farer would be grateful did they but know. In value the work was far beyond the remuneration he received.

During the time he was so occupied he had a narrow escape from death by an accident, the glancing of a double-bitted ax in the hands of a too energetic workman; it struck him between the eyes, inflicting a wound which bled alarmingly, but finally was successfully closed.

The next year he camped at Lake Kichelas in the interests of a mining company, and incidentally enjoyed some fishing and prospecting. It was the last time he visited the mountains.

Gradually some maladies which had haunted him for years increased. As long as he could he exerted himself in helping his family, especially in preparing the site for a new home. He soon after became a great sufferer for several years, struggling against his infirmities, in all exhibiting great fortitude and patience.

His mind was clear to the last and he was able to converse, to read and to give sound and admirable advice and opinions.

Almost to the last day of his life he took interest in the progress of the nation and of the world, following the great movements with absorbing interest.

He expressed a desire to see his friends earnest Christians, his own willingness to leave earthly scenes and his faith in

Jesus.

So he lived and thus he died, passing away on the morning of November 25th, 1903, in the seventy-second year of his age.

He was a great pioneer, a mighty force, commercial, moral and religious, in the foundation-building of the Northwest.

In a set of resolutions presented by the Pioneer Association of the State of Washington occur these words: "The record of no citizen was ever marked more distinctly by acts of probity, integrity and general worth than that of Mr. D. T. Denny, endearing him to all the people and causing them to regard him with the utmost esteem and favor."

On the morning of November 26th, 1903, there appeared in the *Post-Intelligencer,* the following:

"David Thomas Denny, who came to the site of Seattle in 1851, the first of his name on Puget Sound, died at his home, a mile north of Green Lake, at 3:36 yesterday morning. All the members of his family, including John Denny, who arrived the day before from Alaska, were at the bedside. Until half an hour before he passed away Mr. Denny was conscious, and engaged those about him in conversation."

MARRIED IN A CABIN

The story of the early life of the Denny brothers tallies very nearly with the history of Seattle. Mr. and Mrs. David Denny were married in a cabin on the north end of A. A. Denny's claim near the foot of Lenora street, January 23, 1853. The next morning the couple moved to their own cabin—built by the husband's hands—at the foot of what is now Denny Way. The moving was accomplished in a canoe.

Though they professed a great respect for David Denny, the Indians were numerous and never very reliable. In a year or two, therefore, the family moved up nearer the sawmill and little settlement which had grown up near the foot of Cherry street. D. T. Denny had meanwhile staked out a very large portion of what is now North Seattle—a plat of three hundred and twenty acres. Later he made seven additions to the city of Seattle from this claim. In 1857 it was a wilderness of thick brush, but the pioneer moved his family to his farm on the present site of Recreation park in that year. The Indian war had occurred the winter before and the red men were quiet, having received a lesson from the blue jackets which were landed from the United States gunboat Decatur.

Three or four years later the family moved to a cottage at the corner of Second avenue and Seneca street. In the early '70s they moved to the large home at the corner of Dexter and Republican streets, where the children grew up. In 1890 the family took possession of the large house standing on Queen Anne avenue, known as the Denny home, which was occupied by the family until a few years ago, when they moved to Fremont and later to the house where Mr. Denny died, in Licton Park, some distance north of Green Lake.

Until about ten years ago David T. Denny was considered the wealthiest man in Seattle. His large property in the north end of the city had been the source of more and more revenue as the town grew. When the needs of the town became those of a big city he hastened to supply them with energy and money. His mill on the shores of Lake Union was the largest in the city, when Seattle was first known as a milling town. The establishment of an electric light plant and a water supply to a part of the city were among the enterprises which he headed.

The cable and horse car roads were consolidated into a company headed by D. T. Denny more than a decade ago. In the effort to supply the company with the necessary funds Mr.

Denny attempted to convert much of his property into cash. At that time an estimate of his resources was made by a close personal friend, who yesterday said that the amount was considerably over three million dollars, which included his valuable stock in the traction companies. In the hard times of '93 Mr. Denny was unable to realize the apparent value of his property, and a considerable reduction of his fortune was a result. Since then he has been to a great extent engaged in mining in the Cascade mountains, and for the past three years has been closely confined to his home by a serious illness.

Among the gifts of D. T. Denny to the city of Seattle is Denny Park. Denny Way, the Denny school and other public places in Seattle bear his name. D. T. Denny was a liberal Republican always. He was at one time a member of the board of regents of the territorial university, the first treasurer of King county, probate judge for two years and for twelve years a school director of District No. 1, comprising the city of Seattle.

Several of those who were associated with David T. Denny during the time when he was in active business and a strong factor in local affairs have offered estimates of his character and of the part he took in the founding and building of the city. Said Col. William T. Prosser:

"It is sad to think that David T. Denny will no more be seen upon the streets of the city he assisted in founding more than fifty years ago. During all that time he was closely identified with its varying periods of danger, delayed hopes and bitter disappointments, as well as those of marvelous growth, activity and prosperity. The changing features of the city were reflected in his own personal history. The waves of prosperity and adversity both swept over him, yet throughout his entire career he always maintained his integrity and through it all he bore himself as an energetic and patriotic citizen and as a Christian gentleman."

Judge Thomas Burke:

"D. T. Denny had great faith in Seattle, and his salient characteristic was his readiness in pushing forward its welfare. I remember him having an irreproachable character—honest, just in all his dealings and strong in his spirit. In illustration of his strong feeling on the temperance question I remember that he embodied a clause in the early deeds of the property which he sold to the effect that no intoxicating liquors were to be sold upon the premises. Yes, he was a good citizen."

Charles A. Prosch:

"Although Mr. Denny's later years were clouded by financial troubles, reverses did not soil his spirit nor change his integrity. He was progressive to the last and one of the most upright men I know."

D. B. Ward:

"I first met David Denny in 1859 and I have known him more or less intimately ever since. I know him to have possessed strict integrity, unswerving purpose and cordial hospitality. My first dinner in Seattle was eaten at his home—where a baked salmon fresh from the Sound was an oddity to me. His financial troubles some years ago grew out of his undaunted public spirit. He was president of the first consolidated street car system here, and in his efforts to support it most of his property was confiscated. I knew him for a strong, able man."

Judge Orange Jacobs:

"Mr. Denny was a quiet man, but he carried the stamp of truth. He was extremely generous, and as I remember, he possessed a fine mind. In his death I feel a personal, poignant grief."

Rev. W. S. Harrington:

"D. T. Denny was a man of much more than average ability. He thought much and deeply on all questions which affected the welfare of man. He was retiring and his strength was known to few. But his integrity was thorough and transparent and his purpose inflexible. Even though he suffered, his spirit was never bitter toward his fellows, and his benefactions were numerous. Above all, he was a Christian and believed in a religion which he sought to live, not to exhibit. His long illness was borne with a patience and a sweetness which commanded my deep respect and admiration."

Samuel L. Crawford:

"A man with the courage to fight for his convictions of right and with a marvelous capacity for honest work—such is the splendid heritage David T. Denny has left to his sorrowing family. When but 19 years of age he walked from the Columbia river to Puget Sound, driving a small band of stock ahead of him through the brush.

"No sooner had his party settled and the log cabin been completed than David commenced looking for more work, and, like all others who seek diligently, he was successful, for early in December of that year the brig Leonesa, Capt. Daniel S. Howard, stopped at Alki Point, seeking a cargo of piling for San Francisco. David T. Denny, William N. Bell, C. D. Boren, C. C. Terry, J. N. Low, A. A. Denny and Lee Terry took the contract of cutting the piling and loading the vessel, which they accomplished in about two weeks, a remarkably short time, when the weather and the lack of teams and other facilities are taken into consideration.

"Other vessels came for cargo and Mr. Denny became an expert woodsman, helping to supply them with piling from the shores. In 1852 Mr. Denny, in company with his brother

Arthur and some others, came over to Elliott Bay and laid the foundation of Seattle, the great city of the future. Mr. Denny, being a bachelor, took the most northerly claim, adjoining that of W. N. Bell, and built a cabin near the shore, at the foot of what is now Denny Way. The Indians being troublesome, he moved into a small house beside that of his brother on the site of the present Stevens Hotel.

"In the meantime he married a sister of C. D. Boren, and a small family commenced to spring up around him, thus requiring larger quarters. In 1871 Mr. Denny built a large frame house on the southwest shore of Lake Union, on a beautiful knoll. He cleared up a large portion of his claim, and for many years engaged in farming and stock-raising. He afterward built a palatial home on his property at the foot of Queen Anne Hill, midway between Lake Union and the Sound, but this he occupied only a short time. In 1852, in company with his brother Arthur, Mr. Denny discovered Salmon Bay.

"Mr. Denny was a just man and always dealt fairly with the Indians. For this reason the Indians learned to love and respect him, and for many years they have gone to him to settle their disputes and help them out of their difficulties with the whites and among themselves.

"As Seattle grew, David Denny platted much of his claim and sold it off in town lots. He built the Western mill at the south end of Lake Union and engaged extensively in the building and promotion of street railways. He had too many irons in the fire, and when the panic came in 1892-3 it crippled him financially, but he gave up his property, the accumulation of a lifetime of struggle and work, to satisfy his creditors, and went manfully to work in the mountains of Washington to regain his lost fortune. His heroic efforts were rapidly being crowned with success, as he is known to have secured a number of mines of great promise, on which he has done a large amount of development work during the past few years.

"In the death of David T. Denny, Seattle loses an upright, generous worker, who has always contributed of his brain, brawn and cash for the upbuilding of the city of which he was one of the most important founders."

DEXTER HORTON'S TRIBUTE

"'I have known Mr. Denny for fifty years. A mighty tree has fallen. He was one of the best men, of highest character and principle, this city ever claimed as a citizen. That is enough.'

"By Father F. X. Prefontaine, of the Church of Our Lady of Good Help: 'I have known Mr. Denny about thirty-six or thirty-seven years. I always liked him, though I was more intimately acquainted with his brother, Hon. A. A. Denny, and his venerable father, John Denny. His father in his time impressed me as a fine gentleman, a great American. He was a man who was always called upon at public meetings for a speech and he was a deeply earnest man, so much so that tears often showed in his eyes while he was addressing the people.'

"Hon. Boyd J. Tallman, judge of the Superior Court: 'I have only known Mr. Denny since 1889, and I always entertained the highest regard for him. He was a man of firm conviction and principle and was always ready to uphold them. Though coming here to help found the town, he was always ready to advocate and stand for the principle of prohibition and temperance on all occasions. While there were many who could not agree with him in these things, every manly man felt bound to accord to Mr. Denny honesty of purpose and respect for the sincerity of his opinion. I believe that in his death a good man has gone and this community has suffered a great loss.'"

C. B. BAGLEY TALKS

"Clarence B. Bagley, who as a boy and man has known Mr. Denny for almost the full number of years the latter lived at Seattle, was visibly overcome at the news of his death. Mr. Bagley would gladly have submitted a more extended estimate than he did of Mr. Denny's life and character, but he was just hurrying into court to take his place as a juryman.

"'Mr. Denny was one of the best men Seattle ever had. He was a liberal man, ever ready to embark his means in enterprises calculated to upbuild and aid in the progress of Seattle. He was a man of strong convictions, strong almost to obstinacy in upholding and maintaining cherished principles he fully believed.

"'Mr. Denny suffered reverses through his willingness to establish enterprises for the good of the whole city. He built the Western Mill at Lake Union when the location was away in the woods, and eventually lost a great deal of money in it during the duller periods of the city's life. He also lost a great deal of money in giving this city a modern street railway system. His character as an honorable man and Christian always stood out boldly, his integrity of purpose never questioned.'

"Lawrence J. Colman, son of J. M. Colman, the pioneer, said: 'Our family has known Mr. Denny for thirty-one years, ever since coming to Seattle. We regarded him as an absolutely upright, conscientious and Christian man, notwithstanding the reverses that came to him, in whom our confidence was supreme, and one who did not require his character to be upheld, for it shone brightly at all times by its own lustre.'"

SAMUEL COOMBS TALKS

"S. F. Coombs, the well-known pioneer, had known Mr. Denny since 1859, about forty-five years. 'It was to Mr. Denny,' said Mr. Coombs, 'that the Indians who lived here and knew him always went for advice and comfort and to have their disputes settled. Their high estimate of the man was shown in many ways, where the whites were under consideration. Mr. Denny was a man whom I always admired and greatly respected. He afforded me much information of the resident Indians here and around Salmon Bay, as he was intimately acquainted with them all.

"'At one time Mr. Denny was reckoned as Seattle's wealthiest citizen. When acting as deputy assessor for Andrew Chilberg, the city lying north of Mill Street, now Yesler Way, was my district to assess. Denny's holdings, D. T. Denny's plats, had the year previous been assessed by the acre. The law was explicit, and to have made up the assessment by the acre would have been illegal. Mr. Denny's assessed value the year before was fifty thousand dollars. The best I could do was to make the assessment by the lot and block. For the year I assessed two hundred and fifty thousand. Recourse was had to the county commissioners, but the assessment remained about the same. Just before his purchase of the Seattle street car system he was the wealthiest man in King County, worth more than five hundred thousand dollars.

"'Of Mr. Denny it may be said that if others had applied the Golden Rule as he did, he would have been living in his old home in great comfort in this city today.'"

LIFE OF DAVID DENNY

"Fifty-two years and two months ago David Thomas Denny came to Seattle, to the spot where Seattle now stands enthroned upon her seven hills. Mr. Denny, the last but one of the little band of pioneers—some half dozen men first to make this spot their home—has been gathered to his fathers;

'has wrapped the mantle of his shroud about him and laid down to pleasant dreams.' Gone is a man and citizen who perhaps loved Seattle best of all those who ever made Seattle their home. This is attested by the fact that from the time that Mr. Denny first came to Elliott Bay it has been his constant home. Never but once or twice during that long period of time did he go far away, and then for but a very short time. Once he went as far away as New York—and that proved a sad trip—and once, in recent years, to California. Both trips were comparatively brief, and he who first conquered the primeval forest that crowned the hills around returned home full of intense longing to get back and full of love for the old home.

"Mr. Denny lived a rugged, honorable, upright life—the life of a patriarch. He bore patiently a long period of intense suffering manfully and without murmur, and when the end approached he calmly awaited the summons and died as if falling away into a quiet sleep. So he lived, so he died.

"Few indeed who can comprehend the extent of his devotion to Seattle. Living in Seattle for the last two years, yet for that period he never looked once upon the city which he helped to build. About that long ago he moved from his home which he had maintained for some years at Fremont, to the place where he died, Licton Springs, about a mile north of Green Lake. Said Mr. Denny as he went from the door of the old home he was giving up for the new: 'This will be the last time I will ever look upon Seattle,' and Mr. Denny's words were true. He never was able to leave again the little sylvan home his family—his wife, sister and children—had raised for him in the woods. There, dearly loved, he was watched over and cared for by the children and by the wife who had shared with him for two-score-and-ten years the joys and

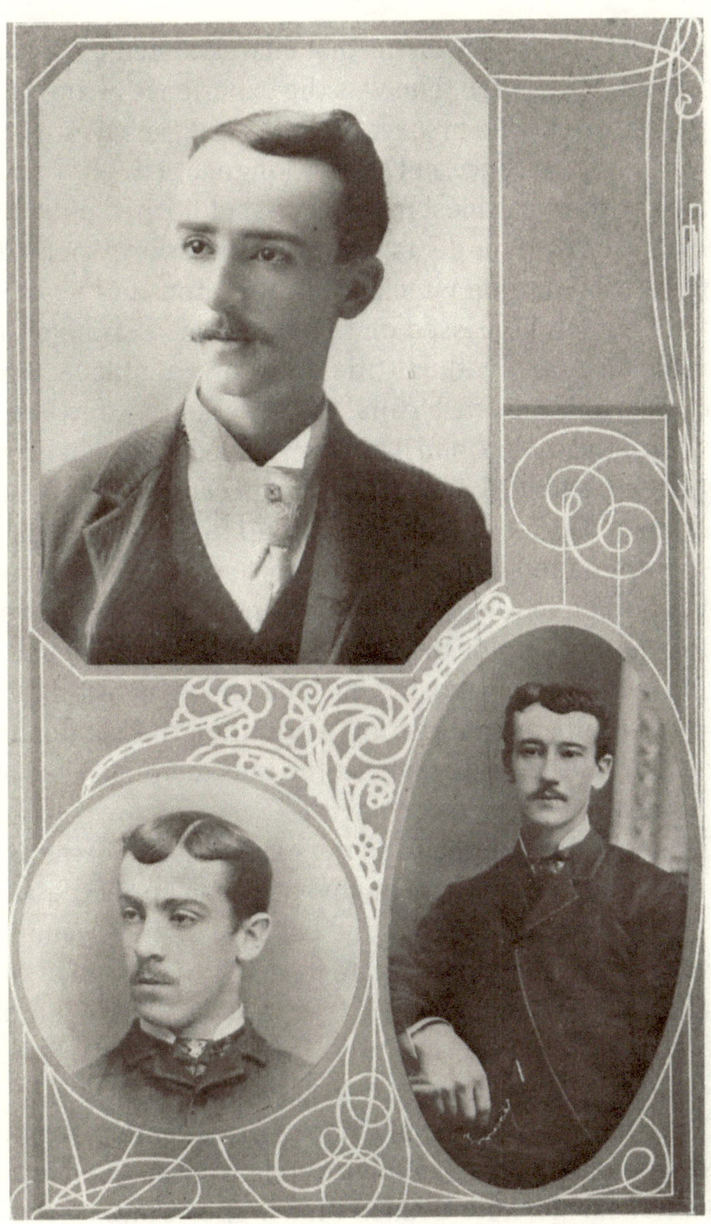

SONS OF D. T. AND LOUISA DENNY
VICTOR W. S., D. THOMAS, JOHN B.

sorrows, the ups and downs that characterized his life in a more marked degree than was the experience of any other of the pioneers who first reached this rugged bay.

"Mr. Denny was once, not so very long ago, a wealthy man—some say the wealthiest in the city—but he died poor, very poor; but he paid his debts to the full. Once the owner in fee simple of land upon which are now a thousand beautiful Seattle homes, he passed on to his account a stranger in a strange land, and without title to his own domicile. When the crisis and the crash came that wrecked his fortune he went stoutly to work, and if he ever repined it was not known outside of the family and small circle of chosen friends. That was about fourteen years ago, and up to two years ago Mr. Denny toiled in an humble way, perhaps never expecting, never hoping to regain his lost fortune. Those last years of labor were spent, for the most part, at the Denny Mine on Gold Creek, a mine, too, in which he had no direct interest or ownership, or in directing work upon the Snoqualmie Pass road. He came down from the hills to his sick bed and to his death.

"Mr. Denny's life for half a century is the history of the town. Without the Dennys there might have been no Seattle. Of all the band that came here in the fall of 1851, they seemed to have taken deepest root and to have left the stamp of their name and individuality which is keen and patent to this day."

CAME FROM ILLINOIS

"The Dennys came from Illinois, from some place near Springfield, and crossing Iowa, rendezvoused at what was then Kanesville, now Council Bluffs. They came by way of Fort Hall and the South Pass, along the south side of the Snake River, where, at or near American Falls, they had their first and only brush with the Indians. There was only desultory firing and no one was injured. The party reached The Dalles August 11, 1851. The party separated there, Low, Boren and A. A. Denny going by river to Portland, arriving August 22. In September, Low and D. T. Denny drove a herd of cattle, those that drew them across the plains, to Chehalis River to get them to a good winter range. These men came on to the Sound and here they arrived before the end of that month. After looking around some, Low went away, having hired Mr. Denny, who was an unmarried man, to stay behind and build Low a cabin. This was done and on September 28th, 1851, the foundation of this first cabin was laid close to the beach at Alki Point.

"A. A. Denny, Low, Boren, Bell and C. C. Terry arrived at Alki Point, joining D. T. Denny. That made a happy little family, twenty-four persons, twelve men and women, twelve children and one cabin. In this they all resided until the men could erect a second log cabin. By this time the immediate vicinity of the point had been stripped of its building logs and the men had to go back and split shakes and carry them out of the woods on their backs. With these they erected two 'shake' or split cedar houses that, with the two log cabins, provided fair room for the twenty-four people.

"During that winter the men cut and loaded a small brig with piles for San Francisco. The piles were cut near the water and rolled and dragged by hand to where they would float to the vessel's side. There were no oxen in the country at that time and the first team that came to Elliott Bay was driven along the beach at low tide from up near Tacoma."

SURROUNDED BY INDIANS

"The first winter spent at Alki Point the settlers were almost constantly surrounded with one thousand Indians armed with old Hudson Bay Company's muskets. This company maintained one of its posts at Nisqually, Pierce County, and traded flintlocks and blankets with the Indians all over Western Washington, taking in trade their furs and skins. The Indians from far and near hearing of the settlement of whites came and camped on the beach nearly the whole winter.

"In addition to the Indians of this bay the Muckleshoots, Green Rivers, Snoqualmies, Tulalips, Port Madisons and likely numerous other bands were on hand. At one time the Muckleshoots and Snoqualmies lined up in front of the little cluster of whites and came near engaging in a battle, having become enraged at one another. The whites acted as peacemakers and no blood was spilled.

"In those days the government gave what was known as donation claims, one hundred sixty acres to a man, and an equal amount to the women. In the spring of 1852 the Dennys, Bell and Boren, came over to this side and took donation claims. Boren located first on the south, his line being at about the line of Jackson Street. A. A. Denny came next and Bell third. Shortly after D. T. Denny located, taking a strip of ground from the bay back to Lake Union and bounded by lines north and south which tally about with Denny Way on the south and Mercer Street on the north. Later Mr. Denny bought the eastern shore of Lake Union, extending from the lake to the portage between Union and Washington.

"Mr. Denny's first house on this side of the bay, built presumably in the spring of 1852, was located on the beach at the foot of what is now Denny Way in North Seattle. This was a one-story log cabin. It was on the bluff overlooking the bay and the woods hemmed it in, and it was only by cutting and slashing that one could open a way back into the forest."

MR. DENNY'S FARM

"Some time later Mr. Denny begun his original clearing for a farm at what is now the vicinity of Third Avenue North and Republican Street, and also in the early years of residence here—about 1860 or 1861—built a home on the site of what is now occupied by modern business houses at Second Avenue and Seneca Street.

"It seems to have been Mr. Denny's plan to work out on his farm at Third Avenue and Republican Street during the dry summer season and to reside down in the settlement in the winter. The farm at Third Avenue and Republican Street grew apace until in after years it became the notable spot in all the district of what is now North Seattle. After the arrival on the coast of the Chinaman it was leased to them for a number of years, and became widely known as the China gardens. Mr. Denny does not seem to have planted orchard to any extent here, but at Second and Seneca he had quite an orchard. Forming what later became a part of the original D. T. Denny farm was a large tract of open, boggy land running well through the center of Mr. Denny's claim from about Third Avenue down to Lake Union. This was overgrown largely with willow and swamp shrubs. In ancient times it was either a lake or beaver marsh, and long after the whites came, ducks frequented the place. The house built at Second Avenue and Seneca Street by Mr. Denny was a small one-story structure of three or four rooms.

"In 1871 Mr. Denny built another homestead of the D. T. Denny family at this place. It was, after its completion, one of the most commodious and important houses in the city. This house was built overlooking Lake Union, instead of the bay. The site selected was on what is now Dexter Avenue and Republican Street. This house still stands, a twelve or fourteen-room house, surrounded by orchard and grounds."

BUILT A NEW HOME

"Mr. Denny lived at the Lake Union home until just after the big fire here in 1889, when he began the erection and completed a fine mansion on Queen Anne Avenue, with fine grounds, but he did not long have the pleasure of residing here. The unfortunate business enterprises in which he soon found himself engulfed, swept away his vast wealth, and 'Honest Dave,' as he had become familiarly to be known, was left without a place wherein to rest his head."

These tributes also recite something of the story of his life:

"He was one of the original locators of donation claims on Elliott Bay, within the present limits of Seattle. The two Dennys, David and his brother, Arthur, now deceased; Dr. Maynard, Carson D. Boren and W. N. Bell, were the first locators of the land upon which the main portion of Seattle now rests. All of them, save Boren, have passed away, and Boren has not lived in Seattle for many years; so it may be said that David Denny was the last of the Seattle pioneers. Of his seventy-one years of life, fifty-two were passed on Puget Sound and fifty-one in the City of Seattle, in the upbuilding of which he bore a prominent part.

"With his original donation claim and lands subsequently acquired, Mr. Denny was for many years the heaviest property owner in actual acreage in Seattle. Most of his holdings had passed into the hands of others before his death. In his efforts to build up the city he engaged in the promotion of many large enterprises, and was carrying large liabilities, although well within the limit of his financial ability, when the panic of ten years ago rendered it impossible to realize upon any property of any value, and left equities in real property covered even by light mortgages, absolutely valueless. In that disastrous period he, among all Seattle's citizens, was stricken the hardest blow, but he never lost the hope or the energy of the born pioneer, nor faith in the destinies of the city which he had helped to found. His name remains permanently affixed to many of the monuments of Seattle, and he will pass into history as one of the men who laid the foundations of one of the great cities of the world, and who did much in erecting the superstructure.

"In the enthusiasms of early life the ambitious men and women of America turn their faces toward 'the setting sun' and bravely assume the task of building homes in uninhabited places and transforming the wilderness into prosperous communities. Those who undertake such work are to be listed among God's noblemen—for without such men little progress would be made in the development of any country.

"For more than a hundred years one of the interesting features of life in the United States is that connected with pioneering. The men and women of energy are usually possessed with an adventurous spirit which chafes under the fixed customs and inflexible conservatism of the older communities, and longs to take a hand in crowding the frontier toward the Pacific.

"The poet has said that only the brave start out West and only the strong success in getting there. Thus it is that those, who, more than a half century ago, elected to cross the American continent were from the bravest of the eastern or middle portion of the United States. Many who started turned back; others died by the wayside. Only the 'strong' reached their destination.

"Of this class was the small party which landed at Alki Point in the late summer of 1851 and began the task of building up a civilization where grew the gigantic forests and where roamed the dusky savage. Of that number was David T. Denny, the last survivor but one, C. D. Boren, of the seven men who composed the first white man's party to camp on the shores of Elliott Bay.

"It requires some stretch of the imagination to view the surroundings that enveloped that band of hardy pioneers and to comprehend the magnitude of the task that towered before them. It was no place for the weak or faint-hearted. There was work to do—and no one shirked.

"Since then more than fifty years have come and gone, and from the humble beginnings made by David T. Denny and the others has grown a community that is the metropolis of the Pacific Northwest and which, a few years hence, will be the metropolis of the entire Pacific Coast. That this has been the product of these initial efforts is due in a large measure to the energy, the example, the business integrity and public spirit of him whose demise is now mourned as that of the last but one of the male survivors of that little party of pioneers of 1851.

"The history of any community can be told in the biographies of a few of the leading men connected with its affairs. The history of Seattle can be told by writing a complete biography of David T. Denny. He was among the first to recognize that here was an eligible site for a great city. He located a piece of land with this object in view and steadfastly he clung to his purpose. When a public enterprise was to be planned that would redound to the growth and prestige of Seattle he was at the front, pledging his credit and contributing of his means.

"Then came a time in the growth of cities on the Pacific Coast when the spirit of speculation appeared to drive men mad. Great schemes were laid and great enterprises planned. Some of them were substantial; some of them were not. With a disposition to do anything honorable that would contribute to the glory of Seattle, David T. Denny threw himself into the maelstrom with all of his earthly possessions and took chances of increasing his already handsome fortune. Then came the panic of 1893 and Mr. Denny was among many other Seattle men who emerged from the cataclysm without a dollar.

"Subsequent years made successful the enterprise that proved the financial ruin of so many of Seattle's wealthy, but it was too late for those who had borne the brunt of the battle. Others came in to reap where the pioneers had sown and the latter were too far along in years to again take up the struggle of accumulating a competence. His declining years were passed in the circle of loving friends who never failed to speak of him as the personification of honesty and integrity and one whose noble traits of character in this respect were worthy of all emulation."

The following is an epitaph written for his tomb:

"David Thomas Denny, Born March 17th, 1832, Died Nov. 25th, 1903. The first of the name to reach Puget Sound, landing at Duwampsh Head, Sept. 25th, 1851. A great pioneer from whose active and worthy life succeeding generations will reap countless benefits."

"He giveth his beloved sleep."

The early days of the State, or rather, Territory, of Washington produced a distinct type of great men, one of whom was David Thomas Denny.

Had Washington a poet to tell of the achievements of her heroic founders and builders a considerable epic would be devoted to the remarkable career and character of this noble man.

At the risk of repetition I append this slight recapitulation:

The first of the name to set foot on Puget Sound, *Oregon Territory*, September 25th, 1851, he then evinced the characteristics more fully developed in after years.

He had crossed the plains and then from Portland proceeded to Puget Sound by the old Hudson Bay trail. He landed at Duwampsh Head where now is West Seattle, and there met and shook hands with Chief Sealth, or old Seattle as the whites called him. He helped to build the first cabin home at Alki Point. He alone was the Committee of Reception when the notable party landed from the *Exact*. He ran the race of the bravest of the brave pioneers.

Beginning at the very bottom of the ladder, he worked with his hands, as did the others, at every sort of work to be found in a country entirely unimproved.

A ready axman, a very Nimrod, a natural linguist, he began the attack on the mighty forest, he slew wild animals and birds for food, he made friends with the native tribes.

He builded, planted, harvested, helped to found schools, churches, government and civilized society. Always and everywhere he embodied and upheld scriptural morality and temperance.

Many now living could testify to his untiring service to the stranded newcomers. Employment, money, credit, hospitality, time, advice, he gave freely to help and encourage the settlers following the pioneers.

He was Probate Judge, County Treasurer, City Councilman, Regent of the University, School Director for twelve years, etc., etc. He administered a number of estates with extreme care and faithfulness.

David T. Denny early realized that Seattle was a strategic site for a great city and by thrifty investments in wild land prepared for settlements sure to come.

After long years of patient toil, upright dealing and wise management, he began to accumulate until his property was worth a fortune.

With increasing wealth his generosity increased and he gave liberally to carry on all the institutions of a civilized community.

David T. Denny gave "Denny Park" to the City of Seattle.

Denny school was named for him, as is perfectly well known to many persons.

As prosperity increased he became more active in building the city and lavished energy, toil, property and money, installing public enterprises and utilities, such as water supply, electric lights, a large sawmill, banks, street railways, laying off additions to the city, grading and improvements, etc., etc.

Then came 1893, the black year of trade. Thousands lost all they possessed. David T. Denny suffered a martyrdom of disappointment, humiliation, calumny, extreme and undeserved reproach from those who crammed themselves with securities, following the great money panic in which his immense holdings passed into the hands of others.

He was a soldier of the Indian war and was on guard near the door of Fort Decatur when the memorable attack took place on January 26th, 1856. The fort was built of timbers hewn by D. T. Denny and two others, taken from his donation claim. These timbers were brought to Seattle, then a little settlement of about three hundred people. There he helped to build the fort.

Many persons have expressed a desire to see a fitting

memorial erected to the memory of Seattle's "Fairy Prince," Founder and Defender, David Thomas Denny.

I feel the inadequacy of these fragmentary glimpses of the busy life of this well known pioneer. I have not made a set arrangement of the material as I wished to preserve the testimony of others, hence there appear some repetitions; an accurate and intimate biography may come in the future.

Logically, his long, active, useful life in the Northwest, might be divided into epochs on this wise:

1st. The log cabin and "claim" era, in which, within my own memory, he was seen toiling early and late, felling the forest giants, cultivating the soil, superintending Indian workers and bringing in game, killed with his rifle.

2nd. The farm-home era, when he built a substantial house on his part of the donation claim, near the south end of Lake Union, obtained cattle (famous Jersey stock of California), horses, etc. The home then achieved by himself and his equally busy wife, was one to be desired, surrounded as it was by beautiful flowers, orchards, wide meadows and pastures, and outside these, the far-spreading primeval forest.

3rd. Town-building. The west end of the claim, belonging to Louisa Denny, was first platted; other plats followed, as may be seen by reference to Seattle records. Commercial opportunities loomed large and he entered upon many promising enterprises. All these flourished for a time.

4th. 1893. The failure of Baring Bros., as he told me repeatedly, began it—theirs being the result of having taken bonds of the Argentine Republic, and a revolution happening along, $100,000,000.00 went by the board; a sizable failure.

Partly on account of this and partly on account of the vast advantage of the lender over the borrower, and partly through the vast anxiety of those who held his securities, they were able to distribute among themselves his hard-earned fortune.

"A certain man went down from Jerusalem to Jericho and fell among thieves, which stripped him of his raiment and wounded him and departed leaving him half dead."

The Deficiency Judgment also loomed large and frequent and his last days were disturbed by those who still pressed their greedy claims, even following after his death, with a false, unjust and monstrous sale of the cemetery in which he lies buried!

But he is with the just men made perfect.

Law, custom and business methods have permitted, from time immemorial, gross injustice to debtors; formerly they were imprisoned; a man might speedily pay his debts, if in prison!

The Deficiency Judgment and renewal of the same gives opportunity for greedy and unprincipled creditors to rob the debtor. There should be a law compelling the return of the surplus. When one class of people make many times their money out of the misfortunes of others, there is manifestly great inequality.

The principles of some are to grab all they can, "skin" all they can, and follow up all they can even to the *graveyard*.

THESE THINGS OUGHT NOT SO TO BE

5th. In the end he laid down all earthly things, and in spite of grief and suffering, showed a clear perception and grasp of justice, mercy and truth.

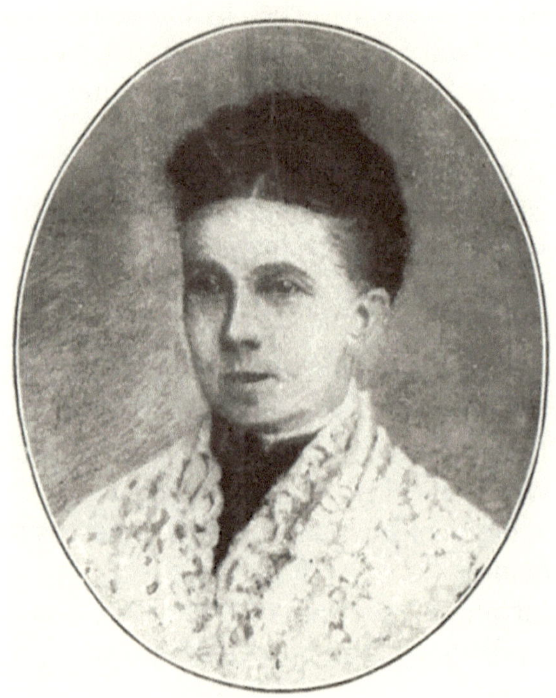

LOUISA B. DENNY

CHAPTER IV

THE FIRST WEDDING ON ELLIOTT BAY

ONCERNING THIS notable occurrence many interesting incidents were recorded by an interviewer who obtained the same from the lips of David Thomas Denny.

"On January 23rd, 1895, Mr. and Mrs. David T. Denny celebrated their forty-second wedding anniversary—and the anniversary of the first wedding in Seattle—in their home at 'Decatur Terrace' (512 Temperance Street), Seattle, with a gathering of children, grandchildren, relatives and friends that represented four distinctive generations.

"One of the notable features of the evening was the large gathering of pioneers who collectively represented more years of residence in Seattle than ever were found together before.

"What added interest to the occasion was the historical fact that Mr. and Mrs. Denny were the first couple married in Seattle, and the transition from the small, uncouth log cabin, built forty-three years ago by the sturdy young pioneer for his bride, to the present beautiful residence with all its modern convenience in which the respected couple are enjoying the fruits of a well spent life, was the subject of many congratulations from the friends of the honored host and hostess who remembered their early trials and tribulations. All present were more or less connected with the history of Seattle, all knew one another's history, and with their children and grandchildren the gathering, unconventional in every respect, with the two-year-old baby romping in the arms of the octogenarian, presented a colossal, happy family reunion.

"The old pioneer days were not forgotten, and one corner of the reception room was made to represent the interior of a cabin, lined with newspapers, decorated with gun, bullet pouch and powder horn and measure, a calico sunbonnet, straw hat and hunting shirt.

"A table was set to represent one in the early fifties, namely, two boards across two boxes, for a table, a smoked salmon, a tin plate full of boiled potatoes, some sea biscuits and a few large clams. Such a meal, when it was had, was supposed to be a feast.

"Many other relics were in sight; a thirty-two pound solid shot, fired by the sloop-of-war Decatur among the Indians during the uprising; a ten-pound shot belonging to Dr. Maynard's cannon; a pair of enormous elk's horns belonging to a six hundred and thirty-pound elk killed by Mr. D. T. Denny, September 7th, 1869, in the woods north west of Green Lake; the first Bible of the family from which the eldest daughter, Miss Emily Inez, learned her letters; an old-fashioned Indian halibut hook, an ingenious contrivance; an old family Bible, once the property of the father of David T. Denny, bearing the following inscription on the inside cover:

The property of J. Denny,
Purchased of J. Strange,
August the 15th, 1829,
Price 62-1/2 cents.
Putnam County, Indiana.

"Also a number of daguerreotypes of Mr. and Mrs. D. T. Denny in the early years of their married life, taken in the fifties, and one of W. G. Latimer and his sister.

"All these and many more afforded food for conversation and reminiscences on the part of the old pioneers present.

"An informal programme introduced the social intercourse of the evening. Harold Denny, a grandson of the hosts and son of Mr. John B. Denny, made an address to his grand-parents, giving them the greeting of the assembly in these words:

"'O fortunate, O happy day,'
The people sing, the people say;
The bride and bridegroom, pioneers,
Crowned now with good and gracious years
Serenely smile upon the scene.
The growing state they helped to found
Unto their praise shall yet redound.
O may they see a green old age,
With every leaf a written page
Of joy and peace from day to day.
In good, new times not far away
May people sing and people say,
'Heaven bless their coming years;
Honor the noble Pioneers."

"The chief diversion was afforded by the sudden entrance of a band of sixteen young men and women gorgeously dressed as Indians, preceded by a runner who announced their approach. They were headed by Capt. D. T. Davies who acted as chief. The band marched in true Indian file, formed a circle and sat down on the floor with their *tamanuse* boards upon which they beat the old time music and sang their Indian songs. After an impressive hush, the chief addressed their white chief, Denny, in the Chinook language, wishing Mr. and Mrs. Denny many returns of the auspicious occasion.

"Mr. Denny, who is an adept in the Indian languages, replied in the same tongue, thanking his dark brethren for their good intentions and speaking of the happy relations that always existed between the whites and the Indians until bad white men and whisky turned the minds and brains of the Indians. The council then broke up and took their departure.

"The marriage certificate of Mr. and Mrs. Denny is written on heavy blue paper and has been so carefully preserved that, beyond the slight fading of the ink, it is as perfect as when first given in the dense forests on the shores of Elliott Bay. It reads as follows:

"'This may certify that David Denny and Louisa Boren were joined in marriage at the residence of Arthur A. Denny in the County of King and Territory of Oregon, by me in the presence of A. A. Denny and wife and others, on this 23rd day of January, 1853. D. S. Maynard, J. P.'

"Another historical event, apropos right here, was the death and burial of D. S. Maynard early in 1873.

"The funeral services were conducted March 15, 1873, by Rev. John F. Damon in Yesler's pavilion, then located at what is now Cherry and Front Streets. The funeral was under the auspices of St. John's lodge, of which Dr. Maynard was a member. The remains were escorted to what is now Denny Park—the gift to the city, of Mr. David T. Denny—and the casket was deposited and kept in the tool house of that place until the trail could be cut to the new Masonic—now Lake

View—cemetery. Maynard's body was the first interred there.

"Miss Louisa Boren, who married Mr. David T. Denny, was the younger sister of A. A. Denny's wife and came across the plains with the Denny's in 1851.

"The house of A. A. Denny, in which the marriage took place, was located near the foot of what is now Bell Street, and was the first cabin built by A. A. Denny when he moved over from Alki Point. Seattle was then a dense forest down to the water's edge, and had at that time, in the spring of 1852, only three cabins, namely: C. D. Boren's, the bride's brother; W. N. Bell's and A. A. Denny's. Boren's stood where now stands the Merchant's National Bank, and Bell's was near the foot of Battery Street.

"At first the forests were so dense that the only means of communication was along the beach at low tide; after three or four months, a trail was beaten between the three cabins. David lived with his brother, but he built himself a cabin previous to his marriage, near the foot of Denny Way, near and north of Bell's house. To this lonely cabin in the woods, he took his bride and they lived there until August, 1853, eking out an existence like the other pioneers, chopping wood, cutting piles for shipment, living on anyhow, but always managing to have enough to eat, such as it was, with plenty of pure spring water.

"In August, of 1853, he built a cabin on the spot where now the Frye Block stands and they passed the winter of 1853 there.

"In the spring of 1854 he built another cabin further east on the donation claim, east of what is now Box Street, between Mercer and Republican, and they moved into it, remaining there until near the time of the Indian outbreak.

"Mr. Denny had acquired a knowledge of the various Indian dialects, and through this learned much of the threatened outbreak, and moved his family in time back to the house on the Frye Block site, which was also near the stockade or fort that stood at the foot of Cherry Street. During the greater part of the winter of 1855 the women in the settlement lived in the fort, and Mrs. Denny passed much of the time there.

"After the Indian trouble was over the Denny's moved out again to their outside cabin. The Indians making the trouble were the Swunumpsh and the Klickitats, from east of the mountains; the Sound Indians, the Duwampsh and the Suquampsh, were friendly and helped the whites a great deal. Sealth or Seattle belonged to the Suquampsh tribe and his men gave the first warning of the approach of the hostile Indians.

"Mr. and Mrs. David T. Denny have had eight children, four daughters and four sons. One son died shortly after birth, and all the others grew to maturity, after which the father and mother were called to mourn the loss of two daughters. Two daughters and three sons survive, namely: Miss Emily Inez, Mrs. Abbie D. Lindsley, Mr. John B. Denny, Mr. D. Thomas Denny and Mr. Victor W. S. Denny.

"The sons are all married and nine out of ten grandchildren were present last evening to gladden the hearts of Grandpa and Grandma Denny. The absent members of the family group were Mrs. John B. Denny and daughter, in New York on a visit.

"'People in these days of modern improvements and plenty know nothing of the hardships the pioneer of forty years ago had to undergo right here,' said Mr. Denny.

"'Nearly forty years of life in a dense forest surrounded by savages and wild beasts, with the hardest kind of work necessary in order to eke out an existence, was the lot of every man and woman here. It was a life of privation, inconveniences, anxieties, fears and dangers innumerable, and required physical and mental strength to live it out. Of course, we all had good health, for in twenty-four years' time we only had a doctor four times. Our colony grew little by little, good men and bad men came in and by the time the Indians wanted to massacre us we had about three hundred white men, women and children. We got our provisions from ships that took our piles and then the Indians also furnished us with venison, potatoes, fish, clams and wild fowl. Flour, sugar and coffee we got from San Francisco. When we could get no flour, we made a shift to live on potatoes.'

"In speaking of cold weather, Mr. Denny recalled the year of 1852, when it was an open winter until March 3, but that night fourteen inches of snow fell and made it the coldest winter, all in that one month. The next severe winter was that of 1861-2, which was about the coldest on record. During those cold spells the pioneers kept warm cutting wood.

"The unique invitations sent out for this anniversary, consisted of a fringed piece of buck-skin stretched over the card and painted '1851, Ankuti. 1895, Okoke Sun.' They were well responded to, and every room in the large house was filled with interested guests, from the baby in arms to the white haired friend of the old people. Pioneers were plenty, and it is doubtful if there ever was a gathering in the City of Seattle that could aggregate so many years of residence in the Queen City of the West on the shores of Elliott Bay.

"Arranged according to families, and classing those as pioneers who came prior to the Indian war of 1855-6, the following list will be found of historical value:

"Rev. and Mrs. D. E. Blaine, pioneers; A. A. Denny, brother

of D. T. Denny; Loretta Denny, sister of D. T. Denny; Lenora Denny, daughter of A. A. Denny; Rev. and Mrs. Daniel Bagley, pioneers of 1852, Oregon, Seattle 1860; Mrs. Clarence B. Bagley, daughter of Thomas Mercer, 1852; C. B. Bagley, pioneer, 1852 Oregon, Seattle 1860; Hillory Butler, pioneer; Mrs. Gardner Kellogg, daughter of Bonney, Pierce County 1853; Walter Graham, pioneer; Rev. Geo. F. Whitworth, pioneer; Thomas Mercer, 1852 Oregon, Seattle 1853; David Graham, 1858; Mrs. Susan Graham, daughter of Thomas Mercer; Mrs. S. D. Libby, wife of Captain Libby, pioneer; George Frye, 1853; Mrs. Katherine Frye, daughter of A. A. Denny; Sophie and Bertie Frye, granddaughters of A. A. Denny; Mrs. Mamie Kauffman Dawson, granddaughter of Wm. N. Bell, pioneer; Mr. and Mrs. D. B. Ward, pioneers (Mrs. Ward, daughter of Charles Byles, of Thurston County, 1853); Mrs. Abbie D. Lindsley, daughter of D. T. and Louisa Denny; the Bryans, all children of Edgar Bryan, a pioneer of Thurston County; J. W. George, pioneer 1852; Orange Jacobs, pioneer of Oregon."

In another chapter it has been shown how D. T. Denny was the first of the name to reach Puget Sound. Not having yet attained his majority he was required to consider, judge and act for himself and others. Like the two spies, who entered the Promised Land in ancient days, Low and Denny viewed the goodly shores of Puget Sound for the sake of others by whom their report was anxiously awaited.

As before stated, Low returned to carry the tidings of the wonderful country bordering on the Inland Sea, while David T. Denny, but nineteen years of age, was left alone, the only white person on Elliott Bay, until the Exact came with the brave families of the first settlers. From that time on he has been in the forefront of progress and effort, beginning at the very foundation of trade, business enterprises, educational interests, religious institutions and reforms. From the early conditions of hard toil in humble occupations, through faith, foresight and persistence, he rose to a leading position in the business world, when his means were lavished in modern enterprises and improvements through which many individuals and the general public were benefited, said improvements being now in daily use in the City of Seattle.

One of these is the Third Street and Suburban Electric Railway, built and equipped by this energetic pioneer and his sons.

The old donation claim having become valuable city property, the taxation was heavy to meet the expenses of extravagant and wasteful administration partly, and partly incidental to the phenomenal growth of the city, consequently both Mr. and Mrs. D. T. Denny have paid into the public treasury a considerable fortune, ten or twelve thousand a year for ten years, twenty thousand for grades, six thousand at a time for school tax and so on—much more than they were able to use for themselves.

* * *

A fascinating volume would recount their hunting adventures, as all, father and sons, are fine shots; game, both large and small, swarmed about the present site of Seattle in the early days.

Indeed, for many years the bounty of Nature failed not; as late as 1879, ruffed grouse or "pheasants," blue grouse, brown and black bears were numerous seven or eight miles north of Seattle, a region then untenanted wilds. The women folk were not always left behind on hunting expeditions, and the pioneer mother, and daughters, too, quite often accompanied them.

Into this primeval wilderness, to a mineral spring known and visited by the Indians in times past and called by them Licton, came the father, mother and eldest son to enjoy all they might discover. The two hunting dogs proved necessary and important members of the party by rousing up a big black bear and her cubs near the spring,—but we will let the pioneer mother, Mrs. Louisa Denny, tell the tale as she has often told it in the yesterdays:

"We were out in the deep forest at the mineral spring the Indians call 'Licton'; the two dogs, Prince and Gyp, treed a black bear cub in a tall fir on the farther side of the brook, a little way along the trail; the hunters pressed up and fired. Receiving a shot, the cub gave a piercing scream and, tumbling down, aroused the old bear, which, though completely hidden by the undergrowth, answered it with an enraged roar that sounded so near that the hunters fled without ceremony. I sat directly in the path, on the ends of some poles laid across the brook for a foot bridge, very calmly resting and not at all excited—as yet. My boy yelled to me, at the top of his voice, 'Get up a tree, mother! get up a tree, quick! The old bear is coming!' Hearing a turmoil at the foot of the big tree, where the dogs, old bear and two cubs were engaged in a general melee, I also thought it best to 'get up a tree.' We dashed across the brook and climbed up a medium sized alder tree—the boy first, myself next, and my husband last and not very far from the ground. We could hear the bear crashing around through the tall bushes and ferns, growling at every step and only a little way off, but she did not come out in sight. The dogs came and lay down under the tree where we were. Two long, weary hours we watched for Bruin, and then, everything being quiet, climbed down, stiff and sore, parted the brushes cautiously and reconnoitered.

One climbed up a leaning tree to get a better view, but there was no view to be had, the woods were so thick. We crept along softly until we reached the foot of the big fir, and there lay the wounded cub, dead! The hunters dragged it a long distance, looking back frequently and feeling very uncertain, as they had no means of knowing the whereabouts of the enemy. I walked behind carrying one of the guns. Perhaps I was cruel in asking them if they looked behind them when they tacked the skin on the barn at home! However, it was certainly a case of discretion better than valor, as one weapon was only a shotgun and the rank undergrowth gave no advantage. It seemed to make everybody laugh when we told of our adventure, but I did not think the experience altogether amusing, and I shall never forget that mother-bear's roar. They have killed plenty of big game since; my two younger boys shot a fine, large black bear whose beautiful skin adorns my parlor floor and is much admired."

This is but one incident in the life of a pioneer woman, the greater portion of whose existence has been spent in the wilds of the Northwest. In perils oft, in watchings many, in often uncongenial toil, Louisa Boren Denny spent the years of her youth and prime, as did the other pioneer mothers.

"What a book the story of my life would make!" she exclaimed in a retrospective mood—yet, like the majority of the class she typifies, she has left the book unwritten, while hand and brain have been busy with the daily duties pressing on her.

A childhood on the beautiful, flower-decked, virgin prairie of Illinois, in the log cabin days of that state, the steadfast pursuit of knowledge until maturity, when she went out to instruct others, the breaking of many ties of friendship to accompany her relatives across the plains, the joy of new scenes so keenly appreciated by the observant mind, the self-denials and suffering inevitable to that stupendous journey and the reaching of the goal on Puget Sound, at once the beginning and the ending of eventful days, might be the themes of its opening chapters.

Her marriage and the rearing of beautiful and gifted children, in the midst of the solemn and noble solitudes of Nature's great domain, where they often wandered together hand in hand, she the gentle teacher, they the happy learners, green boughs and fair blossoms bending near—yes, the toil, too, as well as pleasure, in which the willing hands wrought and tireless feet hastened to and fro in the service of her God, all these things I shared in are indelibly written on my memory's pages, though they be never recorded elsewhere.

AND WHILE SHE WROUGHT, SHE THOUGHT

Many times in the latter years, spoken opinions have shown that she has originated ideas of progress and reform that have been subsequently brought before the public as initiative and original, but were no less original with her.

Mrs. Louisa Denny was a member of the famous grand jury, with several other women of the best standing; during their term the gamblers packed their grip-sacks to leave Seattle, as those "old women on the jury" were making trouble for them.

For many years she was called upon or volunteered to visit the sick, anon to be present at a surgical operation, and with ready response and steady nerve complied.

Generous to a fault, hospitable and kind, in countless unknown deeds of mercy and unrecorded words, she expressed good-will toward humanity, and the recipients, a goodly company, might well arise up and call her "Blessed."

A separate sketch is given in which the life of the first bride of Seattle is more fully set forth.

CHAPTER V

LOUISA BOREN DENNY

THE FIRST bride of Seattle was born in White County, Illinois, on the 1st of June, 1827, and is the daughter of Richard Freeman Boren and Sarah Latimer Boren. Her father, a young Baptist minister, died when she was an infant, and she has often said, "I have missed my father all my life." A religious nature seems to have been inherited, as she has also said, "I cannot remember when I did not pray to God."

Her early youth was spent on the great prairies, then a veritable garden adorned with many beautiful wild flowers, in the log cabin with her widowed, pioneer mother, her sister Mary and brother Carson.

She learned to be industrious and thrifty without parsimony; to be simple, genuine, faithful. In the heat of summer or cold of winter she trudged to school, as she loved learning, showing, as her mind developed, a natural aptitude and taste for the sciences; chemistry, philosophy, botany and astronomy being her especial delights.

Of a striking personal appearance, her fair complexion with a deep rose flush in the cheeks, sparkling eyes, masses of heavy black hair, small and perfect figure, would have attracted marked attention in any circle.

Her temperate and wholesome life, never given to fashion's follies, retained for her these points of beauty far beyond middle life, when many have lost all semblance of their youth and have become faded and decrepit.

Her school life merged into the teacher's and she took her place in the ranks of the pioneer instructors, who were truly heroic.

She taught with patience the bare-foot urchins, some of whom were destined for great things, and boarded 'round as was the primitive custom.

Going to camp meetings in the summer, lectures and singing schools in the winter were developing influences in those days, and primitive pleasures were no less delightful; the husking-bees, quilting parties and sleigh rides of fifty years ago in which she participated.

In 1851, when she was twenty-four years of age, she joined the army of pioneers moving West, in the division composed of her mother's and step-father's people, her mother having married John Denny and her sister Mary, A. A. Denny.

With what buoyant spirits, bright with hope and anticipation, they set out, except for the cloud of sorrow that hovered over them for the parting with friends they left behind. But they soon found it was to be a hard-fought battle. Louisa Boren, the only young, unmarried woman of the party, found many things to do in assisting those who had family cares. Her delight in nature was unlimited, and although she found no time to record her observations and experiences, her anecdotes and descriptions have given pleasure to others in after years.

She possessed dauntless courage and in the face of danger

was cool and collected.

It was she who pleaded for the boat to be turned inshore on a memorable night on the Columbia River, when they came so near going over the falls (the Cascades) owing to the stupefied condition of the men who had been imbibing "Blue Ruin" too freely.

When the party arrived at Alki Point on Puget Sound, although the outlook was not cheerful, she busied herself a little while after landing in observing the luxuriant and, to her, curious vegetation.

She soon made friends with the Indians and succeeded admirably in dealing with them, having patience and showing them kindness, for which they were not ungrateful.

It transpired that the first attempt at building on the site of Seattle, so far as known to the writer, is to be credited to Louisa Boren and another white woman, who crossed Elliott Bay in a canoe with Indian paddlers and a large dog to protect them from wild animals. They made their way through an untouched forest, and the two women cut and laid logs for the foundation of a cabin.

As she was strikingly beautiful, young and unmarried, both white and Indian braves thought it would be a fine thing to win her hand, and intimations of this fact were not wanting. The young Indians brought long poles with them and leaned them up against the cabin at Alki, the significance of which was not at first understood, but it was afterward learned that they were courtship poles, according to their custom.

The white competitors found themselves distanced by the younger Denny, who was the first of the name to set foot on Puget Sound.

On January 23rd, 1853, in the cabin of A. A. Denny, on the east side of Elliott Bay, Louisa Boren was married to David T. Denny.

In order to fulfil law and custom, David had made a trip to Olympia and back in a canoe to obtain a marriage license, but was told that no one there had authority to issue one, so he returned undaunted to proceed without it; neither was there a minister to perform the ceremony, but Dr. Maynard, who was a Justice of the Peace, successfully tied the knot.

Among the few articles of wearing apparel it was possible to transport to these far-off shores in a time of slow and difficult travel, was a white lawn dress, which did duty as a wedding gown.

The young couple moved their worldly possessions in an Indian canoe to their own cabin on the bay, about a mile and a half away, in a little clearing at the edge of the vast forest.

Here began the life of toil and struggle which characterized the early days.

Then came the Indian war. A short time before the outbreak, while they were absent at the settlement, some Indians robbed the cabin; as they returned they met the culprits. Mrs. Denny noticed that one of them had adorned his cap with a white embroidered collar and a gray ribbon belonging to her. The young rascal when questioned said that the other one had given them to him. Possibly it was true; at any rate when George Seattle heard of it he gave the accused a whipping.

The warnings given by their Indian friends were heeded and they retired to the settlement, to a little frame house not far from Fort Decatur.

On the morning of the battle, January 26th, Louisa Boren Denny was occupied with the necessary preparation of food for her family. She heard shots and saw from her window the marines swarming up from their boats onto Yesler's wharf, and rightly judging that the attack had begun she snatched the biscuits from the oven, turned them into her apron, gathered up her child, two years old, and ran toward the fort. Her husband, who was standing guard, met her and assisted them into the fort.

A little incident occurred in the fort which showed her strong temperance principles. One of the officers, perhaps feeling the need of something to strengthen his courage, requested her to pour out some whisky for him, producing a bottle and glass; whether or no his hand was already unsteady from fear or former libations, she very properly refused and has, throughout her whole life, discouraged the use of intoxicants.

A number of the settlers remained in the fort for some time, as it was unsafe for them to return to their claims.

On the 16th of March, 1856, her second child was born in Fort Decatur.

With this infant and the elder of two years and three months, they journeyed back again into the wilderness, where she took up the toilsome and uncertain life of the frontier. "There was nothing," she has said, "that was too hard or disagreeable for me to undertake."

All the work of the house and even lending a hand at digging and delving, piling and burning brush outside, and the work was done without questioning the limits of her "spere."

They removed again to the edge of the settlement and lived for a number of years in a rose-embowered cottage on Seneca Street.

Accumulating cares filled the years, but she met them with the same high courage throughout. Her sons and daughters were carefully brought up and given every available advantage even though it cost her additional sacrifice.

Her half of the old donation claim became very valuable in time as city property, but the enormous taxation robbed her to a considerable extent of its benefits.

The manner of life of this heroic mother, type of her race, was such as to develop the noblest traits of character. The patience, steadfastness, courage, hopefulness and the consideration for the needs and trials of others, wrought out in her and others like her, during the pioneer days, challenge the admiration of the world.

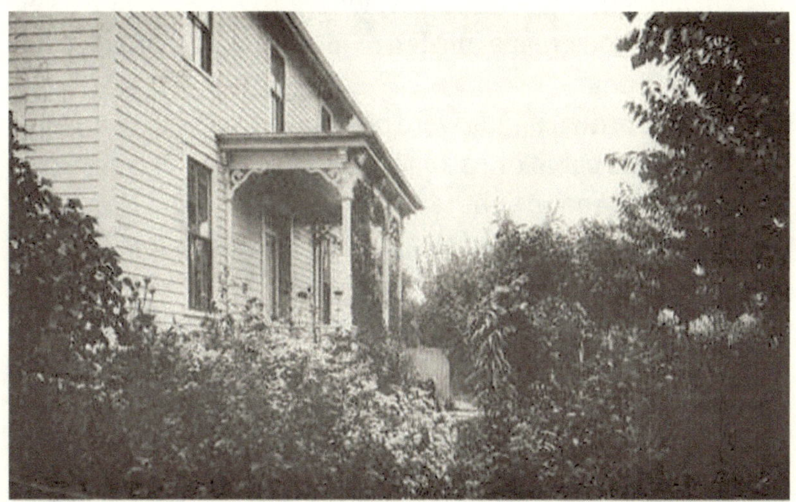

FLOWER GARDEN PLANTED BY LOUISA B. DENNY

I have seen the busy toil, the anxious brow, the falling tears of the pioneer woman as she tended her sick or fretful child, hurried the dinner for the growing family and the hired Indians who were clearing, grubbing or ditching, bent over the washtub to cleanse the garments of the household, or up at a late hour to mend little stockings for restless feet, meanwhile helping the young students of the family to conquer the difficulties that lay before them.

The separation from dearly loved friends, left far behind, wrought upon the mind of the pioneer woman to make her sad to melancholy, but after a few years new ties were formed and new interests grasped to partially wear this away, but never entirely, it is my opinion.

She traveled on foot many a weary mile or rode over the roughest roads in a jolting, springless wagon; in calm or stormy weather in the tip-tilting Indian canoes, or on the back of the treacherous cayuse, carrying her babes with her through dangerous places, where to care for one's self would seem too great a burden to most people, patient, calm, uncomplaining.

The little brown hands were busy from morning to night in and about the cabin or cottage; seldom could a disagreeable task be delegated to another; to dress the fish and clams, dig the potatoes in summer as needed for the table, pluck the ducks and grouse, cook and serve the same, fell to her lot before the children were large enough to assist. Moreover, to milk the cows, feed the horses, chop wood occasionally, shoot at predatory birds and animals, burn brush piles and plant a garden and tactfully trade with the Indians were a few of the accomplishments she mastered and practiced with skill and success.

In the summer time this mother took the children out into the great evergreen forest to gather wild berries for present and future use. While the youngest slept under giant ferns or drooping cedar, she filled brimming pails with the luscious fruit, salmonberry, dewberry or huckleberry in their seasons. Here, too, the older children could help, and there was an admixture of pleasure in stopping to gather the wild scarlet honeysuckle, orange lilies, snowy Philadelphus, cones, mosses and lichens and listening to the "blackberry bird," as we called the olive-backed thrush, or the sigh of the boughs overhead.

The family dog went along, barking cheerfully at every living thing, chasing rabbits, digging out "suwellas" or scaring up pheasants and grouse which the eldest boy would shoot. It was a great treat to the children, but when all returned home, tired after the day's adventure, it was mother's hands prepared the evening meal and put the sleepy children to bed.

Everywhere that she has made her home, even for a few years, she has cultivated a garden of fragrant and lovely flowers, a source of much pleasure to her family and friends. The old-fashioned roses and hollyhocks, honeysuckles and sweet Williams grew and flourished, with hosts of annuals around the cottage on Seneca Street in the '60s, and at the old homestead on Lake Union the old and new garden favorites ran riot; so luxuriant were the Japan and Ascension lilies, the velvety pansies, tea, climbing, moss and monthly roses, fancy tulips, English violets, etc., etc., as to call forth exclamations from passersby. Some were overheard in enthusiastic praise saying, "Talk about Florida! just look at these flowers!"

The great forest, with its wealth of beautiful flowers and fruitful things, gave her much delight; the wild flowers, ferns, vines, mosses, lichens and evergreens, to which she often called our attention when we all went blackberrying or picnicing in the old, old time.

The grand scenery of the Northwest accords with her thought-life. She always keenly enjoys the oft-recurring displays of wonderful color in the western sky, the shimmering waves under moon or sun, the majestic mountains and dark fir forests that line the shores of the Inland Sea.

In early days she was of necessity everything in turn to her family; when neither physician nor nurse was readily obtainable, her treatment of their ailments commanded admiration, as she promptly administered and applied with excellent judgment the remedies at her command with such success that professional service was not needed for thirty years except in case of accident of unusual kind.

She looked carefully to the food, fresh air, exercise and bathing of her little flock with the most satisfying results. She believes in the house for the people, not the people for the house, and has invariably put the health and comfort of her household before her care for things.

Her mind is one to originate and further ideas of reform and eagerly appropriate the best of others' conclusions.

Ever the sympathetic counsellor and friend of her children in work and study, she shared their pastimes frequently as well. She remembers going through the heavy forest which once surrounded Lake Union with her boys trout-fishing in the outlet of the lake; while she poked the fish with a pole from their hiding places under the bank the boys would gig them, having good success and much lively sport.

On one trip they had the excitement of a cougar hunt; that is, the cougar seemed to be hunting them, but they "made tracks" and accomplished their escape; the cougar was afterward killed.

Several other of her adventures are recounted elsewhere. It would require hundreds of pages to set forth a moving picture of the stirring frontier life in which she participated.

Louisa Boren Denny is a pioneer woman of the best type.

Her charities have been many; kind and encouraging words, sympathy and gifts to the needy and suffering; her nature is generous and unselfish, and, though working quietly, her influence is and has ever been none the less potent for good.

"Peace hath her victories no less renowned than war."

Of the victories over environment and circumstances much

might be written. The lack of comforts and conveniences compelled arduous manual toil and the busy "brown hands" found many homely duties to engage their activities. In and out of the cabins the high-browed pioneer mothers wrought, where now the delicate dames, perhaps, indolently occupy luxuriant homes.

It is impossible for these latter to realize the loneliness, wildness and rudeness of the surroundings of the pioneer women. Instead of standing awed before the dauntless souls that preceded them, with a toss of the head they say, "You might endure such things but we couldn't, *we are so much finer clay."*

The friends they left behind were sorely regretted; one pioneer woman said the most cruel deprivation was the rarity of letters from home friends, the anxious waiting month after month for some word that might tell of their well-being. Neither telegraph nor fleet mail service had then been established.

The pioneer woman learned to face every sort of danger from riding rough water in an Indian canoe to hunting blackberries where bears, panthers and Indians roamed the deep forest. One said that she would not go through it again for the whole State of Washington.

Each was obliged to depend almost wholly on herself and was compelled to invent and apply many expedients to feed and clothe herself and little ones. There was no piano playing or fancy work for her, but she made, mended and re-made, cooked, washed and swept, helped put in the garden or clear the land, all the time instructing her children as best she could, and by both precept and example, inculcating those high principles that mark true manhood and womanhood.

The typical band of pioneer women who landed on Alki

Point, all but one of whom sat down to weep, have lived to see a great city built, in less than a half century, the home of thousands who reap the fruits of their struggles in the wilderness.

The heroic endurance with which they toiled and waited, many years, the tide in their affairs, whereby they attained a moderate degree of ease, comfort and freedom from anxiety, all so hardily won, is beyond words of admiration.

The well-appointed kitchen of today, with hot and cold water on tap, fine steel range, cupboards and closets crowded with every sort of cunning invention in the shape of utensils for cooking, is a luxurious contrast to the meager outfit of the pioneer housewife. As an example of the inconvenience and privations of the early '50s, I give the following from the lips of one of the pioneer daughters, Sarah (Bonney) Kellogg:

"When we came to Steilacoom in 1853, we lived overhead in a rough lumber store building, and my mother had to go up and down stairs and out into the middle of the street or roadway and cook for a numerous family by a stump fire. She owned the only sieve in the settlement, a large round one; flour was $25.00 a barrel and had weevils in it at that, so every time bread was made the flour had to be sifted to get them out. The sieve was very much in demand and frequently the children were sent here or there among the neighbors to bring it home.

"We had sent to Olympia for a stove, but it was six weeks before it reached its destination."

Think of cooking outdoors for six weeks for a family of growing children, with only the fewest possible dishes and utensils, too!

Any woman of the present time may imagine, if she will, what it would be to have every picture, or other ornament, every article of furniture, except the barest necessities for existence, the fewest possible in number, every fashionable garment, her house itself with its vines and shrubbery suddenly vanish and raise her eyes to see without the somber forest standing close around; within, the newspapered or bare walls of a log cabin, a tiny window admitting little light, a half-open door, but darkened frequently by savage faces; or to strain her ears to catch the song, whistle or step of her husband returning through the dark forest, fearing but hoping and praying that he may not have fallen on the way by the hand of a foe. She might look down to see her form clad in homely garments of cotton print, moccasins on her feet, and her wandering glance touch her sunbonnet hanging on a peg driven between the logs.

Now and then a wild cry sounds faintly or fully over the water or from the sighing depths of the vast wilderness.

An unusual challenge by ringing stentorian voices may call her to the door to scan the face of the waters and see great canoes loaded with brawny savages, whose intentions are uncertain, paddled swiftly up the bay, instead of the familiar sound of steam whistles and gliding in of steamships to a welcome port.

Should it be a winter evening and her companion late, they seat themselves at a rude table and partake of the simplest food from the barely sufficient dishes, meanwhile striving to reassure each other ere retiring for the night.

So day after day passed away and many years of them, the conditions gradually modified by advancing civilization, yet rendered even more arduous by increasing cares and toils incident upon the rearing and educating of a family with very little, if any, assistance from such sources as the modern mother has at her command. Physicians and nurses, cooks and house-maids were almost entirely lacking, and the mother, with what the father could help her, had to be all these in turn.

In all ordinary, incipient or trifling ailments they necessarily became skillful, and for many years kept their families in health with active and vigorous bodies, clear brains and goodly countenances.

The pioneer women are of sterling worth and character. The patience, courage, purity and steadfastness which were developed in them presents a moral resemblance to the holy women of old.

Pioneer men are generally liberal in their views, as was witnessed when the suffrage was bestowed upon the women of Washington Territory several years ago.

CHAPTER Va

A NATIVE DAUGHTER, BORN IN FORT DECATUR

MADGE DECATUR DENNY

MADGE DECATUR Denny was born in Fort Decatur, in the year of the Indian war, on March 16th, 1856; to those sheltering walls had the gentle mother, Louisa Boren Denny, fled on the day of battle. Ushered into the world of danger and rude alarms, her nature proved, in its development, one well suited to the circumstances and conditions; courage, steadfastness and intrepidity were marked traits in her character. Far from being outwardly indicated, they were rather contrasted by her delicate and refined appearance; one said of her, "Madge is such a dainty thing."

Madge was a beautiful child, and woman, too, with great sparkling eyes, abundant golden-brown curls and rosy cheeks. What a picture lingers in my memory!—of this child with her arms entwined about the slender neck of a pet fawn, her eyes shining with love and laughter, her burnished hair shimmering like a halo in the sunlight as she pattered here and there with her graceful playfellow.

The Indians admired her exceedingly, and both they and the white people of the little settlement often remarked upon her beauty.

In early youth she showed a keen intellectuality, reading with avidity at ten years such books as Irving's *Life of Washington*, *History of France*, *Pilgrim's Progress*, Sir Walter Scott's *Lay of the Last Minstrel* and *Lady of the Lake*. From that time on she read every book or printed page that fell in her way; a very rapid reader, one who seemed to take in a page at a few glances, she ranged happily over the fields of literature like a bright-winged bird. Poetry, fiction, history, bards, wits, essayists, all gave of their riches to her fresh, inquiring young mind.

The surpassing loveliness and grandeur of the "world in the open air" appealed to her pure nature even in extreme youth; her friends recall with wonder that when only two and a half years of age she marked the enchantment of a scene in Oregon, of flowery mead, dark forest and deep canyon, under a bright June sky, by plucking at her mother's gown and lisping, "Look! mother, look! so pitty!" (pretty).

And such a lover of flowers! From this same season when she gathered armfuls of great, golden buttercups, blue violets, scarlet columbines, "flags" and lilies from the sunny slopes of the Waldo Hills, through her youth, on the evergreen banks of Puget Sound where she climbed fearlessly about to pluck the purple lupine, orange honeysuckle, Oregon grape and sweet wild roses, was her love of them exemplified. Very often she walked or rode on horseback some distance to procure the lovely lady's slipper (Calypso borealis), the favorite flower of the pioneer children.

A charming letter writer, she often added the adornment of a tiny group of wild flowers in the corner, a few yellow violets, fairylike twin-flowers or lady's slippers.

At one time she had a large correspondence with curious young Eastern people who wished to know something of the far Northwest; to these she sent accurate and graphic descriptions of tall trees, great mountains, waterfalls, lakes and seas, beasts, birds and fishes. She possessed no mean literary talent; without her knowledge some of her letters strayed into print. A very witty one was published in a newspaper, cut out and pasted in the scrapbook of an elocutionist, and to her astonishment produced as a "funny piece" before an audience among whom she sat, the speaker evidently not knowing its author. A parody on Poe's *Raven* made another audience weep real tears in anguished mirth.

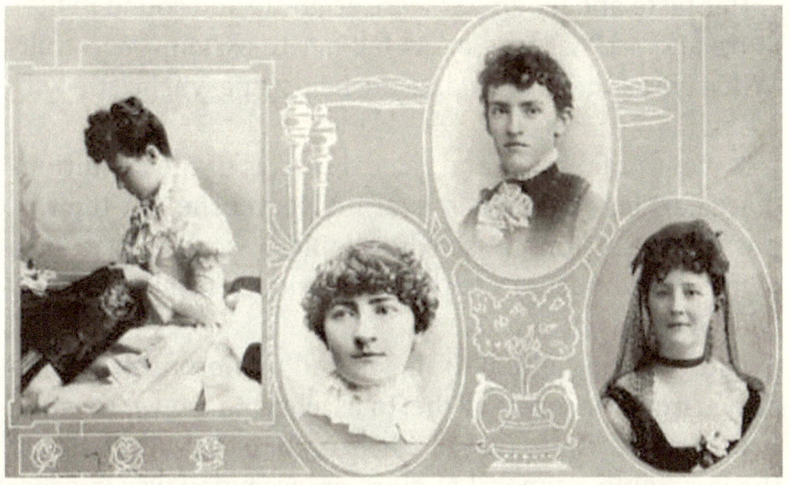

DAUGHTERS OF D. T. AND LOUISA DENNY
EMILY INEZ, MADGE DECATUR, ANNA
LOUISA, MRS. ABBIE DENNY-LINDSLEY

Every felicitous phrase or quaint conceit she met was treasured up, and to these were added not a few of her own invention, and woe betide the wight who accompanied her to opera, concert or lecture, for her *sotto voce* comments, murmured with a grave countenance, were disastrous to their composure and "company manners."

It must be recorded of her that she gave up selfish pleasures to be her mother's helper, whose chief stay she was through many years. In her last illness she said, with much tenderness, "Mother, who will help you now?"

Madge was a true *lady or loaf-giver.* Every creature, within or without the domicile, partook of her generous care, from the pet canary to the housedog, all the human inhabitants and the stranger within the gates.

Moreover, she was genuine, nothing she undertook was slighted or done in a slipshod manner.

Her taste and judgment were accurate and sound in literature and art; her love of art led her to exclaim regretfully, "When we are dead and gone, the landscape will bristle with easels."

A scant population and the exigencies of the conditions placed art expression in the far future, yet she saw the vast possibilities before those who should be so fortunate as to dwell in the midst of such native grandeur, beauty and richness of color.

Like many other children, we had numerous pets, wild things from the forest or the, to us, charming juvenile members of the barnyard flocks. When any of these succumbed to the inevitable, a funeral of more or less pomp was in order, and many a hapless victim of untoward fate was thus tearfully consigned to the bosom of Mother Earth. On one occasion, at the obsequies of a beloved bird or kitten, I forget which, Madge, then perhaps six years of age, insisted upon arranging a litter, draped with white muslin and decorated with flowers, and followed it, as it was borne by two other children, singing with serious though tearless eyes,

> "We're traveling to the grave
> To lay this body down,
> And the last word that I heard him speak
> Was about Jerusalem," etc.

She was so thoroughly in earnest that the older children refrained from laughing at what some might have thought unnecessary solemnity.

Madge had her share of adventures, too; one dark night she came near drowning in Lake Washington. Having visited the Newcastle coal mines with a small party of friends and returned to the lake shore, they were on the wharf ready to go on board the steamer. In some manner, perhaps from inadequate lighting, she stepped backward and fell into the water some distance below. The water was perhaps forty feet deep, the mud unknown. Several men called for "A rope! A rope!" but not a rope could they lay their hands on. After what seemed an age to her, a lantern flashed into the darkness and a long pole held by seven men was held down to her; she grasped it firmly and, as she afterward said, felt as if she could climb to the moon with its assistance—and was safely drawn up, taken to a miner's cottage, where a kind-hearted woman dressed her in dry clothing. She reached home none the worse for her narrow escape.

Her nerves were nerves of steel; she seldom exhibited a shadow of fear and seemed of a spirit to undertake any daring feat. To dare the darkness, climb declivities, explore recesses, seemed pleasures to her courageous nature. At Snoqualmie Falls, in the Archipelago de Haro, in the Jupiter Hills of the Olympic Range, she climbed up and down the steep gorges with the agility of the chamois or our own mountain goat.

The forest, the mountain, the seashore yielded their charm to her, each gave their messages. In a collection which she culled from many sources, ranging from sparkling gayety to profound seriousness, occur these words:

> "I saw the long line of the vacant shore
> The sea-weed and the shells upon the sand
> And the brown rocks left bare on every hand
> As if the ebbing tide would flow no more.
> Then heard I more distinctly than before,
> The ocean breathe and its great breast expand,
> And hurrying came on the defenseless land,
> The insurgent waters with tumultuous roar;
> All thought and feeling and desire, I said
> Love, laughter, and the exultant joy of song
> Have ebbed from me forever! Suddenly o'er me
> They swept again from their deep ocean bed,
> And in a tumult of delight and strong
> As youth, and beautiful as youth, upbore me."

It must have been that "Bird and bee and blossom taught her Love's spell to know," and then she went away to the "land where Love itself had birth."

CHAPTER Vb

LIKE A FOREST FLOWER

ANNA LOUISA DENNY

ANNA WAS the fourth daughter of D. T. and Louisa Boren Denny. In infancy she showed a marked talent for music, signifying by her eyes, head and hands her approval of certain tunes, preferring them to all others. Before she was able to frame words she could sing tunes. When a young girl her memory for musical tones was marvelous, enabling her to reproduce difficult strains while yet unable to read the notes. Possessed of a pure, high, flexible soprano voice, her singing was a delight to her friends. Upon hearing famous singers render favorite airs, her pleasure shone from every feature, although her comments were few. On the long summer camping expeditions of the family, the music books went along with her brothers' cornets, possibly her own flute, and many a happy hour was spent as we drove leisurely along past the tall, dark evergreens, or floated on the silvery waters of the Sound, with perhaps a book of duets open before us, singing sweet songs of bird, blossom and pine tree.

While the other daughters were small and delicately formed, Anna grew up to be a tall, statuesque woman of a truly noble appearance, with a fair face, a high white forehead crowned by masses of brown hair, and a countenance mirthful, sunny, serious, but seldom stern.

A certain draped marble statue in the Metropolitan Museum in New York bears a striking resemblance to Anna, but is not of so noble a type.

Childhood in the wild Northwest braved many dangers both seen and unseen.

While returning late one summer night through the deep forest to our home after having attended a concert in which the children had taken part, Anna, then a little girl of perhaps seven or eight years, had a narrow escape from some wild beast, either a cougar or wildcat. Her mother, who was leading her a little behind the others, said that something grabbed at her and disappeared instantly in the thick undergrowth; grasping her hand more firmly she started to run and the little party, thoroughly frightened, fairly flew along the road toward home.

In this north country it is never really dark on a cloudless summer night, but the heavy forests enshroud the roads and trails in a deep twilight.

Anna, like her sister Madge, was a daring rider and they often went together on long trips through the forest. At one time each was mounted on a lively Indian pony, both of which doubtless had seen strange things and enjoyed many exciting experiences, but were supposed to be quite lamblike and docile. Some reminiscence must have crossed their equine minds, and they apparently challenged each other to a race, so race they must and race they did at a lightning speed on the home run.

They came flying up the lane to the house (the homestead on Lake Union) in a succession of leaps that would have made Pegasus envious had he been "thar or tharabouts." Their riders stuck on like cockleburrs until they reached the gate, when a sudden stop threw Anna to the ground, but she escaped injury, the only damage being a wrecked riding habit.

Anna made no pretension to great learning, yet possessed a well-balanced and cultivated mind. With no ado of great effort she stood first in her class.

At a notable celebration of Decoration Day in Seattle, she was chosen to walk beside the teacher at the head of the school procession; both were tall, handsome young women, carrying the school banner bearing the motto, "Right, then Onward."

It was to this school, which bore his own name, that her father presented a beautiful piano as a memorial of her; it bears the words, from her own lips, "I believe in Jesus," in gold letters across the front.

In 1888 she accompanied her family across the continent to the eastern coast, where she expected to be reunited with a friend, a young girl to whom she was much attached, but it was otherwise ordered; after a brief illness in New York City, she passed away and was brought back to her own loved native land, by the sun-down-seas. Afar in a forest nook she rests, where wildwood creatures pass by, the pine trees wave and the stars sweep over, waiting, watching for the Day toward which the whole creation moves.

* * *

They wandered through the wonderful forest, by lake, fern-embroidered stream and pebble seashore, gazed on the

glistening mountains, the sparkling waves, the burning sun-
sets, shining with such jewel colors as to make them think of
the land of hope, the New Jerusalem. And the majestic snow-
dome of Mountain Rainier which at the first sight thereof
caused a noted man to leap up and shout aloud the joy that
filled his soul; they lived in sight of it for years.

* * *

It might be asked, "Does the environment affect the character and mental development, even the physical configu-
ration?" We answer, "Yes, we believe it does." The fine physique, the bright intellectuality, the lovely character of these
daughters of the West were certainly in part produced and
developed by the wonderful world about them. Simple, pure,
exalted natures ought to be, and we believe are, the rule
among the children of the pioneers of Puget Sound and many
of their successors.

* * *

In this time of gathering up portraits of fair women, I cannot help reverting to the good old times on Puget Sound,
when among the daughters of the white settlers ugliness was
the exception, the majority possessing many points of beauty.
Bright, dark eyes, brilliant complexions, graceful forms, luxuriant hair and fine teeth were the rule. The pure air, mild
climate, simple habits and rational life were amply proved
producers of physical perfection. Old-timers will doubtless
remember the handsome Bonney girls, the Misses Chambers, the Misses Thornton, Eva Andrews, Mary Collins, Nellie
Burnett, Alice Mercer, the Dennys, noticeable for clear white
skin and brilliant color, with abundant dark hair, Gertrude
and Mary Boren with rosy cheeks and blue eyes; Blanche
Hinds, very fair, with large, gray eyes, and others I cannot

now name, as well as a number of beautiful matrons. Every settlement had its favored fair.

Perhaps because women were so scarce, they were petted and indulged and came up with the idea that they were very fine porcelain indeed; they were all given the opportunities in the reach of their parents and were quite fastidious in their dress and belongings.

* * *

Of the other children of D. T. and Louisa Boren Denny, John B. is a well educated and accomplished man of versatility, a lawyer, musician, and practical miner.

D. Thomas is an electrician; was a precocious young business man who superintended the building of an electric street railway when under twenty-five years of age.

Victor W. S., a practical miner, assayer and mining expert, who has been engaged in developing gold and silver mines. Abbie D., an artist and writer, who has published numerous articles, a fine shot with the rifle and an accomplished house-wife; and E. I. Denny, the author of this work, who is not now engaged in writing an autobiography.

All, including the last mentioned, are fond of wild life, hunting, camping and mountain climbing, in which they have had much experience and yearly seek for more.

CHAPTER Vc

ONE OF THE COURAGEOUS YOUTHS

WILLIAM RICHARD BOREN

WILLIAM RICHARD Boren was one of the boy pioneers. He was born in Seattle on the 4th of October, 1854.

The children necessarily shared with their parents and guardians the hardships, dangers, adventures and pleasures of the wild life of the early days.

When his father, Carson D. Boren, went to the gold diggings, William came to the D. T. Denny cottage and remained there for some time. As there was then no boy in the family (there were three little girls) he stepped into usefulness almost immediately. To bring home the cows, weed in the garden, carry flowers and vegetables to market, cut and carry wood, the "chores" of a pioneer home he helped to do willingly and cheerfully.

Every pair of hands must help, and the children learned while very young that they were to be industrious and useful.

It required real fortitude to go on lonely trails or roads

through the dark, thick forest in the deepening twilight that was impenetrable blackness in the wall of sombre evergreens on either hand.

Some children seem to have little fear of anything, but it was different with William; he was afraid; as he graphically described it, he *"felt as if something would catch him in the back."* But he steadfastly traveled the dark trails, showing a remarkable quality of courage.

His sensations cannot be attributed to constitutional timidity altogether, as there were real dangers from wild beasts and savage men in those days.

He would often go long distances from the settlement through the great forest as the shadows were darkening into night, listening breathlessly for the welcome jingle of the bells of the herd, or anxiously to snapping twigs and creaking of lodged trees or voices of night-birds. But when the cattle were gathered up and he could hear the steady tinkle of the leader's bell, although to the eye she was lost in the dusk in the trail ahead, he felt safe.

He calmly faced dangers, both seen and unseen, in after years.

By the time he was twelve or fourteen he had learned to shoot very well with the shotgun and could bring home a fine bunch of blue grouse or "pheasants" (ruffed grouse).

Late one May evening he came into the old kitchen, laden with charming spoils from the forest, a large handful of the sweet favorite of the pioneer children, the lady's slipper or Calypso Borealis, and a bag of fat "hooters" for the stew or pie so much relished by the settlers.

The majority of the pioneer boys were not expected to be particular as to whether they did men's work or women's work, and William was a notable example of versatility, lending a hand with helpless babies, cooking or washing, the most patient and faithful of nurses, lifting many a burden from the tired house-mother.

He was a total abstainer from intoxicants and tobacco, and to the amusement of his friends said he "could not see any sense in jumping around the room," as he described the social dance. It surprised no one, therefore, that he should grow up straight and vigorous, able to endure many hardships.

William was a very Nimrod by the time he reached his majority, a fine shot with the rifle and successful in killing large game. As he came in sight one day on the trail to our camp in the deep forest, he appeared carrying the blackest and glossiest of bear cubs slung over one shoulder. I called to him, "Halt, if you please, and let me sketch you right there." He obligingly consented and in a few moments bear, gun and hunter were transferred to paper. And a good theme it was; with a background of dark firs and cedars, in a mass of brightest green ferns, stood the stalwart figure, clad in vivid scarlet and black, gun on one shoulder and bear cub on the other.

William Boren was an active and useful member of the M. E. or "White Church" in Seattle many years ago. This was the first church established in Seattle.

He removed from the settlement and lived on a ranch for a number of years.

For a time in youth he was in the mining district; while there he imposed upon himself heavy burdens, packing as much as two hundred pounds over the trail.

This was probably overexertion; also in later years, heavy lifting in a logging camp may have helped break his naturally strong constitution.

Many muscular and vigorous persons do not realize the

necessity for caution in exertion. I have seen strong young men balancing their weight against the "hold" of huge stumps, by hanging across a large pole in mid-air.

During his ranch life he was waylaid, basely and cruelly attacked and beaten into insensibility by two ruffians. Most likely this caused the fatal brain trouble from which he died in January, 1899, at the home of his sister, Gertrude Boren, who through a long illness cared for him with affectionate solicitude.

* * *

"O bearded, stalwart, westmost men,
A kingdom won without the guilt
Of studied battle; that hath been
Your blood's inheritance.

Yea, Time, the grand old harvester,
Has gathered you from wood and plain.
We call to you again, again;
The rush and rumble of the car
Comes back in answer. Deep and wide
The wheels of progress have passed on;
The silent pioneer is gone."

CHAPTER VI

ARTHUR A. DENNY

(BORN JUNE 20TH, 1822, DIED JANUARY 9TH, 1889)

A PONDEROUS VOLUME of biography could scarcely set forth the journeyings, experiences, efforts, achievements and character of this well-known pioneer of the Northwest Coast. He was one of the foremost of the steadfast leaders of the pioneers. A long, useful and worthy life he spent among men, the far-reaching influence of which cannot be estimated. When he passed away both private citizens and public officials honored him; those who had known him far back in his youth and through the intervening years said of the eulogies pronounced upon his life, "Well, it is all true, and much more might be said."

A. A. Denny was a son of John Denny and brother of David Thomas Denny; each of them exerted a great influence on the life and institutions of the Northwest.

From sketches published in the local papers I have made these selections:

"The Dennys are a very ancient family of England, Ireland and Scotland. The present branch traces its ancestry from

Ireland to America through great-grandparents, David and Margaret Denny, who settled in Berks County, Pennsylvania, previous to the revolutionary war. There Robert Denny, the grandfather of A. A. Denny was born in 1753. In early life he removed to Frederick County, Virginia, where in 1778 he married Rachel Thomas; and about 1790 removed to and settled in Mercer County, Kentucky.

"There John Denny, father of the deceased, was born May 4, 1793, and was married August 25, 1814, to Sarah Wilson, daughter of Bassel and Ann (Scott) Wilson, who was born in the old town of Bladensburg, near Washington City, February 3, 1797. Her parents came to America in an early day.

"Their paternal and maternal grandparents served in the revolutionary war. The former belonged to Washington's command at the time of Braddock's defeat.

"John Denny was a soldier in the war of 1812, being in Col. Richard M. Johnson's regiment of Kentucky volunteers. He was also an ensign in Capt. McFee's company, and was with Gen. Harrison at the battle of the Thames, when Proctor was defeated and the noted Tecumseh killed. He was a member of the Illinois legislature in 1840 and 1841, with Lincoln, Yates, Bates and others, who afterwards became renowned in national affairs. In politics he was first a Whig and afterward a Republican. For many years he was a Justice of the Peace. He died July 28th, 1875, when 83 years of age. His first wife died March 21st, 1841, when 44 years of age.

"About 1816 John Denny and his family removed to Washington County, Indiana, and settled near Salem, where Arthur A. Denny was born June 20th, 1822. One year later they removed to Putnam County, six miles east from Greencastle, where they remained twelve years, and from there went to Knox County, Illinois. Mr. A. A. Denny has said of his boyhood:

"'My early education began in the log schoolhouse so familiar to the early settler in the West. The teachers were paid by subscription, so much per pupil, and the schools rarely lasted more than half the year, and often but three months. Among the earliest of my recollections is of my father hewing out a farm in the beech woods of Indiana, and I well remember that the first school that I attended was two and a half miles from my home. When I became older it was often necessary for me to attend to home duties half of the day before going to school a mile distant. By close application I was able to keep up with my class.

"'My opportunities to some extent improved as time advanced. I spent my vacations with an older brother at carpenter and joiner work to obtain the means to pay my expenses during term time.'"

A. A. Denny was married November 23, 1843, to Mary Ann Boren, to whom he has paid a graceful and well-deserved tribute in these words:

"She has been kind and indulgent to all my faults, and in cases of doubt and difficulty in the long voyage we have made together she has always been, without the least disposition to dictate, a safe and prudent adviser."

He held many public offices, each and all of which he filled with scrupulous care, from county supervisor in Illinois in 1843 to first postmaster of Seattle in 1853. He was elected to the legislature of Washington Territory, serving for nine consecutive sessions, being the speaker of the third; was registrar of the U. S. Land Office at Olympia from 1861 to 1865. He was a member of the Thirty-ninth Congress, being a delegate from Washington Territory. Even in his age he was given the unanimous vote of the Republicans for U. S. Senator from the State of Washington.

His business enterprises date from the founding of the City of Seattle and are interwoven with its history.

He was a volunteer in the war against the Indians and had some stirring experiences. In his book, *Pioneer Days on Puget Sound*, he gives a very clear and accurate account of the beginning of the trouble with the Indians and many facts concerning the war following.

He found, as many others did, good and true friends, as well as enemies, among the Indians. On page 68 of the work mentioned may be found these words: "I will say further, that my acquaintance and experience with the Puget Sound Indians proved them to be sincere in their friendship, and no more unfaithful and treasonable than the average white man, and I am disposed to believe that the same might be truthfully said of many other Indians."

With regard to the dissatisfied tenderfoot he says: "All old settlers know that it is a common occurrence for parties who have reached here by the easy method of steamer or railway in a palace car to be most blindly unreasonable in their fault-finding, and they are often not content with abusing the country and climate, but they heap curses and abuse on those who came before them by the good old method of ninety or a hundred days crossing the plains, just as though we had sent for them and thus given them an undoubted right to abuse us for their lack of good strong sense. Then we all know, too, that it as been a common occurrence for those same fault-finders to leave, declaring that the country was not fit for civilized people to live in; and not by any means unusual for the same parties to return after a short time ready to settle down and commence praising the country, as though they wanted to make amends for their unreasonable behavior in the first instance."

There are a good many other pithy remarks in this book, forcible for their truth and simplicity.

As the stories of adventure have an imperishable fascination, I give his own account of the discovery of Shilshole or Salmon Bay:

"When we selected our claims we had fears that the range for our stock would not afford them sufficient feed in the winter, and it was not possible to provide feed for them, which caused us a great deal of anxiety. From statements made by the Indians, which we could then but imperfectly understand, we were led to believe that there was prairie or grass lands to the northwest, where we might find feed in case of necessity, but we were too busy to explore until in December, 1852, when Bell, my brother, D. T. Denny, and myself determined to look for the prairie. It was slow and laborious traveling through the unbroken forest, and before we had gone far Bell gave out and returned home, leaving us to proceed alone. In the afternoon we unexpectedly came to a body of water, and at first thought we had inclined too far eastward and struck the lake, but on examination we found it to be tidewater. From our point of observation we could not see the outlet to the Sound, and our anxiety to learn more about it caused us to spend so much time that when we turned homeward it soon became so dark that we were compelled to camp for the night without dinner, supper or blankets, and we came near being without fire also, as it had rained on us nearly all day and wet our matches so that we could only get fire by the flash of a rifle, which was exceedingly difficult under the circumstances."

D. T. Denny remembers that A. A. Denny pulled some of the cotton wadding out of his coat and then dug into a dead fir tree that was dry inside and put it in with what other dry stuff they could find, which was very little, and D. T. Denny fired off his gun into it with the muzzle so close as to set fire to it.

He also relates that he shot a pheasant and broiled it before the fire, dividing it in halves.

A. A. Denny further says:

"Our camp was about midway between the mouth of the bay and the cove, and in the morning we made our way to the cove and took the beach for home. Of course, our failing to return at night caused great anxiety at home, and soon after we got on the beach we met Bell coming on hunt of us, and the thing of most interest to us just then was he had his pockets filled with hard bread.

"This was our first knowledge of Shilshole Bay, which, we soon after fully explored, and were ready to point newcomers in that direction for locations."

Old Salmon Bay Curley had told them there was grass in that region, which was true they afterward learned, but not prairie grass, it was salt marsh, in sufficient quantity to sustain the cattle.

Speaking of the Indians, he tells how they settled around the cabins of the whites at Alki until there were perhaps a thousand, and relates this incident: "On one occasion during the winter, Nelson (Chief Pialse) came with a party of Green River and Muckilshoot Indians, and got into an altercation with John Kanem and the Snoqualmies. They met and the opposing forces, amounting to thirty or forty on a side, drew up directly in front of Low's house, armed with Hudson Bay muskets, the two parties near enough together to have powder-burnt each other, and were apparently in the act of opening fire, when we interposed and restored peace without bloodshed, by my taking John Kanem away and keeping them apart until Nelson and his party left."

His daughter, Lenora Denny, related the same incident to me. She witnessed it as a little child and remembers it perfectly, together with her fright at the preparations for battle, and added that Kanem desired her father at their conference behind the cabin just to let him go around behind the enemy's line of battle and stab their chief; nobody would know who did it and that would be sufficient in lieu of the proposed fight. Mr. Denny dissuaded him and the "war" terminated as above stated.

In the fall of 1855, the Indians exhibited more and more hostility toward the whites, and narrow escapes were not uncommon before the war fairly broke out.

About this time as A. A. Denny was making a canoe voyage from Olympia down the Sound he met with a thrilling experience.

When he and his two Indian canoemen were opposite a camp of savages on the beach, they were hailed by the latter with:

"Who is it you have in the canoe and where are you going?" spoken in their native tongue. After calling back and forth for some little time, two of them put out hastily in a canoe to overtake the travelers, keeping up an earnest and excited argument with one of Mr. Denny's Indians, both of whom he observed never ceased paddling. One of the strangers was dressed up in war-paint and had a gun across his lap; he kept up the angry debate with one of the travelers while the other was perfectly silent.

Finally the pursuers were near enough so that one reached out to catch hold of the canoe when Denny's men paddled quickly out of reach and increased their speed to a furious rate, continuing to paddle with all their might until a long distance from their threatening visitors. Although Mr. Denny did not understand their speech, their voices and gestures were not difficult to interpret; he felt they wished to kill him and thought himself lost.

He afterward learned that his canoeman, who had answered the attacking party, had saved his life by his courage and cunning. The savages from the camp had demanded that Mr. Denny be given up to them that they might kill him in revenge for the killing of some Indians, saying he was a *hyas tyee* (great man) and a most suitable subject for their satisfaction.

He had answered that Mr. Denny was not near so high up nor as great as some others and was always a good friend of the Indians and then carried him to a place of safety by fast and furious paddling. The one who was silent during the colloquy declared afterward that he said nothing for fear they would kill him too.

This exhibition of faithfulness on the part of Indian hirelings is worthy of note in the face of many accusations of treachery on the part of their race.

It is my opinion that Arthur Armstrong Denny led an exemplary life and that he ever desired to do justice to others. If he failed in doing so, it was the fault of those with whom he was associated rather than his own.

A leading trait in his character was integrity, another was the modesty that ever accompanies true greatness, noticeable also in his well known younger brother, D. T. Denny; neither has been boastful, arrogant or grasping for public honors.

A. A. Denny fought the long battle of the pioneer faithfully and well and sleeps in an honored grave.

MARY A. DENNY

Mary Ann Boren (Denny) was born in Tennessee, November 25th, 1822, the first child of Richard Boren and Sarah Latimer Boren (afterward Denny). Her grandfather Latimer, a kind hearted, sympathetic man, sent a bottle of camphor to revive the pale young mother. This camphor bottle was kept in the family, the children resorting to it for the palliation of cuts and bruises throughout their adolescence, and it is now preserved by her own family as a cherished relic, having seen eighty years and more since its presentation.

After the death of her father, leaving her mother a young widow with three small children, they lived in Illinois as pioneers, where Mary shared the toils, dangers and vicissitudes of frontier life. Was not this the school for the greater pioneering of the farthest west?

November 23rd, 1843, she married Arthur A. Denny, a man who both recognized and acknowledged her worth.

When she crossed the plains in 1851 with the Denny company, Mrs. Denny was a young matron of twenty-nine years, with two little daughters. The journey, arduous to any, was peculiarly trying to her with the helpless ones to care for and make as comfortable as such tenting in the wilds might be.

At Fort Laramie her own feet were so uncomfortable in shoes that she put on a pair of moccasins which David T. Denny had bought of an Indian and worn for one day. Mrs. Denny wore them during the remainder of the journey to Portland.

One incident among many serves to show her unfaltering courage; an Indian reached into her wagon to take the gun hung up inside: Mrs. Mary A. Denny pluckily seized a hatchet and drew it to strike a vigorous blow when the savage suddenly withdrew, doubtless with an increased respect for white squaws in general and this one in particular.

The great journey ended, at Portland her third child, Rolland H., was born. If motherhood be a trial under the most favorable circumstances, what must it have been on the long march?

On the stormy and dangerous trip from Portland on the schooner *Exact*, out over the bar and around Cape Flattery to the landing at Alki Point, went the little band with this brave mother and her babe.

On a drizzly day in November, the 13th, 1851, she climbed the bank at Alki Point to the rude cabin, bare of everything now considered necessary to begin housekeeping. They were imperfectly protected from the elements and the eldest child, Catharine, or Kate as she was called, yet remembers how the rain dropped on her face the first night they slept in the unfinished cabin, giving her a decided prejudice against camping out.

The mother's health was poor and it became necessary to provide nourishment for the infant; as there were no cows within reach, or tinned substitutes, the experiment of feeding him on clam juice was made with good effect.

Louisa Boren Denny, her sister, then unmarried, relates the following incident:

"At Alki Point one day, I stood just within the door of the cabin and Mary stood just inside; both of us saw an Indian bob up from behind the bank and point his gun directly at my sister Mary and almost immediately lower it without firing."

Mary A. Denny, when asked recently what she thought might have been his reason for doing so replied, "Well, I don't know, unless it was just to show what he could do; it was Indian Jim; I suppose he did it to show that he could shoot me if he wanted to."

Probably he thought to frighten her at least, but with the customary nerve of the pioneer woman, she exhibited no sign of fear and he went his way.

They afterward learned that on the same evening there had been some trouble with the Indians at the Maple Place and it was thought that this Indian was one of the disaffected or a sympathizer.

Mrs. Mary A. Denny moved about from place to place, living first in the cabin at Alki Point, then a cabin on Elliott Bay, on the north end of their claim, then another cabin near the great laurel tree, on the site of the Stevens Hotel, Seattle. After a time the family went to Olympia. Her husband was in the Land Office, was a member of the Territorial Legislature and Delegate to Congress; all the while she toiled on in her home with her growing family.

They returned to Seattle and built what was for those times a very good residence on the corner of Pike Street and First Avenue, where they had a fine orchard, and there they lived many years.

After having struggled through long years of poverty, not extreme, to be sure, but requiring much patient toil and endurance, their property became immensely valuable and they enjoyed well deserved affluence.

Mrs. Mary A. Denny's family consists of four sons and two daughters; Orion O., the second son, was the second white child born in Seattle. Catherine (Denny) Frye, the elder daughter, was happily married in her girlhood and is the mother of a most interesting family. Rolland H., Orion O., A. Wilson and Charles L. Denny, the four sons, are prominent business men of Seattle.

Mrs. Denny makes her home with Lenora, the younger unmarried daughter, at her palatial residence in Seattle. The last mentioned is a traveled, well read woman of most sympathetic nature, devoted to her friends, one who has shown kindness to many strangers in times past as they were guests in her parents' home.

HENRY VAN ASSELT OF DUWAMISH

I N THE *Post-Intelligencer* of december 8th and 9th, 1902, appeared the following sketches of this well known pioneer: "At the ripe old age of 85, with the friendship and affection of every man he knew in this life, Henry Van Asselt, one of the founders of King County, and one of the four of the first white men to set foot on the shores of Elliott Bay, died yesterday morning at his home, on Fifteenth Avenue, of paralysis. Mr. Van Asselt, with Samuel and Jacob Maple and L. M. Collins, landed in a canoe September 14th, 1851, at the mouth of the Duwamish River, where it enters the harbor of Seattle. They had come from the Columbia River and were more than two months in advance of Arthur Denny, one of the pioneer builders of the city of Seattle. Van Asselt's name is perpetuated through the town of Van Asselt, adjoining the southern limits of the city. He was well known all over the Puget Sound country, and he was the last living member of one of the first bands of white arrivals, on the shores of Elliott Bay.

"Mr. Van Asselt was a Hollander, having been born in

Holland April 11, 1817, two years after the battle of Water-loo. He was in his early youth a soldier in the Holland army during its dispute with Belgium. An expert marksman and an indefatigable huntsman, he came to America in 1850, on a sailing schooner, and a year later was traveling the trail from the Central West to California. Instead of going to the land of gold and sunshine, Van Asselt headed north, reaching the Columbia River in the fall of 1850. A year later found him crossing the Columbia River, after a short sojourn in the mining camps of Northern California. With three companions, L. M. Collins, Jacob and Samuel Maple, Henry Van Asselt made the perilous journey from the Columbia River to the Sound, where, near Olympia, he boarded a canoe, and after two days' traveling reached the mouth of the Duwamish River. Ascending the stream to the junction of the White and Black Rivers, a distance of only a few miles, he staked out a donation land claim of 320 acres in the heart of the richest section of the Duwamish valley."

SAID VALUES INCREASED

"The sturdy Hollander cleared the valley of its primeval forest of firs, and made it truly blossom with farm products of every description. The land today (1902) is worth $1,000 an acre and upwards. At his death, the aged pioneer, the last of his generation, had in his own name some 100 odd acres of this land. Not many weeks ago he had sold twenty-four acres of the old homestead as the site of the new rolling mill and foundry to be constructed by the Vulcan Iron Works.

"Mr. Van Asselt was not the least interesting, by any means, of the old pioneers of King County. In fact, until his death he was the last living member of the first group of white men to set foot on the shores of Elliott Bay. He was a very devout man, and in the late years of his life, when he had retired from active business, it was his custom to spend part of every Sunday at the county jail, reading to the prisoners excerpts from holy writ and giving them words of hopefulness and cheer. This duty was performed for many years as regularly as was his attendance at the Methodist Protestant church, in this city, of which he had been for thirty years a member. It is to be said of the dead pioneer that he was universally loved and respected, and it was his proudest boast that he had never made an enemy in his life. This was literally true.

"Crossing the plains in 1850, young Van Asselt was of great assistance to his party in procuring game and in driving the hostile Indians away, because of his superior marksmanship, which he had acquired as a hunter on the estates of wealthy residents of his native country. He landed at Oregon City, Ore., in September, 1850, and the ensuing winter he spent in mining in California. He accumulated a considerable sum, and, lured by stories of the richness and vastness of the great Northwest, he returned to Portland in 1851, and, crossing the Columbia, made his way to the Sound country. On this trip he was accidentally wounded, the bullet being imbedded in his shoulder. In the days of the Indian troubles on the Sound, Van Asselt was safe from the attacks of the hostiles, who held him in superstitious reverence because of the fact that he carried a bullet in his body. They believed that he could not be killed by a tomahawk. This fact, perhaps, had much to do with his escape from assassination at the hands of the hostiles in the Indian war of 1855.

"Jacob and Samuel Maple, who with L. M. Collins accompanied Mr. Van Asselt to Puget Sound, have been dead many years. Arthur A. Denny has been gathered to his fathers, along with many others of the old pioneers of King County and

Washington. Van Asselt is the last of that hardy race that opened the wilderness on Puget Sound and made it blossom like the rose.

"The news of the death of Van Asselt was received as a sad blow among the people of Van Asselt, where the aged pioneer spent the greater portion of his days in the house which still stands as a monument to his rugged pioneer days. In Van Asselt the people speak the name of the pioneer with reverence on account of the many charities he extended to the poor during his lifetime, and also on account of the many acts which he did in pioneer days to save and maintain the peaceful relations with the savages.

"The marriage of Mr. and Mrs. Van Asselt was celebrated in this county, on Christmas evening 1862. All of those present at the wedding have now passed away with a few exceptions.

"Mr. Van Asselt leaves a wife, Mrs. Mary Jane Maple Van Asselt; a son, Dr. J. H. Van Asselt; two daughters, Mrs. J. H. Benadom, of Puyallup, and Dr. Nettie Van Asselt Burling, and a grandson, Floyd Julian, son of Mrs. Mary Adriane Van Asselt Julian, who died in 1893. Mr. Van Asselt also leaves a brother, Rev. Garrett Van Asselt, of Utrecht, Holland, and several sisters in Holland.

"The following were selected as active pallbearers: William P. Harper, Dexter Horton, D. B. Ward, O. J. Carr, Isaac Parker, M. R. Maddocks. The honorary pallbearers were: Edgar Bryan, Rev. Daniel Bagley, F. M. Guye, Joseph Foster, William Carkeek, Judge Orange Jacobs.

"As illustrative of the regard and esteem in which this pioneer was held by those who knew him best, Dexter Horton, the well known banker and capitalist, who met Mr. Van Asselt in 1852, said last night:

"'Mr. Van Asselt was a man of sterling character. His word

was as good as a government bond. I knew him almost from the beginning of his life here. He was one of the kindliest men I ever met.

"'For fifteen years after I came to Seattle I conducted a general merchandise store here. There were mighty few of us here in those early times and we were all intimately acquainted. I dare say that when a newcomer had resided on the Sound, anywhere from Olympia to the Strait of Fuca, for thirty days, I became acquainted with him. They dropped in here to trade, traveling in Indian canoes. There never was a man of them that I did not trust to any reasonable extent for goods, and my losses on that account in fifteen years' dealing with the early settlers were less than $1,000. This is sufficient testimony as to the character and integrity of the men who, like Van Asselt, faced the privations and dangers of the Western Trail to find homes for themselves on the Pacific Coast.

"'Mr. Van Asselt located on a level farm in the Duwamish valley on his arrival here. He was a man of great energy and thrift, and soon had good and paying crops growing. He used to bring his produce to Seattle, either by Indian canoe, or afterwards, when a trail was cut under the brow of the hill, by teams. This produce was readily disposed of, as we had a large number of men working in the mills and few to supply their necessities.

"'I remember that after he had lived here for several years he moved to town and established a cabinet maker's shop. He was an expert in that line of work. I have an ancient curly maple bureau which he made for me, and Mrs. A. A. Denny has another. They are beautifully fashioned, Van Asselt being well skilled in the trade. Doubtless others among the old-timers here have mementos of his handicraft.

"'Van Asselt was of the type of men who blazed the path for generations that followed them to the Pacific Coast. His integrity was unchallenged, and his charities were numerous and unostentatious. He used to give every worthy newcomer work on his ranch, and many an emigrant in those days got his first start from Henry Van Asselt.'

"Samuel Crawford knew Mr. Van Asselt intimately since 1876. He said last night:

"'Henry Van Asselt, or Uncle Henry, as we all called him, spent the winter of 1850-1851 with my great-great-grandfather, Robert Moore, at Oregon City, Ore., or more properly speaking, on the west shore of the Willamette, just across from Oregon City. Mr. Van Asselt told me this himself. Moore kept a large place, which was a sort of rendezvous for the immigrants, and many a man found shelter at his ranch. He gave them work enough to keep them going, and Van Asselt found employment with him that winter, making shingles from cedar bolts with a draw knife.

"'Mr. Van Asselt was one of the best men that ever lived. His word was as good as gold, and he never overlooked a chance to do a friend a favor. While he spoke English with difficulty, on occasion he could make a good speech, and he always took a deep interest in public affairs. There was probably no important public question involving the interests of Seattle and the Puget Sound country but that Mr. Van Asselt had his say. He did not care for public office, however, but preferred to go along in his quiet way, doing all the good that was possible. He firmly believed in the future of Seattle, which he loved dearly, and I remember many years ago of his purchase of two blocks of ground on Renton Hill, in the vicinity of the residence where he passed the last years of his life. This was nearly twenty years ago.'

"Thomas W. Prosch had known Mr. Van Asselt for many years. He, too, paid a tribute to his fine character, and rugged honesty. 'Six years ago,' said Mr. Prosch, 'I went to talk with Mr. Van Asselt regarding his early experiences on the Sound. He told me of his long and arduous trip across the plains in 1850, and of his escapades with the Indians then and afterward. He said himself that he believed he led a charmed life, as the Indians took many a shot at him, but without avail. He was a dead shot himself, and the Indians had great respect for his skill. He was a very determined man, and undoubtedly had a great influence over the savages.

"'Mr. Van Asselt told me that he met Hill Harmon, a well known Oregon settler, in the spring of 1851, and together they crossed the Columbia and came to Olympia. From there they went with two or three others to Nesqually, where they met Luther M. Collins, one of the first settlers in King County. Collins endeavored to persuade them to locate near him, but they wanted a better place. Finally Collins brought them to the Duwamish valley and located them here. One of the party bought Collins' place at Nesqually, and he came here to locate with Van Asselt and the others. Collins' family was the first white family to establish a home in King County.'"

CHAPTER VIII

THOMAS MERCER

THOMAS MERCER was born in Harrison county, Ohio, March 11, 1813, the eldest of a large family of children. He remained with his father until he was twenty-one, gaining a common school education and a thorough knowledge of the manufacture of woolen goods. His father was the owner of a well appointed woolen mill. The father, Aaron Mercer, was born in Virginia and was of the same family as General Mercer of revolutionary fame. His mother, Jane Dickerson Mercer, was born in Pennsylvania of an old family of that state.

The family moved to Princeton, Ill., in 1834, a period when buffalo were still occasionally found east of the Mississippi river, and savage Indians annoyed and harassed outlying settlements in that region. A remarkable coincidence is a matter of family tradition. Nancy Brigham, who later became Mr. Mercer's wife, and her family, were compelled to flee by night from their home near Dixon at the time of the Black Hawk war, and narrowly escaped massacre. In 1856, about twenty years later, her daughters, the youngest only eight years old, also made a midnight escape in Seattle, two thousand miles away from the scene of their mother's adventure, and they endured the terrors of the attack upon the village a few days later when the shots and shouts of the thousand painted devils rang out in the forest on the hillside from a point near the present gas works to another near where Madison street ends at First Avenue.

CROSSING THE PLAINS

In April, 1852, a train of about twenty wagons, drawn by horses, was organized at Princeton to cross the plains to Oregon. In this train were Thomas Mercer, Aaron Mercer, Dexter Horton, Daniel Bagley, William H. Shoudy, and their families. Some of these still live in or near Seattle and others settled in Oregon. Mr. Mercer was chosen captain of the train and discharged the arduous duties of that position fearlessly and successfully. Danger and disease were on both sides of the long, dreary way, and hundreds of new made graves were often counted along the roadside in a day. But this train seemed to bear a charmed existence. Not a member of the original party died on the way, although many were seriously ill. Only one animal was lost.

As the journey was fairly at an end and western civilization had been reached at The Dalles, Oregon, Mrs. Mercer was taken ill, but managed to keep up until the Cascades were reached. There she grew rapidly worse and soon died. Several members of the expedition went to Salem and wintered there, and in the early spring of 1853 Mercer and Dexter Horton came to Seattle and decided to make it their home. Mr. Horton entered immediately upon a business career, the success of which is known in California, Oregon and Washington, and Mr. Mercer settled upon a donation claim whose eastern end was the meander line of Lake Union and the western end, half way across to the bay. Mercer street is the dividing line between his and D. T. Denny's claims, and all of these tracts were included within the city limits about fifteen years ago.

Mr. Mercer brought one span of horses and a wagon from the outfit with which he crossed the plains and for some time all the hauling of wood and merchandise was done by him. The wagon was the first one in King county. In 1859 he went to Oregon for the summer and while there married Hester L. Ward, who lived with him nearly forty years, dying last November. During the twenty years succeeding his settlement here he worked hard clearing the farm and carrying on dairying and farming in a small way and doing much work with his team. In 1873 portions of the farm came into demand for homes and his sales soon put him in easy circumstances and in later years made him independent, though the past few years of hard times have left but a small part of the estate.

The old home on the farm that the Indians spared when other buildings in the county not protected by soldiers were burned, is still standing and is the oldest building in the county. Mr. D. T. Denny had a log cabin on his place which was not destroyed—these two alone escaped. The Indians were asked, after the war, why they did not burn Mercer's house, to which they replied, "Oh, old Mercer might want it again." Denny and Mercer had always been particularly kind to the natives and just in their dealings, and the savages seem to have felt some little gratitude toward them.

In the early '40s Mr. Mercer and Rev. Daniel Bagley were co-workers in the anti-slavery cause with Owen Lovejoy, of Princeton, who was known to all men of that period in the great Middle West. Later Mr. Mercer joined the Republican party and has been an ardent supporter of its men and measures down to the present. He served ten years as probate judge of King county, and at the end of that period declined a renomination.

In early life he joined the Methodist Protestant church and has ever been a consistent member of that body. Rev. Daniel Bagley was his pastor fifty-two years ago at Princeton, and continued to hold that relation to him in Seattle from 1860 until 1885, when he resigned his Seattle pastorate.

To Mr. Mercer belongs the honor of naming the lakes adjacent to and almost surrounding the city. At a social gathering or picnic in 1855 he made a short address and proposed the adoption of "Union" for the small lake between the bay and the large lake, and "Washington" for the other body of water. This proposition was received with favor and at once adopted. In the early days of the county and city he was always active in all public enterprises, ready alike with individual effort and with his purse, according to his ability, and no one of the city's thousands has taken a keener interest or greater pride than he in the recent development of the city's greatness, although he could no longer share actively in its accomplishment. He was exceedingly anxious to see the canal completed between salt water and the lakes.

His oldest daughter, Mrs. Henry Parsons, lives near Olympia, and is a confirmed invalid. The second daughter was the first wife of Walter Graham, of this place, but died in 1862. The next younger daughters, Mrs. David Graham and Mrs. C. B. Bagley, lived near him and cared for him entirely since the death of Mrs. Mercer last November. In all the collateral branches the aged patriarch leaves behind him here in King county fully half a hundred of relatives of greater or lesser degrees of kinship.

His generosity and benevolence have ever been proverbial. The churches, Y. M. C. A., orphanages and other objects of public benevolence and private charity have good cause to remember his liberality. In a period of five years he gave away at least $20,000 in public and private donations.

Judge Mercer was a charter member of the Pioneers' Association, and took great interest in its affairs. He always made a special effort to attend the annual meeting, until the last two years, when his health would not permit.

Another of the band of hardy pioneers who laid the foundation of the great commonwealth bounded by California on the south, British Columbia on the north, the Rocky Mountains on the east and the illimitable Pacific toward the setting sun, has gone to rest.

"Judge Thomas Mercer died yesterday morning, May 25th, at 5:15 o'clock, after a brief illness, at his home in North Seattle, within a stone's throw of the old homestead where he and his four motherless daughters, all mere children, settled in the somber and unbroken forest two score and five years ago, when the Seattle of today consisted of a sawmill, a trading post and less than a half hundred white people."—(From *Post-Intelligencer* of May 26th, 1898.)

For many years we looked across the valley to see the smoke from the fire on the Mercer hearthstone winding skyward, for they were our only neighbors. Even for this, we were not so solitary, nor quite so lonely as we must have been with no human habitation in our view. And then we felt the kindly presence, sympathy we knew we could always claim, the cheerful greetings and friendly visits.

When his aged pastor, Rev. Daniel Bagley, with snowy locks, stood above his bier and a troop of silver-haired pioneers in tearful silence harkened, he told of fifty years of friendship;

how they crossed the plains together, and of the quiet, steady, Christian life of Thomas Mercer.

He said, "Whatever other reasons may have been given, that he understood some Indians to say the reason they did not burn Mercer's house during the war, was that Mercer was *klosh tum-tum*, (kind, friendly, literally a good heart), and he *wawa-ed Sahale Tyee* (prayed to the Heavenly Chief or Great Spirit). Thus did he let his light shine; even the savages beheld it."

In closing a touching, suggestive and affectionate tribute, he quoted these lines:

> "O what hath Jesus bought for me!
> Before my ravish'd eyes
> Rivers of life divine I see,
> And trees of Paradise;
> I see a world of spirits bright,
> Who taste the pleasures there;
> They all are robed in spotless white,
> And conqu'ring palms they bear."

HESTER L. MERCER

When a child I often visited this good pioneer woman—so faithful, cheerful, kind, self-forgetful.

With busy hands she toiled from morning to night, scarcely sitting down without some house-wifely task to occupy her while she chatted.

Of a very lively disposition, her laugh was frequent and merry.

A more generous, frank and warm-hearted nature was hard to find, the demands made upon it were many and such as to exhaust a shallow one. Her experiences were varied and thrilling, as the following account from the Seattle

Post-Intelligencer of November 13th, 1897, will show:

"There is something in the life of this pioneer woman that makes a lasting impression upon the minds of those who consider it. Mrs. Mercer's general life differed somewhat from the lives of many pioneer women in that she was always a pioneer. Many had given up an existence in the thickly settled portions of the east to accept the burdensome, half-civilized life of the west. They had at least once known the joys of civilization. It was not so with Mrs. Mercer. She was a pioneer from the time she was ushered into the world.

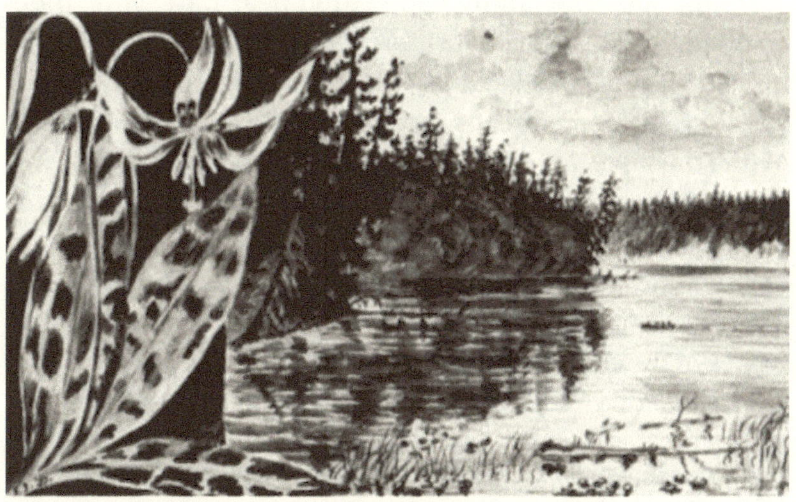

ERYTHRONIUM OF LAKE UNION

"She was born in Kentucky. Go back 75 years in the life of that state and you will get something of its early history. Those who lived there that long ago were pioneers. Her father and mother were Jesse and Elizabeth Ward. They were of that staunch, sturdy people that struggled to obtain a home and accumulate a little fortune in the southern country. Jesse Ward at the age of 18 joined a regiment of Kentucky volunteers which was a part of Jackson's army at the defense of New Orleans in 1814.

"Mrs. Mercer was born in Hartford, the county seat of Ohio county, Kentucky. She was but a little tot when her mother died.

"Her father married again, and children, issues of the second marriage, had been born before Mr. Ward and his family said good-bye to old Kentucky or in reality, young Kentucky, and moved to Arkansas. That was in 1845. There they lived until 1853 and Hester Mercer had a chance of proving her true womanhood. The family had settled near Batesville, Independence county. At that time the county had much virgin soil and it was not a hard matter to figure up the population of the state. Mrs. Mercer seemed to be the head of the family. While the male members of the family were at work clearing land and establishing what they thought would be a permanent home, she was busily occupied in making clothes for herself and others of the family. And what a task it was in those days to make clothes. Crude machinery, in the settled states of the east, turned out with what was considered wonderful rapidity, cloth for garments. But the common people of the West knew nothing of the details of such luxuries.

"Mrs. Mercer, then Hester Ward, took the wool from the sheep, cleaned it, wove it, dyed the cloth, cut and made it into clothing for her father and brothers. When she wanted a gown she could have it, that is, after she had gone into the fields, picked the necessary cotton, developed it into dress goods and turned the goods into a garment.

"Mr. D. B. Ward, a half brother of Mrs. Mercer, has in his possession pieces of the goods out of which she made her gowns when a girl.

"In 1853, Mr. Ward, having heard so much of the great

opportunities that were offered to the pioneer who would accept life in the far West, started with his family and a party of other pioneers across the great Western plains. Stories without end could be told of the adventures and incidents, the results of that long journey. There were nine children of Mr. Ward in his party. The start was made March 9, 1853, and on September 30, Waldo Hills, near Salem, Oregon, was reached.

"The Indians, of course, figured in the life of the Wards while they were crossing the plains, just as they seemed to come into the life of every other band of pioneers that undertook the journey. When about eight miles, by the emigrant route, east of the North Platte, Mr. Ward's party encountered a big band of Arapahoes. Every one was a warrior. They were in full war regalia and dangling from their belts were dozens of scalps. They had been in battle with their enemies, the Blackfeet and Snake River Indians the day before. Crowned with victory, they were on their way home to celebrate.

"The Ward party had been resting in the woods and were about breaking camp to continue their journey when the Indian braves made their appearance. They insisted that they were friendly, but their behavior was not wholly consistent. They crowded in and about the wagons, wanted this and that and finally became impudent because their requests were denied.

"The Ward party had an old bugler with them; when he placed his lips to the bugle something that bordered on music came from the instrument. While the Indians were making their presence known the old bugler grabbed up his bugle and let out several blasts, which echoed and re-echoed around. The leaves trembled, the trees seemed to shake and the Indian braves, who did not fear an encounter with a thousand Blackfeet, were dumbfounded. Their heads went up in the air, the ears of their horses shot forward. The leader of the braves murmured a few words in his native tongue and then like the wind those 400 braves were gone. If the Great White Father had appeared, as they probably expected he would, he would have had to travel many miles to find the Arapahoes.

"The Ward party was soon out of the woods, when they met another band. The old chief was with them. He was mounted on a white mule and produced a copy of a treaty with the government to show that his people loved the white men.

"Down in the valley through which the pioneers were compelled to travel they saw many little tents. Other Indians were camped there. The old chief and his party accompanied the emigrants. Every Indian showed an ugly disposition. The emigrants were compelled to stop in the midst of the tents in the valley. The old chief explained through an interpreter that his people had just come back from a great battle. They were hungry, he said, and wanted food and the emigrants would have to give it to them, for were not these whites, he said, passing through the sacred land of the Indian?

"The Ward party was a small one, it could muster but 22 men. Each man was well armed, but the Indians were mixing up with them and it would have been impossible to get together for united action. It was necessary to submit to the wishes of the Indians. Bacon, sugar, flour and crackers were given up and the old chief divided them among his people.

"While this division was being made young braves were busying themselves by annoying the members of the party. Among the white people was a young woman who had charge of two horses attached to a light covered wagon. Several of the braves took a fancy to her. They gave the whites to understand that any woman who could drive horses was all right and must not go any farther. Mr. Ward and his men had a hard time keeping the Indians from stealing the girl. Once they crowded about her and for a time it was thought she would be taken by force. The white men and several of the women went to her rescue. Mrs. Mercer was in the rescue party. She shoved the Indians right and left and in the end the girl was rescued and smuggled into a closed wagon, where she remained concealed for some hours.

"Another young woman in the party had beautiful auburn hair. An Indian warrior took a fancy to her, thought she was the finest woman he had ever seen, and said that his people would compromise if she were given to him for a wife. Again there was trouble and the girl had to be hidden in a closed wagon.

"The Indians kept up their annoyance of the party for some time, but finally their hunger got the better of them and they sat down to eat the food which the Ward party had under compulsion given them.

"The Indian chief consented that the white people should take their departure. They were quick to do so and were soon some distance from the Indian camp.

"After the Wards reached Oregon, Hester settled down to pioneer life with the other members of the family, but in the fall of 1859, Thomas Mercer, then probate judge of King county, Washington Territory, wooed and won her and they were married. The wedding was one of the important affairs of early days. Rev. Daniel Bagley, of this city, performed the ceremony. After Mr. and Mrs. Mercer came to Seattle they took up their residence in a little house on First Avenue, near Washington Street. The Mercer home at present occupies a block of the old donation claim. The home is on Lombard

Street between Prospect and Villard Avenues.

"When Mr. and Mrs. Mercer came to Seattle, John Denny and wife and James Campbell and wife accompanied them. The three families swelled the population to thirteen families.

"D. B. Ward, a half brother of Mrs. Mercer, also came with them.

"'Seattle was not a very big city in those days,' said Mr. Ward recently in discussing the matter. 'I remember that soon after my arrival I thought I would take a walk up in the woods. I went to the church, which stood where at present is the Boston National Bank building. I found windows filled with little holes. It was a great mystery to me. I went down town and made inquiry about it and was told that every hole represented a bullet fired by the Indians during the fight three years before.'

"Mrs. Mercer was a woman of many grand qualities; she never permitted any suffering to go on about her if she were in a position to relieve it. She was a good friend of the poor and did many kind acts of which the world knew but little."

In the latter years of her life she was a patient, uncomplaining invalid, and finally entered into rest on the 12th of November, 1897, having lived in Seattle for thirty-nine years. She was buried with honor and affection; the pallbearers were old pioneers averaging a forty years' residence in the same place; D. T. Denny, the longest, being one of the founders, for forty-five years; they were Dexter Horton, T. D. Hinckley, D. T. Denny, Edgar Bryan, David Kellogg and Hans Nelson.

Mr. Mercer, at the age of 84 (in 1897), still survives her, passing a peaceful old age in the midst of relatives and friends.

CHAPTER IX

DR. HENRY A. SMITH, THE BRILLIANT WRITER

THIS WELL known pioneer joined the "mighty nation moving west" in 1852. From Portland, the wayside inn of weary travelers, he pushed on to Puget Sound, settling in 1853 on Elliott Bay, at a place known for many years as Smith's Cove.

Being a gifted writer he has made numerous contributions to northwestern literature, both in prose and poetry.

In a rarely entertaining set of papers entitled "Early Reminiscences," he brings vividly to the minds of his readers the "good old times" on Elliott Bay, as he describes the manner of life, personal adventure, odd characters and striking environment of the first decade of settlement. In them he relates that after the White River massacre, he conveyed his mother to a place of safety, by night, in a boat with muffled oars.

To quote his own words: "Early the next morning I persuaded James Broad and Charley Williamson, a couple of harum-scarum run-away sailors, to accompany me to my ranch in the cove, where we remained two weeks securing crops. We always kept our rifles near us while working in the field, so as to be ready for emergencies, and brave as they seemed their faces several times blanched white as they sprang for their guns on hearing brush crack near them, usually caused by deer. One morning on going to the field where we were digging potatoes, we found fresh moccasin tracks, and judged from the difference in the size of the tracks that at least half a dozen savages had paid the field a visit during the night. As nothing had been disturbed we concluded that they were waiting in ambush for us and accordingly we retired to the side of the field farthest from the woods and began work, keeping a sharp lookout the while. Soon we heard a cracking in the brush and a noise that sounded like the snapping of a flintlock. We grabbed our rifles and rushed into the woods where we heard the noise, so as to have the trees for shelter, and if possible to draw a bead on the enemy. On reaching shelter, the crackling sound receded toward Salmon Bay. But fearing a surprise if we followed the sound of retreat, we concluded to reach the Bay by way of a trail that led to it, but higher up; we reached the water just in time to see five redskins land in a canoe, on the opposite side of the Bay where the Crooks' barn now stands. After that I had hard work to keep the runaways until the crop was secured, and did so only by keeping one of them secreted in the nearest brush constantly on guard. At night we barred the doors and slept in the attic, hauling the ladder up after us. Sometimes, when the boys told blood-curdling stories until they became panicky by their own eloquence, we slept in the woods, but that was not often.

"In this way the crops were all saved, cellared and stacked, only to be destroyed afterward by the torch of the common enemy.

"Twice the house was fired before it was finally consumed,

and each time I happened to arrive in time to extinguish the flames, the incendiaries evidently having taken to their heels as soon as the torch was applied."

While yet new to the country he met with an adventure not uncommon to the earliest settlers in the great forest, recorded as follows:

"I once had a little experience, but a very amusing one, of being 'lost.' In the summer of 1854, I concluded to make a trail to Seattle. Up to that time I had ridden to the city in a 'Chinook buggy.' One bright morning I took a compass and started for Seattle on as nearly a straight line as possible. After an hour's travel the sun was hid by clouds and the compass had to be entirely relied upon for the right course. This was tedious business, for the woods had never been burned, and the old fallen timber was almost impassable. About noon I noticed to my utter astonishment, that the compass had reversed its poles. I knew that beds of mineral would sometimes cause a variation of the needle and was delighted at the thought of discovering a *valuable* iron mine so near salt water. A good deal of time was spent in breaking bushes and thoroughly marking the spot so that there would be no difficulty in finding it again, and from that on I broke bushes as I walked, so as to be able to easily retrace my steps. From that place I followed the compass *reversed*, calculating, as I walked, the number of ships that would load annually at Seattle with pig-iron, and the amount of ground that would be eventually covered at the cove with furnaces, rolling mills, foundries, tool manufacturing establishments, etc.

"As night came on I became satisfied that I had traveled too far to the east, and had passed Seattle, and the prospect of spending a night in the woods knocked my iron calculations into pi. Soon, however, I was delighted to see a clearing ahead, and a shake-built shanty that I concluded must be the ranch that Mr. Nagle had commenced improving some time before, and which, I had understood, lay between Seattle and Lake Washington. When I reached the fence surrounding the improvements, I seated myself on one of the top rails for a seat and to ponder the advisability of remaining with my new neighbor over night, or going on to town. While sitting thus, I could not help contrasting his improvements with my own. The size of the clearing was the same, the house was a good deal like mine, the only seeming difference was that the front of his faced the west, whereas the front of mine faced the east. While puzzling over this strange coincidence, my own mother came out of the house to feed the poultry that had commenced going to roost, in a rookery for all the world like my own, only facing the wrong way. 'In the name of all that's wonderful!' I thought, 'what is she doing here? and how did she get here ahead of me?' Just then the world took a spin around, my ranch wheeled into line, and, lo! I was sitting on my own fence, and had been looking at my own improvements without knowing them." And from this he draws a moral and adorns the tale with the philosophic conclusion that people cannot see and think alike owing to their point of view, and we therefore must be charitable.

Until accustomed to it and schooled in wood-craft, the mighty and amazing forest was bewildering and mysterious to the adventurous settler; however, they soon learned how not to lose themselves in its labyrinthine depths.

Dr. Smith is a past master in description, as will be seen by this word-picture of a fire in a vast pitchy and resinous mass of combustible material. I have witnessed many, each a magnificent display.

"Washington beats the world for variety and magnificence

of awe inspiring mountains and other scenery. I have seen old ocean in her wildest moods, have beheld the western prairie on fire by night, when the long, waving lines of flame flared and flashed their red light against the low, fleecy clouds till they blossomed into roseate beauty, looking like vast spectral flower gardens, majestically sweeping through the heavens; have been in the valley of the river Platte, when all the windows of the sky and a good many doors opened at once and the cloud-masked batteries of the invisible hosts of the air volleyed and thundered till the earth fairly reeled beneath the terrific cannonade that tore its quivering bosom with red-hot bombs until awe-stricken humanity shriveled into utter nothingness in the presence of the mad fury of the mightiest forces of nature. But for magnificence of sublime imagery and awe-inspiring grandeur a forest fire raging among the gigantic firs and towering cedars that mantle the shores of Puget Sound, surpasses anything I have ever beheld, and absolutely baffles all attempts at description. It has to be seen to be comprehended. The grandest display of forest pyrotechnics is witnessed when an extensive tract that has been partly cleared by logging is purposely or accidentally fired. When thus partly cleared, all the tops of the fir, cedar, spruce, pine and hemlock trees felled for their lumber remain on the ground, their boughs fairly reeking with balsam. All inferior trees are left standing, and in early days when only the very choicest logs would be accepted by the mills, about one-third would be left untouched, and then the trees would stand thicker, mightier, taller than in the average forest of the eastern and middle states.

"I once witnessed the firing of a two thousand acre tract thus logged over. It was noon in the month of August, and not a breath of air moved the most delicate ferns on the hillsides.

The birds had hushed their songs for their midday siesta, and the babbling brook at our feet had grown less garrulous, as if in sympathy with the rest of nature, when the torch was applied. A dozen or more neighbors had come together to witness the exhibition of the unchained element about to hold high carnival in the amphitheater of the hills, and each one posted himself, rifle in hand, in some conspicuous place at least a quarter of a mile from the slashing in order to get a shot at any wild animal fleeing from the 'wrath to come.'

"The tract was fired simultaneously on all sides by siwashes, who rapidly circled it with long brands, followed closely by rivers of flame in hot pursuit.

"As soon as the fire worked its way to the massive winrows of dry brush, piled in making roads in every direction, a circular wall of solid flame rose half way to the tops of the tall trees. Soon the rising of the heated air caused strong currents of cooler air to set in from every side. The air currents soon increased to cyclones. Then began a race of the towering, billowy, surging walls of fire for the center. Driven furiously on by these ever-increasing, eddying, and fiercely contending tornadoes, the flames lolled and rolled and swayed and leaped, rising higher and higher, until one vast, circular tidal wave of liquid fire rolled in and met at the center with the whirl and roar of pandemoniac thunder and shot up in a spiral and rapidly revolving red-hot cone, a thousand feet in mid-air, out of whose flaring and crater-like apex poured dense volumes of tarry smoke, spreading out on every side, like unfolding curtains of night, till the sun was darkened and the moon was turned to blood and the stars seemed literally raining from heaven, as glowing firebrands that had been carried up by the fierce tornado of swirling flame and carried to immense distances by upper air currents, fell back in showers to the ground. The vast tract, but a few moments before as quiet as a sleeping infant in its cradle, was now one vast arena of seething, roaring, raging flame. The long, lithe limbs of the tall cedars were tossing wildly about, while the strong limbs of the sturdier firs and hemlocks were freely gyrating like the sinewy arms of mighty giant athletes engaged in mortal combat. Ever and anon their lower, pitch-dripping branches would ignite from the fervent heat below, when the flames would rush to the very tops with the roar of contending thunders and shoot upward in bright silvery volumes from five to seven hundred feet, or double the height of the trees themselves. Hundreds of these fire-volumes flaring and flaming in quick succession and sometimes many of them simultaneously, in conjunction with the weird eclipse-like darkness that veiled the heavens, rendered the scene one of awful grandeur never to be forgotten.

"So absorbed were we all in the preternatural war of the fiercely contending elements that we forgot our guns, our game and ourselves.

* * *

"The burnt district, after darkness set in, was wild and weird in the extreme. The dry bark to the very tops of the tall trees was on fire and constantly falling off in large flakes, and the air was filled ever and anon with dense showers of golden stars, while the trees in the environs seemed to move about through the fitful shadows like grim brobdignags clad in sheeny armor."

Having witnessed many similar conflagrations I am able to say that the subject could scarcely be better treated.

Through the courtesy of the author, Dr. H. A. Smith, I have been permitted to insert the following poem, which has no doubt caused many a grim chuckle and scowl of sympathy, too, from the old pioneers of the Northwest:

THE MORTGAGE
The man who holds a mortgage on my farm
And sells me out to gratify his greed,
Is shielded by our shyster laws from harm,
And ever laud for the dastard deed!
Though morally the man is really worse
Than if he knocked me down and took my purse;
The last would mean, at most, a moment's strife,
The first would mean the struggle of a life,
And homeless children wailing in the cold,
A prey to want and miseries manifold;
Then if I loot him of his mangy pup
The guardians of the law will lock me up,
And jaundiced justice fly into a rage
While pampered Piety askance my rags will scan,
And Shylock shout, 'Behold a dangerous man!'
But notwithstanding want to Heaven cries,
And villains masquerade in virtue's guise,
And Liberty is moribund or dead—
Except for men who corporations head—
One little consolation still remains,
The human race will one day rend its chains.

In transcribing Indian myths and religious beliefs, Dr. Smith displays much ability. After having had considerable acquaintance with the native races, he concludes that "Many persons are honestly of the opinion that Indians have no ideas above catching and eating salmon, but if they will lay aside prejudice and converse freely with the more intelligent natives, they will soon find that they reason just as well on all subjects that attract their attention as we do, and being free from pre-conceived opinions, they go directly to the heart of theories and reason both inductively and deductively with surprising clearness and force."

Dr. Smith exhibits in his writings a broadly charitable mind which sees even in the worst, still some lingering or smothered good.

Dr. Smith is one of a family of patriots; his great-grandfather, Copelton Smith, who came from Germany to America in 1760 and settled in or near Philadelphia, Pa., fought for liberty in the war of the Revolution under General Washington. His father, Nicholas Smith, a native of Pennsylvania, fought for the Stars and Stripes in 1812. Two brothers fought for Old Glory in the war of the Rebellion, and he himself was one of the volunteers who fought for their firesides in the State, then Territory of Washington.

"A family of fighters," as he says, "famous for their peaceful proclivities when let alone."

The varied experiences of life in the Northwest have developed in him a sane and sweet philosophy, perhaps nowhere better set forth in his writings than in his poem "Pacific's Pioneers," read at a reunion of the founders of the state a few years ago, and with which I close this brief and inadequate sketch:

PACIFIC'S PIONEERS
A greeting to Pacific's Pioneers,
Whose peaceful lives are drawing to a close,
Whose patient toil, for lo these many years,
Has made the forest blossom as the rose.

And bright-browed women, bonny, brave and true,
And laughing lasses, sound of heart and head,
Who home and kindred bade a last adieu
To follow love where fortune led.

I do not dedicate these lines alone
To men who live to bless the world today,
But I include the nameless and unknown
The pioneers who perished by the way.

Not for the recreant do my numbers ring,
The men who spent their lives in sport and spree,
Nor for the barnacles that always cling
To every craft that cruises Freedom's sea.

But nearly all were noble, brave and kind,
And little cared for fame or fashion's gyves;
And though they left their Sunday suits behind
They practiced pure religion all their lives.

Their love of peace no people could excel,
Their dash in war the poet's pen awaits;
Their sterling loyalty made possible
Pacific's golden galaxy of states.

They had no time to bother much about
Contending creeds that vex the nation's Hub,
But then they left their leather latches out
To every wandering Arab short of grub.

Cut off from all courts, man's earthly shield
    from harm,
They looked for help to Him whose court's above,
And learned to lean on labor's honest arm,
And live the higher law, the law of love.

Not one but ought to wear a crown of gold,
If crowns were made for men who do their best
Amid privations cast and manifold
That unborn generations may be blest.

Among these rugged pioneers the rule
Was equal rights, and all took special pride
In 'tending Mother Nature's matchless school,
And on her lessons lovingly relied.

And this is doubtless why they are in touch
With Nature's noblemen neath other skies;
And though of books they may not know as much
Their wisdom lasts, as Nature never lies.

And trusting God and His unerring plan
As only altruistic natures could
Their faith extended to their fellow man,
The image of the Author of all good.

Since Nature here has done her best to please
By making everything in beauty's mold,
Loads down with balm of flowers every breeze,
And runs her rivers over reefs of gold,

It seems but natural that men who yearn
For native skies, and visit scenes of yore,
Are seldom satisfied till they return
To roam the Gardens of the Gods once more!

And since they fell in love with nature here
How fitting they should wish to fall asleep
Where sparkling mountain spires soar and spear
The stainless azure of the upper deep.

And yet we're saddened when the papers say
Another pioneer has passed away!
And memory recalls when first, forsooth,
We saw him in the glorious flush of youth.

How plain the simple truth when seen appears,
No wonder that faded leaves we fall!
This is the winter of the pioneers
That blows a wreath of wrinkles to us all!

A few more mounds for faltering feet to seek,
When, somewhere in this lovely sunset-land
Like some weird, wintry, weather-beaten peak
Some rare old Roman all alone will stand.

But not for long, for ere the rosy dawn
Of many golden days has come and gone,
Our pine-embowered bells will shout to every shore
'Pacific's Pioneers are now no more!'

But lovely still the glorious stars will glow
And glitter in God's upper deep like pearls
And mountains too will wear their robes of snow
Just as they did when we were boys and girls.

Ah well, it may be best, and is, no doubt,
As death is quite as natural as birth
And since no storms can blow the sweet stars out,
Why should one wish to always stay on earth?

Especially as God can never change,
And man's the object of His constant care
And though beyond the Pleiades we range
His boundless love and mercy must be there.

FAMOUS INDIAN CHIEFS

SEALTH OR "Old Seattle," a peaceable son of the forest, was of a line of chieftains, his father, Schweabe, or Schweahub, a chief before him of the Suquampsh tribe inhabiting a portion of the west shore of Puget Sound, his mother, a Duwampsh of Elliott Bay, whose name was Wood-sho-lit-sa.

Sealth's birthplace was the famous Oleman House, near the site of which he is now buried. Oleman House was an immense timber structure, long ago inhabited by many Indians; scarcely a vestige of it now remains. It was built by Sealth's father. Chief Sealth was twice married and had three sons and five daughters, the last of whom, Angeline, or Ka-ki-is-il-ma, passed away on May 31, 1896. In an interview she informed me that her grandfather, Schweabe, was a tall, slim man, while Sealth was rather heavy as well as tall. Sealth was a hunter, she said, but not a great warrior. In the time of her youth there were herds of elk near Oleman House which Sealth hunted with the bow or gun.

The elk, now limited to the fastnesses of the Olympic

Mountains, were also hunted in the cove south of West Seattle, by Englishmen, Sealth's cousin, Tsetseguis, helping, with other Indians, to carry out the game.

Angeline further said that her father, "Old Seattle," as the white people called him, inherited the chiefship when a little boy. As he grew up he became more important, married, obtained slaves, of whom he had eight when the Dennys came, and acquired wealth. Of his slaves, Yutestid is living (1899) and when reminded of him she laughed and repeated his name several times, saying, "Yutestid! Yutestid! How was it possible for me to forget him? Why, we grew up together!" Yutestid was a slave by descent, as also were five others; the remaining two he had purchased. It is said that he bought them out of pity from another who treated them cruelly.

Sealth, Keokuk, William and others, with quite a band of Duwampsh and Suquampsh Indians, once attacked the Chimacums, surrounded their large house or rancheree at night; at some distance away they joined hands forming a circle and gradually crept up along the ground until quite near, when they sprang up and fired upon them; the terrified occupants ran out and were killed by their enemies. On entering they found one of the wounded crawling around crying "Ah! A-ah!" whom they quickly dispatched with an ax.

A band of Indians visited Alki in 1851, who told the story to the white settlers, imitating their movements as the attacking party and evidently much enjoying the performance.

About the year 1841, Sealth set himself to avenge the death of his nephew, Almos, who was killed by Owhi. With five canoe loads of his warriors, among whom was Curley, he ascended White River and attacked a large camp, killed more than ten men and carried the women and children away into captivity.

At one time in Olympia some renegades who had planned to assassinate him, fired a shot through his tent but he escaped unhurt. Dr. Maynard, who visited him shortly after, saw that while he talked as coolly as if nothing unusual had occurred, he toyed with his bow and arrow as if he felt his power to deal death to the plotters, but nothing was ever known of their punishment.

Sealth was of a type of Puget Sound Indian whose physique was not by any means contemptible. Tall, broad shouldered, muscular, even brawny, straight and strong, they made formidable enemies, and on the warpath were sufficiently alarming to satisfy the most exacting tenderfoot whose contempt for the "bowlegged *siwash*" is by no means concealed. Many of the old grizzly-haired Indians were of large frame and would, if living, have made a towering contrast to their little "runts" of critics.

Neither were their minds dwarfed, for evidently not narrowed by running in the grooves of other men's thoughts, they were free to nourish themselves upon nature and from their magnificent environment they drew many striking comparisons.

Not versed in the set phrases of speech, time-worn and hackneyed, their thoughts were naive, fresh, crude and angular as the frost-rended rocks on the mountain side. A number of these Indians were naturally gifted as orators; with great, mellow voices, expressive gestures, flaming earnestness, piteous pathos and scorching sarcasm, they told their wrongs, commemorated their dead and declared their friendship or hatred in a voluminous, polysyllabic language no more like Chinook than American is like pigeon English.

The following is a fragment valuable for the intimation it gives of their power as orators, as well as a true description of the appearance of Sealth, written by Dr. H. A. Smith, a well known pioneer, and published in the Seattle Sunday Star of October 29, 1877:

"Old Chief Seattle was the largest Indian I ever saw, and by far the noblest looking. He stood nearly six feet in his moccasins, was broad-shouldered, deep-chested and finely proportioned. His eyes were large, intelligent, expressive and friendly when in repose, and faithfully mirrored the varying moods of the great soul that looked through them. He was usually solemn, silent and dignified, but on great occasions moved among assembled multitudes like a Titan among Lilliputians, and his lightest word was law.

"When rising to speak in council or to tender advice, all eyes were turned upon him, and deep-toned, sonorous and eloquent sentences rolled from his lips like the ceaseless thunders of cataracts flowing from exhaustless fountains, and his magnificent bearing was as noble as that of the most civilized military chieftain in command of the force of a continent. Neither his eloquence, his dignity nor his grace was acquired. They were as native to his manhood as leaves and blossoms are to a flowering almond.

"His influence was marvelous. He might have been an emperor but all his instincts were democratic, and he ruled his subjects with kindness and paternal benignity.

"He was always flattered by marked attentions from white men, and never so much as when seated at their tables, and on such occasions he manifested more than anywhere else his genuine instincts of a gentleman.

"When Governor Stevens first arrived in Seattle and told the natives that he had been appointed commissioner of Indian affairs for Washington Territory, they gave him a demonstrative reception in front of Dr. Maynard's office near the water front on Main Street. The bay swarmed with canoes and the shore was lined with a living mass of swaying, writhing, dusky humanity, until Old Chief Seattle's trumpet-toned voice rolled over the immense multitude like the reveille of a bass drum, when silence became as instantaneous and perfect as that which follows a clap of thunder from a clear sky.

"The governor was then introduced to the native multitude by Dr. Maynard, and at once commenced in a conversational, plain and straightforward style, an explanation of his mission among them, which is too well understood to require recapitulation.

"When he sat down, Chief Seattle arose, with all the dignity of a senator who carries the responsibilities of a great nation on his shoulders. Placing one hand on the governor's head, and slowly pointing heavenward with the index finger of the other, he commenced his memorable address in solemn and impressive tones:

"'Yonder sky has wept tears of compassion on our fathers for centuries untold, and which to us, looks eternal, may change. Today it is fair, tomorrow it may be overcast with clouds. My words are like the clouds that never set. What Seattle says the chief Washington can rely upon, with as much certainty as our pale-face brothers can rely upon the return of the seasons. The son of the white chief says his father sends us greetings of friendship and good-will. This is kind, for we know he has little need of our friendship in return, because his people are many. They are like the grass that covers the vast prairie, while my people are few and resemble the scattering trees of a storm-swept plain.

"'The great, and I presume good, white chief sends us word that he wants to buy our lands, but is willing to allow us to reserve enough to live on comfortably. This indeed appears generous, for the red man no longer has rights that he need respect, and the offer may be wise also, for we are no longer in need of a great country.

"'There was a time when our people covered the whole land as the waves of a wind-ruffled sea covers its shell-paved shore. That time has long since passed away with the greatness of tribes almost forgotten. I will not mourn over our untimely decay, or reproach my pale-face brothers with hastening it, for we, too, may have been somewhat to blame.

"'When our young men grew angry at some real or imaginary wrong and disfigured their faces with black paint, their hearts also are disfigured and turned black, and then cruelty is relentless and knows no bounds, and our old men are not able to restrain them.'

"He continued in this eloquent strain and closed by saying: 'We will ponder your proposition and when we have decided we will tell you, but should we accept it I here and now make this first condition: That we shall not be denied the privilege, without molestation, of visiting at will the graves of our ancestors and friends. Every part of this country is sacred to my people; every hillside, every valley, every plain and grove has been hallowed by some fond memory or some sad experience of my tribe.

"'Even the rocks that seem to lie dumb, as they swelter in the sun, along the silent seashore in solemn grandeur, thrill with memories of past events, connected with the fate of my people and the very dust under our feet responds more lovingly to our footsteps than to yours, because it is the ashes of our ancestors and their bare feet are conscious of the sympathetic touch, for the soil is rich with the life of our kindred. At night when the streets of your cities and villages shall be silent and you think them deserted they will throng with the returning hosts that once filled and still love this beautiful land. The white man will never be alone. Let him be just and deal kindly with my people, for the dead are not altogether powerless.'"

Concerning the well-known portrait of Sealth, Clarence Bagley has this to say:

"It was in the early summer of 1865 that the original picture which is now so much seen of the old chief was taken. I think I probably have a diary giving the day upon which the old chief sat for his picture. An amateur artist named E. M. Sammis had secured a camera at Olympia and coming to Seattle established himself in a ramshackle building at the southeast corner of what is now Main and First Avenue South. Old Chief Seattle used often to hang about the gallery and scrutinize the pictures with evident satisfaction. I myself spent not a little time in and about the gallery and on the particular day the picture of the old chief was taken, was there. It occurred to the photographer to get a picture of the chief. The latter was easily persuaded to sit and it is a wrong impression, that has become historic, that the Indians generally were afraid of the photographer's art, considering it black magic.

"The chief's picture was taken and I printed the first copy taken from the negative. There may possibly have been photographs taken of the old chief at a later date, but I do not remember any, certainly none earlier, that I ever knew of."

With regard to Sealth's oratory, D. T. Denny relates that when the chief with his *tillicum* camped on the "Point" near the site of the New England Hotel, often in the evening he would stand up and address his people. D. T. Denny's home was near the site of the Stevens Hotel (Marion and First Avenue, Seattle), and many Indians were camped near by.

When these heard Chief Sealth's voice, they would turn their heads in a listening attitude and evidently understood what he was saying, although he was about three-fourths of a mile away, such was the resonance and carrying power of his voice.

My father has also related to me this incident: Sealth and his people camped alongside the little white settlement at Alki. While there one of his wives died and A. A. Denny made a coffin for the body, but they wrapped the same in so many blankets that it would not go in and they were obliged to remove several layers, although they probably felt regret as the number of wrappings no doubt evidenced wealth and position.

D. T. Denny was well acquainted with George Seattle, or See-an-ump-kun, one of Sealth's sons, who was a friendly, good-natured Indian, married to a woman of the Sklallam tribe. The other surviving son when the whites arrived, was called Jim Seattle.

Thlid Kanem was a cousin of Sealth.

On the 7th of June, 1866, the famous old chieftain joined the Great Majority.

He had outlived many of his race, doubtless because of his temperate habits.

If, as the white people concluded, he was born in 1786, his age was eighty years. It might well have been greater, as they have no records and old Indians show little change often in twenty or twenty-five years, as I have myself observed.

In 1890 some leading pioneers of Seattle erected a monument to his memory over his grave in the Port Madison reservation. A Christian emblem it is, a cross of Italian marble adorned with an ivy wreath and bears this legend:

"SEATTLE
Chief of the Suqamps and Allied Tribes,
Died June 7, 1866.
The Firm Friend of the Whites, and for Him the
City of Seattle was Named by Its
Founders."
Also on the side opposite,
"Baptismal name, Noah Sealth, Age probably
80 years."

LESCHI

Leschi was a noted Nesqually-Klickitat chief, who at the head of a body of warriors attacked Seattle in 1856.

Other chiefs implicated were, Kitsap, Kanasket, Quiemuth, Owhi and Coquilton.

Leschi being accused of influencing the Indians at Seattle, who were friendly, in January, 1856, an attempt was made to capture him by Captain Keyes of Fort Steilacoom. Keyes sent Maloney and his company in the Hudson Bay Company's steamer *Beaver* to take him prisoner.

They attempted to land but Leschi gathered up his warriors and prepared to fight. Being at a decided disadvantage, as but a few could land at a time, the soldiers were obliged to withdraw. Keyes made a second attempt in the surveying steamer *Active*; having no cannon he tried to borrow a howitzer from the *Decatur* at Seattle, but the captain refused to loan it and Keyes returned to get a gun at the fort. Leschi prudently withdrew to Puyallup, where he continued his warlike preparations. Followed by quite an army of hostile Indians, he landed on the shore of Lake Washington, east of Seattle, at a point near what is now called Leschi Park, and on the 26th of January, 1856, made the memorable attack on Seattle.

The cunning and skill of the Indian in warfare were no

match for the white man's cannon and substantial defenses and Leschi was defeated. He threatened a second attack but none was ever made. By midsummer the war was at an end.

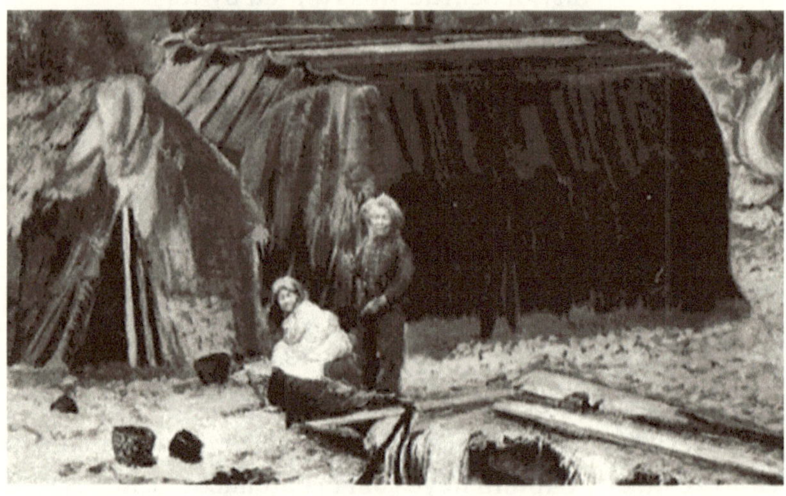

TYPES OF INDIAN HOUSES

By an agreement of a council held in the Yakima country, between Col. Wright and the conquered chiefs, among whom were Leschi, Quiemuth, Nelson, Stahi and the younger Kitsap, they were permitted to go free on parole, having promised to lead peaceable lives. Leschi complied with the agreement but feared the revenge of white men, so gave himself up to Dr. Tolmie, as stated elsewhere. Dr. Tolmie was Chief Factor of the Hudson Bay Company. He came from Scotland in 1833 with another young surgeon and served in the medical department at Fort Vancouver several years. Dr. Tolmie was a prominent figure at Fort Nesqually, a very influential man with the Indians and distinguished for his ability; he lived in Victoria many years, where he died at a good old age.

A special term of court was held to try Leschi for a murder

which it could not be proven he committed and the jury failed to agree. He was tried again in March, 1857, convicted and sentenced to be hanged on the 10th of June. The case was carried up to the supreme court and the verdict sustained. Again he was sentenced to die on the 22nd of January, 1858. A strong appeal was made by those who wished to see justice done, to Gov. McMullin, who succeeded Gov. Stevens, but a protest prevailed, and when the day set for execution arrived, a multitude of people gathered to witness it at Steilacoom. But the doomed man's friends saw the purpose was revenge and a sharp reproof was administered. The sheriff and his deputy were arrested, for selling liquor to the Indians, before the hour appointed, and held until the time passed. Greatly chagrined at being frustrated, the crowd held meetings the same evening and by appealing to the legislature and some extraordinary legislation in sympathy with them, supplemented by "ground and lofty tumbling" in the courts, Leschi was sentenced for the third time.

On the 19th of February, 1858, worn by sickness and prolonged imprisonment he was murdered in accordance with the sentiment of his enemies.

No doubt the methods of *savage* warfare were not approved, but that did not prevent their hanging a man on parole.

On July 3rd, 1895, a large gathering of Indians assembled on the Nesqually reservation. Over one thousand were there. They met to remove the bones of Leschi and Quiemuth to the reservation. The ceremonies were very impressive; George Leschi, a nephew of Leschi and son of Quiemuth, made a speech in the Indian tongue. He said the war was caused by the whites demanding that the Nesqually and Puyallup Indians be removed to the Quiniault reservation on the Pacific Coast, and their reservation thrown open for settlement. It

was in battling for the rights of their people and to preserve
the lands of their forefathers, he said, that the war was inau-
gurated by the Indian chiefs.

PAT KANEM

The subject of this sketch was one of the most interesting
characters brought into prominence by the conflict of the
two races in early days of conquest in the Northwest. That
he was sometimes misunderstood was inevitable as he was
self-contained and independent in his nature and probably
concealed his motives from friend and foe alike.

The opinion of the Indians was not wholly favorable to
him as he became friendly to the white people, especially
so toward some who were influential.

Pat Kanem was one of seven brothers, his mother a Snoqualmie of which tribe he was the recognized leader, his
father, of another tribe, the Soljampsh.

It is said that he planned the extermination or driving
out of the whites and brought about a collision at old Fort
Nesqually in 1849, when Leander Wallace was killed, he
and his warriors having picked a quarrel with the Indians
in that vicinity who ran to the fort for protection. It seems
impossible to ascertain the facts as to the intention of the
Snoqualmies because of conflicting accounts. Some who
are well acquainted with the Indians think it was a quarrel,
pure and simple, between the Indians camped near by and
the visiting Snoqualmies, without any ulterior design upon
the white men or upon the fort itself. Also, Leander Wallace
persisted in boasting that he could settle the difficulty with
a club and contrary to the persuasions of the people in the
fort went outside, thereby losing his life.

Four of Pat Kanem's brothers were arrested; and although

one shot killed Wallace, two Indians were hung, a proceeding which would hardly have followed had they been white men. John Kanem, one of Pat Kanem's brothers, often visited Mr. and Mrs. D. T. Denny afterward, and would repeat again and again, "They killed my brother" (Kluskie mem-a-loose nika ow).

A Snoqualmie Indian in an interview recently said that Qushun (Little Cloud) persuaded Pat Kanem to give up his brother so that he might surely obtain and maintain the chiefship. Whatever may have been his attitude at first toward the white invaders he afterward became their ally in subduing the Indian outbreak.

As A. A. Denny recounts in his valuable work *Pioneer Days on Puget Sound,* Pat Kanem gave him assurance of his steadfast friendship before the war and further demonstrated it by appearing according to previous agreement, accompanied by women and children of the tribe, obviously a peace party, with gifts of choice game which he presented on board to the captain of the *Decatur.*

With half a hundred or more of his warriors, his services were accepted by the governor and they applied themselves to the gruesome industry of taking heads from the hostile ranks. Eighty dollars for a chief's head and twenty for a warrior's were the rewards offered.

Lieut. Phelps, gratefully remembered by the settlers of Seattle, thus described his appearance at Olympia, after having invested some of his pay in Boston *ictas* (clothes): "Pat Kanem was arrayed in citizen's garb, including congress gaiters, white kid gloves, and a white shirt with standing collar reaching half-way up his ears, and the whole finished off with a flaming red neck-tie."

Pat Kanem died while yet young; he must have been

regarded with affection by his people. Years afterward when one of his tribe visited an old pioneer, he was given a photograph of Pat Kanem to look at; wondering at his silence the family were struck by observing that he was gazing intently on the pictured semblance of his dead and gone chieftain, while great tears rolled unchecked down the bronze cheeks. What thoughts of past prosperity, the happy, roving life of the long ago and those who mingled in it, he may have had, we cannot tell.

STUDAH

Studah, or Williams, was one of three sons of a very old Duwampsh chief, Queaucton, who brought them to A. A. Denny asking that he give them "Boston" names. He complied by calling them Tecumseh, Keokuk and William.

The following sketch was written by Rev. G. F. Whitworth, a well-known pioneer:

"William, the chief of the surviving Indians of the Duwampsh tribe, died at the Indian camp on Cedar River on Wednesday, April 1. He was one of the few remaining Indians who were at all prominent in the early settlement of this country, and is almost, if not actually, the last of those who were ever friendly to the whites. His father, who died about the time that the first white settlements were made in this country, was the principal or head chief of the Duwamish Indians. He left three sons, Tecumseh, Keokuk and William. All of whom are now dead. Tecumseh, presumably the eldest son, succeeded his father, and was recognized as chief until he was deposed by Capt. (now Gen.) Dent, U. S. A., who acted under authority of the United States government in relation to the Indians, at that time. He had some characteristics which seemed to disqualify him for the office, while on the other hand William seemed pre-eminently fitted to fill the position, and was therefore chief and had been recognized both by whites and Indians up to the time of his death.

"At the time of the Indian war, he, like Seattle and Curley, was a true friend of the whites. The night before Seattle was attacked there was a council of war held in the woods back of the town, and William attended that council, and his voice was heard for peace and against war. He was always friendly to the whites, and for nearly forty years he has been faithful in his friendship to E. W. Smithers, to whom I am indebted for much of the information contained in this article.

"Those who knew William will remember that he was distinguished for natural dignity of manner. He was an earnest and sincere Catholic, was a thoroughly good Indian, greatly respected by his tribe, and having the confidence of those among the whites who knew him. William was an orator and quite eloquent in his own language. On one occasion shortly after Capt. Hill, U. S. A., came to the territory, some complaints had been made to the superintendent, which were afterwards learned to be unfounded, asking to have the Duwamish Indians removed from Black River to the reservation. Capt. Hill was sent to perform this service, and went with a steamer to their camp, which was on Mr. Smither's farm, a little above the railroad bridge. The captain was accompanied by United States Agent Finkbonner, and on his arrival at the camp addressed the Indians, through an interpreter, informing them of the nature of his errand, and directing them to gather their *ictas* without delay and go on board the steamer, to be at once conveyed to the reservation. William and his Indians listened respectfully to the captain, and when he had closed his remarks William made his reply.

"His speech was about an hour in length, in which his

eloquence was clearly exhibited. He replied that the father at Olympia or the Great Father at Washington City, had no right to remove his tribe. They were peaceful, had done no wrong. They were under no obligation to the government, had received nothing at its hands, and had asked for nothing; they had entered into no treaty; their lands had been taken from them. This, however, was their home. He had been born on Cedar River, and there he intended to remain, and there his bones should be laid. They were not willing to be removed. They could not be removed. He might bring the soldiers to take them, but when they should come he would not find them, for they would flee and hide themselves in the 'stick' (the woods) where the soldiers could not find them. Capt. Hill found himself in a dilemma, out of which he was extricated by Mr. Smithers, who convinced the captain that the complaints were unfounded, and that with two or three exceptions those who had signed the complaint and made the request did not reside in that neighborhood, but lived miles away. They were living on Mr. Smithers' land with his consent, and when he further guaranteed their good behavior, and Mrs. Smithers assured him that she had no fears and no grievance, but that when Mr. Smithers was away she considered them a protection rather than otherwise, the captain concluded to return without them, and to report the facts as he found them.

"William's last message was sent to Mr. Smithers a few days before he died, and was a request that he would see that he was laid to rest as befitted his rank, and not allow him to be buried like a seedy old vagrant, as many of the newcomers considered him to be.

"It is hardly necessary for me to say that this request was faithfully complied with, and that on Friday, April 3, his remains were interred in the Indian burying ground near Renton. The funeral was a large one, Indians from far and near coming to render their last tribute of respect to his memory.

"From the time of his birth until his death he had lived in the region of Cedar and Black Rivers, seventy-nine years.

"His successor as chief will be his nephew, Rogers, who is a son of Tecumseh."

"ANGELINE"

Ka-ki-is-il-ma, called Angeline by the white settlers, about whom so much has been written, was a daughter of Sealth.

In an interview, some interesting facts were elicited.

Angeline saw white people first at Nesqually, "King George" people, the Indians called the Hudson Bay Company's agents and followers.

She saw the brothers of Pat Kanem arrested for the killing of Wallace; she said that Sealth thought it was right that the two Snoqualmies were executed.

When a little girl she wore deerskin robes or long coats and a collar of shells; in those days her tribe made three kinds of robes, some of *suwella*, *shulth* or mountain beaver fur, and of deer-skins; the third was possibly woven, as they made blankets of mountain sheep's wool and goat's hair.

Angeline was first married to a big chief of the Skagits, Dokubkun by name; her second husband was Talisha, a Duwampsh chief. She was a widow of about forty-five when Americans settled on Elliott Bay. Two daughters, Chewatum or Betsy and Mamie, were her only children known to the white people, and both married white men. Betsy committed suicide by hanging herself in the shed room of a house on Commercial Street, tying herself to a rafter by a red bandanna handkerchief. Betsy left an infant son, since grown up, who lived with Angeline many years. Mary or Mamie married Wm. DeShaw and has been dead for some time.

It has been said that some are born great, some achieve greatness, while others have greatness thrust upon them. Of the last described class, Angeline was a shining representative. Souvenir spoons, photographs, and cups bearing her likeness have doubtless traveled over a considerable portion of the civilized world, all of the notoriety arising therefrom certainly being unsought by the poor old Indian woman.

Newspaper reporters, paragraphers, and magazine writers have never wearied of limning her life, recounting even the smallest incidents and making of her a conspicuous figure in the literature of the Northwest.

It quite naturally follows that some absurd things have been written, some heartless, others pathetic and of real literary value, although it has been difficult for the tenderfoot to avoid errors. Upon the event of her death, which occurred on Sunday, May 31st, 1896, a leading paper published an editorial in which a brief outline of the building of the city witnessed by Angeline was given and is here inserted:

"Angeline, as she had been named by the early settlers, had seen many wonders. Born on the lonely shores of an unknown country, reared in the primeval forest, she saw all the progress of modern civilization. She saw the first cabin of the pioneer; the struggles for existence on the part of the white man with nature; the hewing of the log, then the work of the sawmill, the revolt of the aboriginal inhabitants against the intruder and the subjugation of the inferior race; the growth from one hut to a village; from village to town; the swelling population with its concomitants of stores, ships and collateral industries; the platting of a town; the organization of government; the accumulation of commerce; the advent of railroads and locomotives; of steamships and great engines of maritime warfare; the destruction of a town by fire and the marvelous energy which built upon its site, a city. Where there had been a handful of shacks she saw a city of sixty thousand people; in place of a few canoes she saw a great fleet of vessels, stern-wheelers, side-wheelers, propellers, whalebacks, the Charleston and Monterey. She saw the streets lighted by electricity; saw the telephone, elevators and many other wonders.

* * *

"Death came to her as it does to all; but it came as the precursor of extinction, it adds another link in the chain which exemplifies the survival of the fittest."

These comments are coldly judicial and exactly after the mind of the unsympathetic tenderfoot or the "hard case" of early days. In speaking of the "survival of the fittest" and the "subjugation of the inferior race" a contrast is drawn flattering to the white race, but any mention of the incalculable injury, outrages, indignities and villainies practiced upon the native inhabitants by evil white men is carefully avoided. Angeline "saw" a good many other things not mentioned in the above eulogy upon civilization. She saw the wreck wrought by the white man's drink; the Indians never made a fermented liquor of their own.

Angeline said that her father, Sealth, once owned all the land on which Seattle is built, that he was friendly to the white people and wanted them to have the land; that she was glad to see fine buildings, stores and such like, but not the saloons; she did not like it at all that the white people built saloons and Joe, her grandson, would go to them and get drunk and then they made her pay five dollars to get him out of jail!

However, I will not dwell here on the dark side of the poor Indians' history, I turn therefore to more pleasant reminiscence.

Ankuti (a great while ago) when the days were long and happy, in the time of wild blackberries, two pioneer women with their children, of whom the writer was one, embarked with Angeline and Mamie in a canoe, under the old laurel (madrona) tree and paddled down Elliott Bay to a fine blackberry patch on W. N. Bell's claim.

After wandering about a long while they sat down to rest on mossy logs beside the trail. They sat facing the water, the day was waning, and as they thought of their return one of them said, "O look at the canoe!" It was far out on the shining water; the tide had come up while the party wandered in the woods and the canoe, with its stake, was quite a distance from the bank. Mamie ran down the trail to the beach, took off her moccasins and swam out to the canoe, her mother and the rest intently watching her. Then she dived down to the bottom; as her round, black head disappeared beneath the rippling surface, Angeline said "Now she's gone." But in a few moments we breathed a sigh of relief as up she rose, having pulled up the stake, and climbed into the canoe, although how she did it one cannot tell, and paddled to the shore to take in the happy crew. This little incident, but more especially the scene, the forms and faces of my friends, the dark forest, moss-cushioned seats under drooping branches, and the graceful canoe afloat on the silvery water—and *it did* seem for a few, long moments that Mamie was gone as Angeline said in her anxiety for her child's safety showing she too was a human mother—all this has never left my memory!

Angeline lived for many years in her little shanty near the water front, assisted often with food and clothing from kindly white friends. She had a determination to live, die and be buried in Seattle, as it was her home, and that, too, near her old pioneer friends, thus typifying one of the dearest wishes of the Indians.

She was one of the good Indian washerwomen, gratefully remembered by pioneer housewives. These faithful servitors took on them much toil, wearing and wearisome, now accomplished by machinery or Chinese.

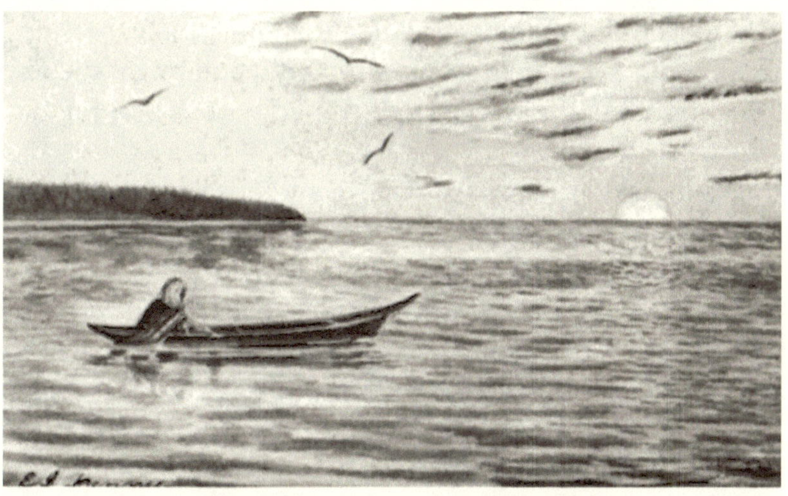

LAST VOYAGE OF THE LUMEI

The world is still deceived by the external appearance; but even the toad "ugly and venomous" was credited with a jewel in its head.

Now Angeline was ugly and untidy, and all that, but not as soulless as some who relegated her to the lowest class of living creatures.

A white friend whom she often visited, Mrs. Sarah Kellogg,

said to the writer, "Angeline lived up to the light she had; she was honest and would never take anything that was offered her unless she needed it. I always made her some little present, saying, 'Well, Angeline, what do you want? Some sugar?' 'No, I have plenty of sugar, I would like a little tea.' So it was with anything else mentioned, if she was supplied she said so. I had not seen her for quite a while at one time, and hearing she was sick sent my husband to the door of her shack to inquire after her. Sure enough she lay in her bunk unable to rise. When asked if she wanted anything to eat, she replied, 'No, I have plenty of muck-amuck; Arthur Denny sent me a box full, but I want some candles and matches.'

"She told me that she was getting old and might die any time and that she never went to bed without saying her prayers.

"During a long illness she came to my house quite often, but was sent away by those in charge; when I was at last able to sit up, I saw her approaching the house and went down to the kitchen to be ready to receive her. As usual I inquired after her wants, when she somewhat indignantly asked, 'Don't you suppose I can come to see you without wanting something?'

"One day as she sat in my kitchen a young white girl asked before her, in English, of course, 'Does Angeline know anything about God?' She said quickly in Chinook, 'You tell that girl that I know God sees me all the time; I might lie or steal and you would never find it out, but God would see me do it.'"

In her old age she exerted herself, even when feeble from sickness, to walk long distances in quest of food and other necessities, stumping along with her cane and sitting down now and then on a door-step to rest.

All the trades-people knew her and were generally kind to her.

At last she succumbed to an attack of lung trouble and passed away. Having declared herself a Roman Catholic, she was honorably buried from the church in Seattle, Rev. F. X. Prefontaine officiating, while several of the old pioneers were pallbearers.

A canoe-shaped coffin had been prepared on which lay a cross of native rhododendrons and a cluster of snowballs, likely from an old garden. A great concourse of people were present, many out of curiosity, no doubt, while some were there with real feeling and solemn thought. Her old friend, Mrs. Maynard, stood at the head of the grave and dropped in a sprig of cedar. She spoke some encouraging words to Joe Foster, Betsy's son, and Angeline's sole mourner, advising him to live a good life.

And so Angeline was buried according to her wish, in the burying ground of the old pioneers.

YUTESTID

After extending numerous invitations, I was pleasantly surprised upon my return to my home one day to find Mr. and Mrs. Yutestid awaiting an interview.

In the first place this Indian name is pronounced *Yute-stid* and he is the only survivor (in 1898) of Chief Sealth's once numerous household. His mother was doubtless a captive, a Cowichan of British Columbia; his father, a Puget Sound Indian from the vicinity of Olympia. He was quite old, he does not know how old, but not decrepit; Angeline said they grew up together.

He is thin and wiry looking, with some straggling bristles for a beard and thick short hair, still quite black, covering a head which looks as if it had been flattened directly on top as well as back and front as they were wont to do. This peculiar cranial development does not affect his intelligence, however, as we have before observed in others; he is quick-witted and knows a great many things. Yutestid says he can speak all the leading dialects of the Upper Sound, Soljampsh, Nesqually, Puyallup, Snoqualmie, Duwampsh, Snohomish, but not the Sklallam and others north toward Vancouver.

Several incidents related in this volume were mentioned and he remembered them perfectly, referred to the naming of "New York" on Alki Point and the earliest settlement, repeating the names of the pioneers. The murder at Bean's Point was committed by two Soljampsh Indians, he said, and they were tried and punished by an Indian court.

He remembers the hanging of Pat Kanem's brothers, Kussass and Quallawowit.

"Long ago, the Indians fight, fight, fight," he said, but he declared he had never heard of the Duwampsh campaign attributed to Sealth.

Yutestid was not at the battle of Seattle but at Oleman House with Sealth's tribe and others whom Gov. Stevens had ordered there. He chuckled as he said "The bad Indians came into the woods near town and the man-of-war (Decatur) mamoked pooh (shot) at them and they were frightened and ran away."

Lachuse, the Indian who was shot near Seneca Street, Seattle, he remembered, and when I told him how the Indian doctor extracted the buckshot from the wounds he sententiously remarked, "Well, sometimes the Indian doctors did very well, sometimes they were old humbugs, just the same as white people."

Oleman House was built long before he was born, according to his testimony, and was adorned by a carved wooden figure, over the entrance, of the great thunder bird, which performed the office of a lightning rod or at least prevented thunder bolts from striking the building.

When asked what the medium of exchange was *ankuti* (long ago), he measured on the index finger the length of pieces of abalone shell formerly used for money.

In those days he saw the old women make feather robes of duck-skins, also of deer-skins and dog-skins with the hair on; they made bead work, too; beaded moccasins called *Yachit.*

The old time ways were very slow; he described the cutting of a huge cedar for a canoe as taking a long time to do, by hacking around it with a stone hammer and "chisel."

Before the advent of the whites, mats served as sails.

I told him of having seen the public part of Black Tamanuse and they both laughed at the heathenism of long ago and said, "We don't have that now."

Yutestid denied that *his* people ate dog when making black tamanuse, but said the Sklallams did so.

"If I could speak better English or you better Chinook I could tell you lots of stories," he averred. Chinook is so very meager, however, that an interpreter of the native tongue will be necessary to get these stories.

They politely shook hands and bade me "Good-bye" to jog off through the rain to their camping place, Indian file, he following in the rear contentedly smoking a pipe. Yutestid is industrious, cultivating a patch of ground and yearly visiting the city of Seattle with fruit to sell.

THE CHIEF'S REPLY

Yonder sky through ages weeping
Tender tears o'er sire and son,
O'er the dead in grave-banks sleeping,
Dead and living loved as one,
May turn cruel, harsh and brazen,

Burn as with a tropic sun,
But my words are true and changeless,
Changeless as the season's run.

Waving grass-blades of wide prairie
Shuttled by lithe foxes wary,
As the eagle sees afar,
So the pale-face people are;
Like the lonely scattering pine-trees
On a bleak and stormy shore,
Few my brother warriors linger
Faint and failing evermore.

Well I know you could command us
To give o'er the land we love,
With your warriors well withstand us
And ne'er weep our graves above.
See on Whulch the South wind blowing
And the waves are running free!
Once my people they were many
Like the waves of Whulch's sea.

When our young men rise in anger,
Gather in a war-bent band,
Face black-painted and the musket
In the fierce, relentless hand,
Old men pleading, plead in vain,
Their dark spirits none restrain.

If to you our land we barter,
This we ask ere set of sun,
To the graves of our forefathers,
Till our days on earth are done,
We may wander as our hearts are
Wandering till our race is run.

Speak the hillsides and the waters,
Speak the valleys, plains and groves,
Waving trees and snow-robed mountains,
Speak to him where'er he roves,
To the red men's sons and daughters
Of their joys, their woes and loves.

By the shore the rocks are ringing
That to you seem wholly dumb,
Ever with the waves are singing,
Winds with songs forever come;
Songs of sorrow for the partings
Death and time make as of yore,
Songs of war and peace and valor,
Red men sang on Whulch's shore.

See! the ashes of our fathers,
Mingling dust beneath our feet,
Common earth to you, the strangers,
Thrills us with a longing sweet.
Fills our pulses rhythmic beat.
At the midnight in your cities
Empty seeming, silent streets
Shall be peopled with the hosts
Of returning warriors' ghosts.
Tho' I shall sink into the dust,
My warning heed; be kind, be just,
Or ghosts shall menace and avenge.

PART III

INDIAN LIFE AND SETTLERS'
BEGINNINGS

CHAPTER I

SAVAGE DEEDS OF SAVAGE MEN

A T BEAN'S Point, opposite Alki on Puget Sound, an Indian murdered, at night, a family of Indians who were camping there.

The Puyallups and Duwampsh came together in council at Bean's Point, held a trial and condemned and executed the murderer. Old Duwampsh Curley was among the members of this native court and likely Sealth and his counsellors.

One of the family escaped by wading out into the water where he might have become very cool, if not entirely cold, if it had not been that Captain Fay and George Martin, a Swedish sailor, were passing by in their boat and the Indian begged to be taken in, a request they readily granted and landed him in a place of safety.

Again at Bean's Point an Indian was shot by a white man, a Scandinavian; the charge was a liberal one of buckshot.

Some white men who went to inquire into the matter

309

followed the Indian's trail, finding ample evidence that he had climbed the hill back of the house, where he may have been employed to work, and weak from his wounds had sat down on a log and then went back to the water; but his body was never found. It was supposed that the murderer enticed him back again and when he was dead, weighted and sunk him in the deep, cold waters of the Sound.

At one time there was quite a large camp of Indians where now runs Seneca Street, Seattle, near which was my home. It was my father's custom to hire the Indians to perform various kinds of hard labor, such as grubbing stumps, digging ditches, cutting wood, etc. For a while we employed a tall, strong, fine-looking Indian called Lachuse to cut wood; through a long summer day he industriously plied the ax and late in the twilight went down to a pool of water, near an old bridge, to bathe. As he passed by a clump of bushes, suddenly the flash and report of a gun shattered the still air and Lachuse fell heavily to the ground with his broad chest riddled with buckshot.

There was great excitement in the camp, running and crying of the women and debate by the men, who soon carried him into the large Indian house. He was laid down in the middle of the room and the medicine man, finding him alive, proceeded to suck the wounds while the tamanuse noise went on.

A distracted, grey-haired lum-e-i, his mother, came to our house to beg for a keeler of water, all the time crying, *"Mameloose Lachuse! Achada!"*

Two of the little girls of our family, sleeping in an old-fashioned trundle bed, were so frightened at the commotion that they pulled the covers up over their heads so far that their feet protruded below.

The medicine man's treatment seems to have been effective, aided by the tamanuse music, as Lachuse finally recovered.

The revengeful deed was committed by a Port Washington Indian, in retaliation for the stealing of his *klootchman* (wife) by an Indian of the Duwampsh tribe, although it was not Lachuse, this sort of revenge being in accordance with their heathen custom.

"Jim Keokuk," an Indian, killed another Indian in the marsh near the gas works; he struck him on the head with a stone. Jim worked as deck hand on a steamer for a time, but he in turn was finally murdered by other Indians, wrapped with chains and thrown overboard, which was afterward revealed by some of the tribe.

There were many cases of retaliation, but the Indians were fairly peaceable until degraded by drink.

The beginning of hostilities against the white people on the Sound, by some historians is said to have been the killing of Leander Wallace at old Fort Nesqually. One of them gives this account:

"Prior to the Whitman massacre, Owhi and Kamiakin, the great chiefs of the upper and lower Yakima nations, while on a visit to Fort Nesqually, had observed to Dr. Tolmie that the Hudson Bay Company's posts with their white employes were a great convenience to the natives, but the American immigration had excited alarm and was the constant theme of hostile conversation among the interior tribes. The erection in 1848, at Fort Nesqually, of a stockade and blockhouse had also been the subject of angry criticism by the visiting northern tribes. So insolent and defiant had been their conduct that upon one afternoon for over an hour the officers and men of the post had guns pointed through the loopholes at a number of Skawhumpsh Indians, who, with their weapons ready for assault, had posted themselves under cover of adjacent stumps and trees.

"Shortly before the shooting of Wallace, rumors had reached the fort that the Snoqualmies were coming in force to redress the alleged cruel treatment of Why-it, the Snoqualmie wife of the young Nesqually chief, Wyampch, a dissipated son of Lahalet.

"Dr. Tolmie treated such a pretext as a mere cloak for a marauding expedition of the Snoqualmies.

"Sheep shearing had gathered numbers of extra hands, chiefly Snohomish, who were occupying mat lodges close to the fort, besides unemployed stragglers and camp followers.

"On Tuesday, May 1, 1849, about noon, numbers of Indian women and children fled in great alarm from their lodges and sought refuge within the fort. A Snoqualmie war party, led by Pat Kanem, approached from the southwestern end of the American plains. Dr. Tolmie having posted a party of Kanakas in the northwest bastion went out to meet them.

"Tolmie induced Pat Kanem to return with him to the fort, closing the gate after their entrance."

The following is said to be the account given by the Hudson Bay Company's officials:

"The gate nearest the mat lodges was guarded by a white man and an Indian servant. While Dr. Tolmie was engaged in attending a patient, he heard a single shot fired, speedily followed by two or three others. He hastily rushed to the bastion, whence a volley was being discharged at a number of retreating Indians who had made a stand and found cover behind the sheep washing dam of Segualitschu Creek. Through a loop-hole the bodies of an Indian and a white man were discernible at a few yards distance from the north gate where the firing had commenced.

"He hastened thither and found Wallace breathing his last, with a full charge of buckshot in his stomach. The dying man was immediately carried inside of the fort.

"The dead Indian was a young Skawhumpsh, who had accompanied the Snoqualmies.

"The Snohomish workers, as also the stragglers, had been, with the newly arrived Snoqualmies, in and out of the abandoned lodges, chatting and exchanging news. A thoughtless act of the Indian sentry posted at the water gate, in firing into the air, had occasioned a general rush of the Snohomish, who had been cool observers of all that had passed outside.

"Walter Ross, the clerk, came to the gate armed, and seeing Kussass, a Snoqualmie, pointing his gun at him, fired but missed him. Kussass then fired at Wallace. Lewis, an American, had a narrow escape, one ball passing through his vest and trousers and another grazing his left arm.

"Quallawowit, as soon as the firing began, shot through the pickets and wounded Tziass, an Indian, in the muscles of his shoulder, which soon after occasioned his death.

"The Snoqualmies as they retreated to the beach killed two Indian ponies and then hastily departed in their canoes.

"At the commencement of the shooting, Pat Kanem, guided by Wyampch, escaped from the fort, a fortunate occurrence, as, upon his rejoining his party the retreat at once began.

"When Dr. Tolmie stooped to raise Wallace, and the Snoqualmies levelled their guns to kill that old and revered friend, an Indian called 'the Priest' pushed aside the guns, exclaiming 'Enough mischief has already been done.'

"The four Indians of the Snoqualmie party whose names were given by Snohomish informers to Dr. Tolmie, together with Kussass and Quallawowit, were afterward tried for the murder of Wallace."

Their names were Whyik, Quallawowit, Kussass, Stahow-
ie, Tatetum and Quilthlimkyne; the last mentioned was a
Duwampsh.

Eighty blankets were offered for the giving up of these
Indians.

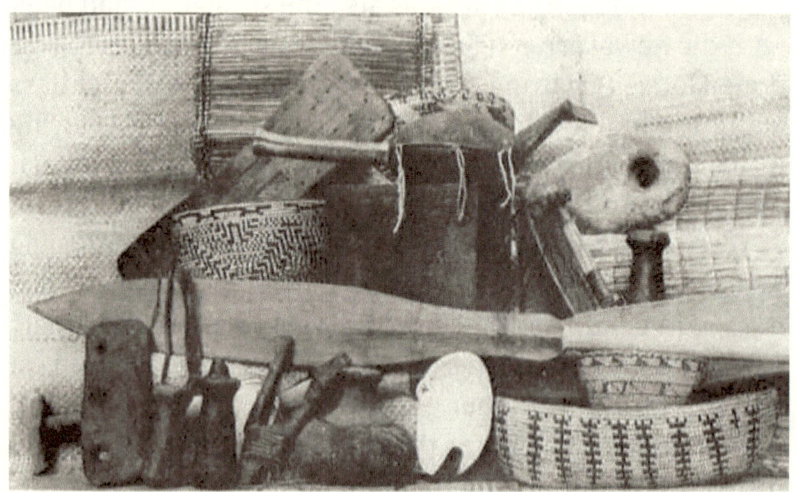

A FEW ARTIFACTS OF PUGET SOUND INDIANS

The Snoqualmies came to Steilacoom, where they were to
be tried, in war paint and parade.

The officials came from far; down the Columbia; up the
Cowlitz, and across to Puget Sound, about two hundred miles
in primitive style, by canoe, oxcart or cayuse.

The trial occupied two days; on the third day, the two condemned, Kussass and Quallawowit, were executed.

One shot Wallace, *two* Indians were hung; Leschi, a leader
in the subsequent war of 1855, looked on and went away
resenting the injustice of taking two lives for one. Other Indians no doubt felt the same, thus preparing the way for their
deadly opposition to the white race.

It certainly seems likely that the "pretext" of the Sno-qualmies was a valid one as Wyampch, the young Nesqually chief, was a drunkard, and Why-it, his Snoqualmie wife, was no doubt treated much as Indian wives generally in such a case, frequently beaten and kicked into insensibility.

The Snoqualmies had been quarreling with the Nesquallies before this and it is extremely probable that, as was current-ly reported among old settlers, the trouble was among the Indians themselves.

There are two stories also concerning Wallace; first, that he was outside quietly looking on, which he ought to have known better than to do; second, that he was warned not to go outside but persisted in going, boasting that he could settle the difficulty with a club, paying for his temerity with his life.

A well known historian has said that the "different tribes had been successfully treated with, but the Indians had acted treacherously inasmuch as it was well known that they had long been plotting against the white race to destroy it. This being true and they having entered upon a war without cause, however, he (Gov. Stevens) might sympathize with the restlessness of an inferior race who perceived that destiny was against them, he nevertheless had high duties toward his own."

Now all this was true, yet there were other things equally true. Not all the treachery, not all the revenge, not all the cruelty were on the side of the "inferior" race. Even all the inferiority was not on one side. The garbled translation by white interpreters, the lying, deceit, nameless and number-less impositions by lawless white men must have aroused and fostered intense resentment. That there were white sav-ages here we have ample proof.

When Col. Wright received the conquered Spokane chiefs in council with some the pipe of peace was smoked. After it was over, Owhi presented himself and was placed in irons for breaking an agreement with Col. Wright, who bade him summon his son, Qualchin, on pain of death by hanging if his son refused to come.

The next day Qualchin appeared not knowing that the order had been given, and was seized and hung without trial. Evidently Kamiakin, the Yakima chief, had good reason to fear the white man's treachery when he refused to join in the council.

The same historian before mentioned tells how Col. Wright called together the Walla Wallas, informed them that he knew that they had taken part in recent battles and ordered those who had to stand up; thirty-five promptly rose. Four of these were selected and hung. Now these Indians fought for home and country and volunteered to be put to death for the sake of their people, as it is thought by some, those hung for the murder of Whitman and his companions, did, choosing to do so of their own free will, not having been the really guilty ones at all.

Quiemuth, an Indian, after the war, emerged from his hiding place, went to a white man on Yelm prairie requesting the latter to accompany him to Olympia that he might give himself up for trial. Several persons went with him; reached Olympia after midnight, the governor placed him in his office, locking the door. It was soon known that the Indian was in the town and several white men got in at the back door of the building. The guard may have been drowsy or their movements very quiet; a shot was fired and Quiemuth and the others made a rush for the door where a white man named Joe Brannan stabbed the Indian fatally, in revenge for the death of his brother who had been killed by Indians some time before.

Three of the Indian leaders in Western Washington were assassinated by white men for revenge. Leschi, the most noted of the hostile chiefs on the Sound, was betrayed by two of his own people, some have said.

I have good authority for saying that he gave himself up for fear of a similar fate.

He was tried three times before he was finally hung after having been kept in jail a long time. Evidently there were some obstructionists who agreed with the following just and truthful statement by Col. G. O. Haller, a well-known Indian fighter, first published in the *Seattle Post-Intelligencer*:

"The white man's aphorism 'The first blow is half the battle,' is no secret among Indians, and they practice it upon entering a war. Indeed, weak nations and Indian tribes, wrought to desperation by real or fancied grievances, inflict while able to do so horrible deeds when viewed by civilized and Christ-like men. War is simply barbarism. And when was war refined and reduced to rules and regulations that must control the Indian who fights for all that is dear to him—his native land and the graves of his sires—who finds the white man's donation claim spread over his long cultivated potato patch, his hog a trespasser on his old pasture ground and his old residence turned into a stable for stock, etc.?

"Leschi, like many citizens during the struggle for secession, appealed to his instincts—his attachment to his tribe—his desire, at the same time to conform to the requirements of the whites, which to many of his people were repulsive and incompatible. He decided and struck heavy blows against us with his warriors. Since then we have learned a lesson.

"Gen. Lee inflicted on the Union army heavy losses of life

and destruction of property belonging to individuals. When he surrendered his sword agreeing to return to his home and become a law-abiding citizen, Gen. Grant protected him and his paroled army from the vengeance of men who sought to make treason odious. This was in 1866 and but the repetition of the Indian war of 1856.

"Col. Geo. Wright, commanding the department of the Columbia, displayed such an overwhelming force in the Klickitat country that it convinced the hostile Indians of the hopelessness of pursuing war to a successful issue, and when they asked the terms of peace, Col. Wright directed them to return to their former homes, be peaceful and obey the orders of the Indian agents sent by our government to take charge of them, and they would be protected by the soldiers.

"The crimes of war cannot be atoned by crimes in cold blood after the war. Two wrongs do not make a right.

"Leschi, though shrewd and daring in war, adopted Col. Wright's directions, dropped hostilities, laid aside his rifle and repaired to Puget Sound, his home.

"Like Lee, he was entitled to protection from the officers and soldiers. But Leschi, on the Sound, feared the enmity of the whites, and gave himself up to Dr. Tolmie, an old friend, at Nesqually—not captured by two Indians of his own tribe and delivered up. Then began a crusade against Leschi for all the crimes of his people in war.

"On the testimony of a perjured man, whose testimony was demonstrated, by a survey of the route claimed by the deponent, to be a falsehood, he was found guilty by the jury, not of the offense alleged against him, for it was physically impossible for Leschi to be at the two points indicated in the time alleged; hence he was a martyr to the vengeance of unforgiving white men."

I remember having seen the beautiful pioneer woman spoken of in the following account first published in a Seattle paper. The Castos were buried in the old burying ground in a corner next the road we traveled from our ranch to school.

This is the article, head-lines and all:

JOHN BONSER'S DEATH RECALLS AN INDIAN MASSACRE

BEAUTIFUL ABBIE CASTO'S FATE

HOW DEATH CAME UPON THREE PIONEERS OF SQUAK VALLEY—SWIFT VENGEANCE ON THE MURDERERS

"The death of John Bonser, one of the earliest pioneers of Oregon, at Sauvie's Island, near Portland, recently, recalls one of the bloodiest tragedies that ever occurred in King County and one which will go down in history as the greatest example the pioneers had of the evil effect of giving whisky to the Indians. The event is memorable for another reason, and that is that the daughter of John Bonser, wife of William Casto, and probably the most beautiful woman in the territory, was a victim.

"'I don't take much stock in the handsome, charming women we read about,' said C. B. Bagley yesterday, 'but Mrs. Casto, if placed in Seattle today with face and form as when she came among us in 1864, would be among the handsomest women in the city, and I shall never forget the sensation created in our little settlement when messengers arrived from Squak valley, where the Castos moved, with the news that Mrs. Casto, her husband and John Holstead had been killed by Indians, and that a friendly Klickitat had slain the murderers.

"The first impression was that there had been an uprising among the treacherous natives and a force, consisting of nearly all the able-bodied men in the community, started for the scene of the massacre.

"It is a hard matter for the people of metropolitan Seattle to carry themselves back, figuratively speaking, to 1864, and imagine the village of that period with its thirty families.

"The boundaries were limited to a short and narrow line extending along the water front not farther north than Pike Street. The few houses were small and unpretentious and the business portion of the town was confined to Commercial Street, between Main and Yesler Avenue.

"At that time and even after the great fire in 1889, Yesler Avenue was known as Mill Street, the name having originated from the fact that Yesler's mill was located at its foot. Where the magnificent Dexter Horton bank building now stands stood a small wooden structure occupied by Dexter Horton as a store, and where the National Bank of Commerce building, at the corner of Yesler Avenue and Commercial Street, stood the mill store of the Yesler-Denny Company. S. B. Hinds, a name forgotten in commercial circles, kept store on Commercial Street, between Washington and Main Streets. Charles Plummer was at the corner of Main and Commercial, and J. R. Williamson was on the east side of Commercial Street, a half block north. This comprised the entire list of stores at that time. The forests were the only source to which the settlers looked for commercial commodities, and these, when put in salable shape, were often-times compelled to await means of transportation to markets. Briefly summed up, spars, piles, lumber and hop-poles were about all the sources of income.

"At that time there was no 'blue book,' and, in fact women were scarce. It is not surprising then that the arrival of William Casto, a man aged 38 years and a true representative of the Kentucky colonel type, with his young wife, the daughter of John Bonser, of Sauvies Island, Columbia River, near

Portland, should have been a memorable occasion. Mrs. Casto was a natural not an artificial beauty—one of those women to whom all apparel adapts itself and becomes a part of the wearer. Every movement was graceful and her face one that an artist would have raved about—not that dark, imperious beauty that some might expect, but the exact opposite. Her eyes were large, blue and expressive, while her complexion, clear as alabaster, was rendered more attractive by a rosy hue. She was admired by all and fairly worshipped by her husband. It was one of those rare cases where disparity in ages did not prevent mutual devotion.

"In the spring of the year that Casto came to Seattle he took up a ranch in the heart of Squak valley, where the Tibbetts farm now lies. Here he built a small house, put in a garden and commenced clearing. In order to create an income for himself and wife he opened a small trading post and carried on the manufacture of hoop poles. The valley was peculiarly adapted to this business, owing to the dense growth of hazel bush, the very article most desired.

"'Casto did most of his trading with San Francisco merchants and frequently received as much as $1,500 for a single shipment. Such a business might be laughed at in 1893, but at that time it meant a great deal to a sparsely settled community where wealth was largely prospective. It is a notable fact that, even in the early days when North Seattle was a howling wilderness and large game ran wild between the town limits and Lake Washington, the advantages of that body of water were appreciated and a successful effort was made by Henry L. Yesler, L. V. Wyckoff and others to connect the one with the other by a wagon road. The lake terminus was at a point called Fleaburg, now known as the terminus of the Madison Street cable line. Fleaburg was a small Indian settlement, and according to tradition derived its name from innumerable insects that made life miserable for the inhabitants and visitors. The many miles of travel this cut saved was greatly appreciated by the Squak settlers, because it was not only to their advantage in a commercial sense, but also made them feel that they were much nearer to the mother settlement. Another short cut was made by means of a foot path starting from Coal Creek on the eastern shore of the lake. This was so rough that only persons well acquainted with the country would have taken advantage of it. While it was not practical, yet it furnished means of reaching the settlement, in case of necessity, in one day, whereas the water route took twice as long.

"'Even at that time the great fear of the settlers, who were few in number, was the Indians. If a young man in Seattle went hunting his mother cautioned him to 'be very careful of the Indians.' Many people now living in or about the city will remember that in the fall of 1864 there were fears of an Indian uprising. How the rumors started or on what they were founded would be hard to state, nevertheless the fact remains that there was a general feeling of uneasiness. During the summer there had been trouble on the Snohomish River between white men and members of the Snohomish tribe. Three of the latter were killed, and among them a chief. These facts alone would have led a person well versed in the characteristics of the Washington Indian to look for trouble of some kind, although to judge from what direction and in what manner would have been difficult.

"'Casto at that time had several of the Snohomish Indians working for him, but the thought of fear never entered his mind. He had great influence over his workmen and was looked up to by them as a sort of white *tyee* or chief. Any one

that knew Casto could not but like him, he was so free-heart-
ed, kind and considerate of every person he met, whether as a
friend and equal or as his servant. He had one fault, however,
which goes hand in hand the world over with a free heart—
he loved liquor and now and then drank too much. He also
got in the habit of giving it to the Indians in his employ. On
several occasions the true Indian nature, under the influence
of stimulants, came out, and it required all his authority to
avoid bloodshed. His neighbors, who could be numbered
on the fingers of both hands, with some to spare, cautioned
him not to give 'a redskin whisky and arouse the devil,' but
he laughed at them, and when they warned him of treachery,
thought they spoke nonsense. He would not believe that the
men whom he treated so kindly and befriended in every conceivable manner would do him harm under any conditions.
He reasoned that his neighbors did not judge the character of
the native correctly and underestimated his influence. There
was no reason why he should not give his Indians liquor if
he so desired.

"'He acted on this decision on the afternoon of November 7,
1864, and then went to his home for supper. The Indians got
gloriously drunk and then commenced to thirst for blood.
In the crowd were two of the Snohomish tribe, bloodthirsty
brutes, and still seeking revenge for the death of their tribes-
men and chief on the Snohomish river the summer previous.
Their resolve was made. Casto's life would atone for that of
the chief, his wife and friend, John Holstead, for the other
two. They secretly took their guns and went to Casto's house.
The curtain of the room wherein all three were seated at the
supper table was up, and the breast of Casto was in plain
view of the assassins. There was no hesitation on the part of
the Indians. The first shot crashed through the window and

pierced Casto in a vital spot. He arose to his feet, staggered and fell upon a lounge. His wife sprang to his assistance, but the rifle spoke again and she fell to the floor. The third shot hit Holstead, but not fatally, and the Indians, determined to complete their bloody work, ran to the front door. They were met by Holstead, who fought like a demon, but at length fell, his body stabbed in more than twenty places. Not content with the slaughter already done, the bloodthirsty wretches drove their knives into the body of Casto's beautiful wife in a manner most inhuman. Having finished their bloody work of revenge they left the house, never for a moment thinking their lives were in danger. In this particular they made a fatal error.

"The shots fired had attracted a Klickitat Indian named Aleck to the scene. As fate had it, he was a true friend to the white man and held Casto, his employer, in high regard. It took him but a brief period to comprehend the situation, and he determined to avenge the death of his master, wife and friend. He concealed himself, and when the bloody brutes came out of the house he crept up behind them. One shot was enough to end the earthly career of one, but the other took to his heels. Aleck followed him with a hatchet he had drawn from his belt, and, being fleeter of foot, caught up. Then with one swift blow the skull of the fleeing Indian was cleft, and as he fell headlong to the ground Aleck jumped on him, and again and again the bloody hatchet drank blood until the head that but a few minutes before had human shape looked like a chipped pumpkin.

"While this series of bloody deeds was being enacted the few neighbors became wild with alarm, and, thinking that an Indian war had broken out, started for Seattle immediately. The band was made up of a Mr. Bush and family and three or four single men who had ranches in the valley.

"They reached Seattle the morning of the 9th and told the news, stating their fears of an Indian uprising. A party consisting of all the able-bodied men in the town immediately started for the scene of the tragedy by the short cut, and arrived there in the evening. The sight that met their eyes was horrible. In the bushes was found the body of the Indian who had been shot, and not far distant were the remains of the other, covered with blood and dirt mixed. In the house the sight was even more horrible. Holstead lay in the front room in a pool of clotted blood, his body literally punctured with knife wounds, and in the adjoining room, on a sofa, half reclining, was the body of Casto. On the floor, almost in the middle of the room, was Mrs. Casto, beautiful even in death, and lying in a pool of blood.

"The coroner at that time was Josiah Settle, and he, after looking around and investigating, found that the only witnesses he had were an old squaw, who claimed to have been an eye witness to the tragedy, and Aleck, the Klickitat. The inquest was held immediately, and the testimony agreed in substance with facts previously stated. The jury then returned the following verdict:

"'Territory of Washington, County of King, before Josiah Settle, Coroner.

"'We, the undersigned jurors summoned to appear before Josiah Settle, the coroner of King county, at Squak, on the 9th day of November, 1864, to inquire into the cause of death of William Casto, Abbie Casto and John Holstead, having been duly sworn according to law, and having made such inquisition after inspecting the bodies and hearing the testimony adduced, upon our oath each and all do say that we find that the deceased were named William Casto, Abbie Casto and

John Holstead; that William Casto was a native of Kentucky, Abbie Casto was formerly a resident of Sauvies Island, Columbia county, Ore., and John Holstead was a native of Wheeling, Va., and that they came to their deaths on the 7th of November, 1864, in this county, by knives and pistols in the hands of Indians, the bodies of the deceased having been found in the house of William Casto, at Squak, and we further find that we believe John Taylor and George, his brother, Indians of the Snoqualmie tribe, to have been the persons by whose hands they came to their deaths.'

"The bodies were brought to Seattle and buried in what is now known as the Denny Park, then a cemetery, North Seattle. Since then they have been removed to the Masonic cemetery.

"The news of the murder was sent to John Bonser, in Oregon, and he came to the town at once. For several weeks after the event the columns of the Seattle *Gazette* were devoted in part to a discussion of the question of selling and giving liquor to the Indians, the general conclusion being that it was not only against the law but a dangerous practice.

"Out of the killing by Aleck of the two Snohomish Indians grew a feud which resulted in the death of Aleck's son. The old man was the one wanted, but he was too quick with the rifle and they never got him. He died a few years ago, aged nearly ninety years."

So we see that whisky caused the death of six persons in this case.

The Lower Sound Indians were, if anything, more fierce and wild than those toward the south.

George Martin, the Swedish sailor who accompanied Capt. Fay, in 1851, said that he saw Sklallam Indians dancing a war dance at which there appeared the head of one of their enemies, which they had roasted; small pieces of it were touched to their lips, but were not eaten.

In an early day when Ira W. Utter lived on Salmon Bay, or more properly *Shilshole* Bay, he was much troubled by cougars killing his cattle, calves particularly. Thinking strychnine a good cure he put a dose in some lights of a beef, placed on a stick with the opposite end thrust in the ground. "Old Limpy," an Indian, spied the tempting morsel, took it to his home, roasted and ate the same and went to join his ancestors in the happy hunting grounds.

This Indian received his name from a limp occasioned by a gunshot wound inflicted by Lower Sound Indians on one of their raids. He was just recovering when the white people settled on Elliott Bay.

The very mention of these raids must have been terrifying to our Indians, as we called those who lived on the Upper Sound. On one occasion as a party of them were digging clams on the eastern shore of Admiralty Inlet, north of Meadow Point, they were attacked by their northern enemies, who shot two or three while the rest *klatawaw-ed* with all the *hyak* (hurry) possible and hid themselves.

CHAPTER II

PIONEER JOKES AND ANECDOTES

I N EARLY days, the preachers came in for some rather severe criticisms, although the roughest of the frontiersmen had a genuine reverence for their calling.

Ministers of the Gospel, as well as others, were obliged to turn the hand to toil with ax and saw. Now these tools require frequent recourse to sharpening processes and the minister with ax on shoulder, requesting the privilege of grinding that useful article on one of the few grindstones in the settlement occasioned no surprise, but when he prepared to grind by putting the handle on "wrong side to," gave it a brisk turn and snapped it off short, the disgust of the owner found vent in the caustic comment, "Well, if you're such a blame fool as that, I'll never go to hear you preach in the world!"

James G. Swan tells of an amusing experience with a Neah Bay Indian chief, in these words:

"I had a lively time with old Kobetsi, the war chief, whose name was Kobetsi-bis, which in the Makah language means frost. I had been directed by Agent Webster to make a survey of the reservation as far south as the Tsoess river, where

328

Kobetsi lived, and claimed exclusive ownership to the cranberry meadows along the bank of that river. He was then at his summer residence on Tatoosh Island. The Makah Indians had seen and understood something of the mariner's compass, but a surveyor's compass was a riddle to them.

"A slave of Kobetsi, who had seen me at work on the cranberry meadows, hurried to Tatoosh Island and reported that I was working a tamanuse, or magic, by which I could collect all the cranberries in one pile, and that Peter had sold me the land. This enraged the old ruffian, and he came up to Neah Bay with sixteen braves, with their faces painted black, their long hair tied in a knot on top of their heads with spruce twigs, their regular war paint, and all whooping and yelling. The old fellow declared he would have my head. Peter and the others laughed at him, and I explained to him what I had been about. He was pacified with me, but on his return to Tatoosh Island he shot the slave dead for making a fool of his chief."

The same writer is responsible for this account of a somewhat harsh practical joke; the time was November, 1859, the place Port Angeles Bay, in a log cabin where Captain Rufus Holmes resided:

"Uncle Rufus had a chum, a jolly, fat butcher named Jones, who lived in Port Townsend, and a great wag. He often visited Uncle Rufus for a few days' hunt and always took along some grub. On one occasion he procured an eagle, which he boiled for two days and then managed to disjoint. When it was cold he carefully wrapped the pieces in a cabbage leaf and took it to Uncle Rufus as a wild swan, but somewhat tough. The captain chopped it up with onions and savory herbs and made a fine soup, of which he partook heartily, Jones contenting himself with some clam fritters and fried salmon, remarking that it was his off day on soup. After dinner the wretched wag informed him that he had been eating an eagle, and produced the head and claws as proof. This piece of news operated on Uncle Rufus like an emetic, and after he had earnestly expressed his gastronomic regrets, Jones asked with feigned anxiety, 'Did the soup make you sick, Uncle Rufus?'

"Not to be outdone, the captain made reply, 'No, not the soup, but the thought I had been eating one of the emblems of my country.'"

A young man of lively disposition and consequently popular, was the victim of an April fool joke in the "auld lang syne." Very fond he was of playing tricks on others but some of the hapless worms turned and planned a sweet and neat revenge, well knowing it was hard to get ahead of the shrewd and witty youth. A "two-bit" piece, which had likely adorned the neck or ear of an Indian belle, as it had a hole pierced in it, was nailed securely to the floor of the postoffice in the village of Seattle, and a group of loungers waited to see the result. Early on the first, the young man before indicated walked briskly and confidently in. Observing the coin he stooped airily and essayed to pick it up, remarking, "It isn't everybody that can pick up two bits so early in the morning!" "April Fool!" and howls of laughter greeted his failure to pocket the coin. With burning face he sheepishly called for his mail and hurried out with the derisive shout of "It isn't everybody that can pick up two bits so early in the morning, Ha! ha! ha!" ringing in his ears.

Such fragments of early history as the following are frequently afloat in the literature of the Sound country:

THEY VOTED THEMSELVES GUNS
HOW PIONEER LEGISLATORS EQUIPPED THEM-
SELVES TO FIGHT THE INDIANS

"If the state legislature should vote to each member of both houses a first-class rifle, a sensation indeed would be created. But few are aware that such a precedent has been established by a legislature of Washington Territory. It has been so long ago, though, that the incident has almost faded from memory, and there are but few of the members to relate the circumstances.

"It was in 1855, when I was a member of the council, that we passed a law giving each legislator a rifle," said Hon. R. S. Robinson, a wealthy old pioneer farmer living near Chimacum in Jefferson County, while going to Port Townsend the other night on the steamer Rosalie. Being in a reminiscent humor, he told about the exciting times the pioneers experienced in both dodging Indians and navigating the waters of Puget Sound in frail canoes.

"It was just preceding the Indian outbreak of 1855-6, the settlers were apprehensive of a sudden onslaught," continued Mr. Robinson. "Gov. Stevens had secured from the war department several stands of small arms and ammunition, which were intended for general distribution, and we thought one feasible plan was to provide each legislator with a rifle and ammunition. Many times since I have thought of the incident, and how ridiculous it would seem if our present legislature adopted our course as a precedent, and armed each member at the state's expense. Things have changed considerably. In those days guns and ammunition were perquisites. Now it is stationery, lead pencils and waste baskets."

Among other incidents related by a speaker whose subject

was "Primitive Justice," was heard this story at a picnic of the pioneers:

"An instance in which I was particularly interested being connected with the administration of the sheriff's office occurred in what is now Shoshone County, Idaho, but was then a part of Washington Territory. A man was brought into the town charged with a crime; he was taken before the justice at once, but the trial was adjourned because the man was drunk. The sheriff took the prisoner down the trail, but before he had gone far the man fell down in a drunken sleep. A wagon bed lay handy and this was turned over the man and weighted down with stones to prevent his escape. The next morning he was again brought before the justice, who, finding him guilty, sentenced him to thirty days con- finement *in the jail from whence he had come* and to be fed on bread and water."

No doubt this was a heavy punishment, especially the water diet.

An incident occurred in that historic building, the Yesler cook house, never before published.

A big, powerful man named Emmick, generally known as "Californy," was engaged one morning in a game of fist- icuffs of more or less seriousness, when Bill Carr, a small man, stepped up and struck Emmick, who was too busy with his opponent just then to pay any attention to the imperti- nent meddler. Nevertheless he bided his time, although "Bill" made himself quite scarce and was nowhere to be seen when "Californy's" bulky form cast a shadow on the sawdust. After a while, however, he grew more confident and returned to a favorite position in front of the fire in the old cook house. He was just comfortably settled when in came "Californy," who pounced on him like a wildcat on a rabbit, stood him on his head and holding him by the heels "chucked" him up and down like a dasher on an old-fashioned churn, until Carr was much subdued, then left him to such reflections as were possible to an all but cracked cranium. It is safe to say he did not soon again meddle with strife.

This mode of punishment offers tempting possibilities in cases where the self-conceit of small people is offensively thrust upon their superiors.

The village of Seattle crept up the hill from the shore of Elliott Bay, by the laborious removal of the heavy forest, cutting, burning and grubbing of trees and stumps, grading and building of neat residences.

In the clearing of a certain piece of property between Fourth and Fifth streets, on Columbia, Seattle, now in the heart of the city, three pioneers participated in a somewhat unique experience. One of them, the irrepressible "Gard" or Gardner Kellogg, now well known as the very popular chief of the fire department of Seattle, has often told the story, which runs somewhat like this:

Mr. and Mrs. Gardner Kellogg were dining on a Sunday, with the latter's sister and her husband, Mr. and Mrs. O. C. Shorey, as they often did, at their home on Third Avenue. It was a cold, drizzly day, but in spite of that "Gard" and Mr. Shorey walked out to the edge of the clearing, where the dense young fir trees still held the ground, and the former was soon pushing up a stump fire on his lots.

As he poked the fire a bright thought occurred to him and he observed to his companion that he believed it "would save a lot of hard work, digging out the roots, to bring up that old shell and put it under the stump."

The "old shell" was one that had been thrown from the sloop-of-war *Decatur* during the Indian war, and had buried itself in the earth without exploding. In excavating for the Kellogg's wood house it had been unearthed.

Mr. Shorey thought it might not be safe if some one should pass by: "O, nobody will come out this way this miserable day; it may not go off anyway," was the answer.

So the shell was brought up and they dug under the roots of the stump, put it in and returned to the Shorey residence.

When they told what they had done, it was, agreed that it was extremely unlikely that anyone would take a pleasure walk in that direction on so gloomy a day.

Meanwhile a worthy citizen of the little burgh had gone roaming in search of his stray cow. As before stated, it was a chilly, damp day, and the man who was looking for his cow, Mr. Dexter Horton, for it was none other than he, seeing the fire, was moved to comfort himself with its genial warmth.

He advanced toward it and spread his hands benignantly as though blessing the man that invented fire, rubbed his palms together in a mute ecstasy of mellow satisfaction and then reversed his position, lifted his coat-tails and set his feet wide apart, even as a man doth at his own peaceful hearth-stone. The radiant energy had not time to reach the marrow when a terrific explosion took place. It threw earth, roots and splinters, firebrands and coals, yards away, hurled the whilom fire-worshiper a considerable distance, cautioned him with a piece of hot iron that just missed his face, cov-ered him with the debris, mystified and stupefied him, but fortunately did not inflict any permanent injury.

As he recovered the use of his faculties the idea gained upon him that it was a mean, low-down trick anyhow to blow up stumps that way. He was very much disgusted and refused very naturally to see anything funny about it; but as time passed by and he recovered from the shock, the ludicrous side appeared and he was content to let it be regarded as a pioneer pleasantry.

The innocent perpetrator of this amazing joke has no doubt laughed long and loud many times as he has pictured to himself the vast astonishment of his fellow townsman, and tells the story often, with the keenest relish, to appreciative listeners.

Yes, to be blown up by an old bomb-shell on a quiet Sunday afternoon, while resting beside a benevolent looking stump-fire that not even remotely suggested warlike demonstrations, was rather tough.

HOW BEAN'S POINT WAS NAMED

Opposite Alki Point was a fine prairie of about forty acres to which C. C. Terry at first laid claim. Some of the earliest settlers of the first mentioned locality crossed the water, taking their cattle, ploughed and planted potatoes on this prairie. Terry subsequently settled elsewhere and the place was settled on by a large man of about sixty years, a Nova Scotian, it was supposed, who bore the name of *Bean*. This lonely settler was a sort of spiritualist; in Fort Decatur, while one of a group around a stove, he leaned his arm on the wall and when a natural tremor resulted, insisted that the "spirits" did it. After the war he returned to his cabin and while in his bed, probably asleep, was shot and killed by an Indian. Since then the place has been known as Bean's Point.

Dr. H. A. Smith, the happiest story-teller of pioneer days, relates in his "Early Reminiscences" how "Dick Atkins played the dickens with poor old Beaty's appetite for cheese" in this engaging manner:

"One day when he (Dick Atkins) was merchandising on Commercial Street, Seattle, as successor to Horton & Denny, he laid a piece of cheese on the stove to fry for his dinner. A dozen loafers were around the stove and among them Mr. Beaty, remarkable principally for his appetite, big feet and good nature. And he on this occasion good-naturedly took the cheese from the stove and cooled and swallowed it without waiting to say grace, while Dick was in the back room, waiting on a customer. When the cheese was fairly out of sight, Beaty grew uneasy and skedadled up the street. When Atkins returned and found his cheese missing, and was told what became of it, he rushed to the door just in time to catch sight of Beaty's coat-tail going into Dr. Williamson's store. Without returning for his coat or hat, off he darted at full speed. Beaty had fairly got seated, when Dick stood before him and fairly screamed:

"'Did you eat that cheese?'

"'Wal—yes—but I didn't think you'd care much.'

"'Care! Care! good thunder, no! but I thought *you* might care, as I had just put a DOUBLE DOSE OF ARSENIC in it to kill rats.'

"'Don't say!' exclaimed Beaty, jumping to his feet, 'thought it tasted mighty queer; what can I do?'

"'Come right along with me; there is only one thing that can save you.'

"And down the street they flew as fast as their feet would carry them. As soon as they had arrived at the store, Atkins drew off a pint of rancid fish-oil and handed it to Beaty saying, 'Swallow it quick! Your life depends upon it!'

"Poor Beaty was too badly frightened to hesitate, and after a few gags, pauses and wry faces he handed back the cup, drained to the bitter dregs. 'There now,' said Dick, 'go home and to bed, and if you are alive in the morning come around and report yourself.'

"After he was gone one of the spectators asked if the cheese was really poisoned.

"'No,' replied Dick, 'and I intended telling the gormand it was not, but when I saw that look of gratitude come into his face as he handed back the empty cup, my heart failed me, and my revenge became my defeat.' 'No, gentlemen, Beaty is decidedly ahead in this little game. I never before was beaten at a game of cold bluff after having stacked the cards myself. I beg you to keep the matter quiet, gentlemen.' But it was always hard for a dozen men to keep a secret."

These same "Early Reminiscences" contain many a merry tale, some "thrice told" to the writer of this work, of the people who were familiar figures on the streets of Seattle and other settlements, in the long ago, among them two of the Rev. J. F. DeVore, with whom I was acquainted.

"When he lived in Steilacoom, at a time when that city was even smaller than it is now, a certain would-be bully declared, with an oath, that if it were not for the respect he had for the 'cloth,' he would let daylight through his portly ministerial carcass. Thereupon the 'cloth' was instantly stripped off and dashed upon the ground, accompanied with the remark, 'The "cloth" never stands in the way of a good cause. I am in a condition, now sir, to be enlightened.' But instead of attempting to shed any light into this luminary of the pulpit, whose eyes fairly blazed with a light not altogether of this world, the blustering bully lit out down the street at the top of his speed."

The following has a perennial freshness, although I have heard it a number of times:

"When Olympia was a struggling village and much in need of a church, this portly, industrious man of many talents took upon himself the not overly pleasant task of raising subscriptions for the enterprise, and in his rounds called on Mr. Crosby, owner of the sawmill at Tumwater, and asked how much lumber he would contribute to the church. Mr. Crosby eyed the 'cloth' a moment and sarcastically replied, 'As much as *you*, sir, will raft and take away between this and sundown.' 'Show me the pile!' was the unexpected rejoinder. Then laying off his coat and beaver tile he waded in with an alacrity that fairly made Mr. Crosby's hair bristle. All day, without stopping a moment, even for dinner, his tall, stalwart form bent under large loads of shingles, sheeting, siding, scantling, studding and lath, and even large sills and plates were rolled and tumbled into the bay with the agility of a giant, and before sundown Mr. Crosby had the proud satisfaction of seeing the 'cloth' triumphantly poling a raft toward Olympia containing lumber enough for a handsome church and a splendid parsonage besides.

"Mr. Crosby was heard to say a few days afterward that no ten men in his employ could, or would, have done that day's work. Meeting the divine shortly afterwards, Mr. Crosby said, 'Well, parson, you can handle more lumber between sunrise and dark than any man I ever saw.'

"'Oh,' said the parson, 'I was working that day for my Maker.'

"Moral: Never trust pioneer preachers with your lumber pile, simply because they wear broadcloth coats, for most of them know how to take them off, and then they can work as well as pray."

This conjuror with the pen has called up another well known personality of the earliest times in the following sketch and anecdote:

"Dr. Maynard was of medium size. He had blue eyes, a square forehead, a strong face and straight black hair, when worn short, but when worn long, as it was when whitened by the snows of many winters, it was quite curly and fell in ringlets over his shoulders. Add to this description, a long, gray beard, and you will see him as he appeared on our streets when on his last legs. When 'half seas over,' he overflowed with generous impulses, would give away anything within reach and was full of extravagant promises, many of which were out of his power to fulfill. He once owned Alki Point and sometimes would move there in order to 'reform,' but seldom remained longer than a month or six weeks. Alki Point was covered with huge logs and stumps, excepting a little cleared ground near the bay where the house stood. But when the doctor saw it through his telescopic wine-glasses it was transformed into a beautiful farm with broad meadows covered with lowing herds and prancing steeds whose 'necks were clothed with thunder.'

"One day, in the fall of 1860, while viewing his farm through his favorite glasses, David Stanley, the venerable Salmon Bay hermit, happened along, when Maynard gave him a glowing description of his Alki Point farm as he himself beheld it just then, and wound up by proposing to take the old man in partnership, and offered him half of the fruit and farm stock for simply looking after it and keeping the fences in repair. The temptation to gain sudden riches was too much for even his unworldliness of mind, and he made no delay in embarking for Alki Point with all his worldly effects. His object in living alone, was, he said, to comply with the injunction to keep one's self 'unspotted from the world,' but the doctor assured him that the change would not seriously interfere with his meditations, inasmuch as few people landed at Alki Point, notwithstanding its many attractions.

"The day of his departure for the Mecca of all his earthly hopes turned out very stormy. It was after dark before he reached the point, and on trying to land his boat filled with water. He lost many of his fowls and came near losing his life in the boiling surf. After getting himself and his 'traps' ashore, he built a fire, dried his blankets, fried some bacon, ate a hearty supper and turned in.

"The excitement of the day, however, prevented sleep, and he got up and sat by the fire till morning. As soon as it was light he strolled out to look at the stock, but to his surprise, only a bewildering maze of logs and interminable stumps were to be seen where he expected to behold broad fields and green pastures. The only thing he could find resembling stock were—to use his own language—'an old white horse, stiff in all his joints and blind in one eye, and a little, runty, scrubby, ornery, steer calf.' After wandering about over and under logs till noon, he concluded he had missed the doctor's farm, and returned to the beach with the intention of pulling further around, but seeing some men in a boat a short distance from shore, he hailed it and inquired for Dr. Maynard's farm. Charley Plummer was one of the party and he told the old man that he had the honor of being already upon it. Stanley explained his object in being there, and after a fit of rib-breaking laughter, Mr. Plummer advised him to return to Salmon Bay as soon as possible, which he did the very next day.

"The old man had a keen sense of the ludicrous, and joined heartily in the laugh, saying he had been taken in a great many times in his life, but never in so laughable manner as on this occasion. A few days afterward as Charley Plummer was sitting in Dr. Maynard's office the hermit put in an appearance. 'Good afternoon, doctor,' said he, with an air of profound respect. 'Why, how do you do, Uncle Stanley, glad to see you—how does the poultry ranch prosper? By the way, have you moved to Alki Point yet?' 'O, yes, I took my traps, poultry and all, over there several days ago, and had the pleasure of meeting Mr. Plummer there. Did he mention the circumstances?' 'No,' said the doctor, 'he just came in. How did you find things?'

"'To tell the truth, doctor, I couldn't rest until I could see you and thank you from the bottom of my heart for the inestimable blessing you have conferred upon me.'

"At this demonstration of satisfaction uttered with an air of profound gratitude, the doctor leaned back complacently in his easy chair, while an expression of benignant self-approval illuminated his benevolent face.

"'Yes,' continued he, 'I can never be sufficiently grateful for the benefit your generosity has already been to me individually, besides it bids fair to prove a signal triumph for religion and morality, and it may turn out to be a priceless contribution to science.'

"At the utterance of this unexpected 'rhapsody' the doctor turned with unalloyed delight, and seeing that the old man hesitated, he encouraged him by saying, 'Go on, Uncle, go right along and tell all about it, although I can't understand exactly how it can prove a triumph for religion or science.'

"'Well,' continued the old man with solemn countenance, 'my orthodoxy has been a little shaky of late, in fact I have seriously doubted the heavenly origin of various forms of inspiration, but when I got to Alki Point and looked around my skepticism fell from my eyes as did the scales from the eyes of Saul of old.'

"'Yes,' interrupted the doctor, 'the scenery over there is really grand and I have often felt devotional myself while contemplating the grand mountain scenery—'

"'Scenery? Well—yes, I suppose there is some scenery scattered around over there, but it isn't that.'

"'No, well what was it, uncle?'

"'Why, sir, as I was saying, when I get a chance to fairly look around I was thoroughly satisfied that nothing but a miracle, in fact, nothing short of the ingenuity and power of the Almighty could possibly have piled up so many logs and stumps to the acre as I found on your *farm*.'

"Here the doctor's face perceptibly lengthened and a very dry laugh, a sort of hysterical cross between a chuckle and a suppressed oath, escaped him, but before he had time to speak the old man went on:

"'So much for the triumph of religion, but science, sir, will be under much weightier obligations to us when you and I succeed in making an honest living from the progeny of an old blind horse and a little, miserable runty steer calf.'

"This was too much for the doctor and springing to his feet he fairly shouted, 'There, there, old man, not another word! come right along and I will stand treat for the whole town and we will never mention Alki Point again.'

"'No, thank you,' said the hermit, dryly, 'I never indulge, and since you have been the means of my conversion you ought to be the last man in the world to lead me into temptation, besides our income from the blind horse and runty steer calf will hardly justify such extravagance.'

"Hat and cane in hand he got as far as the door, when Maynard called to him saying, 'Look here, old man, I hope you're not offended, and if you will say nothing about this little matter, I'll doctor you the rest of your life for nothing.'

"After scratching his head a moment the hermit looked up and naively answered, 'No, I'm not mad, only astonished, and as for your free medicine, if it is all as bitter as the free dose you have just given me, I don't want any more of it,' and he bowed himself out and was soon lost to the doctor's longing gaze. With eyes still fixed on the door he exclaimed, 'Blast my head if I thought the old crackling had so much dry humor in him. Come, Charley, let's have something to brave our nerves.'"

Among the unfortunate victims of the drink habit in an early day was poor old Tom Jones. Nature had endowed him with a splendid physique, but he wrecked himself, traveling downward, until he barely lived from hand to mouth. He made a house on the old Conkling place, up the bay toward the Duwampsh River, his tarrying place. Having been absent from his customary haunts for a considerable time, it was reported that he was dead. In the village of Seattle, some marauder had been robbing henroosts and Tom Jones was accused of being the guilty party. Grandfather John Denny told one of his characteristic stories about being awakened by a great commotion in his henhouse, the lusty cocks crowing "Tom Jo-o-o-ones is dead! Tom Jo-o-o-ones is dead!" rejoicing greatly that they were henceforth safe.

D. T. Denny gathered up seven men and went to investigate the truth of the report of his demise. They found him rolled up in his blankets, in his bunk, not dead but helplessly sick. When they told him what they had come for—to hold an inquest over his dead body, the tears rolled down his withered face. They had him moved nearer town and cared for, but he finally went the way of all the earth.

Another of the army of the wretched was having an attack of the "devil's trimmings," as Grandfather John Denny called them, in front of a saloon one day and a group stood around waiting for him to "come to"; upon his showing signs of returning consciousness, *all but one* filed into the saloon to get a nerve bracer. D. T. Denny, who relates the incident, turned away, he being the only temperance man in the group.

CHAPTER III

TRAILS OF COMMERCE

SAMUEL L. Simpson wrote this sympathetic poem concerning the old Hudson Bay Company's steamer *Beaver,* the first steam vessel on the North Pacific Coast. She came out from London in 1836 and is well remembered by Puget Sound pioneers. In 1889 she went on the rocks in Burrard Inlet, British Columbia.

THE *BEAVER'S* REQUIEM
Forlorn in the lonesome North she lies,
That never again will course the sea,
All heedless of calm or stormy skies,
Or the rocks to windward or a-lee;
 For her day is done
 And her last port won
Let the wild, sad waves her minstrel be.

She will roam no more on the ocean trails,
Where her floating scarf of black was seen
Like a challenge proud to the shrieking gales
By the mighty shores of evergreen;
 For she lies at rest
 With a pulseless breast
In the rough sea's clasp and all serene.

How the world has changed since she kissed the tide
Of the storied Thames in the Georgian reign,
And was pledged with wine as the bonny bride
Of the West's isle-gemmed barbaric main—
    With a dauntless form
    That could breast the storm
As she wove the magic commercial chain.

For Science has gemmed her brow with stars
From many and many a mystic field,
And the nations have stood in crimsoned wars
And thrones have fallen and empires reeled
    Since she sailed that day
    From the Thames away
Under God's blue sky and St. George's shield.

And the world to which, as a pioneer,
She first came trailing her plume of smoke,
Is beyond the dreams of the clearest seer
That ever in lofty symbols spoke—
    In the arts of peace,
    In all life's increase,
And all the gold-browed stress invoke.

A part of this was a work of hers,
In a daring life of fifty years;
But the sea-gulls now are her worshipers,
Wheeling with cries more sad than tears,
    Where she lies alone
    And the surges moan—
And slowly the north sky glooms and clears.

And may we not think when the pale mists glide,
Like the sheeted dead by that rocky shore,
That we hear in the rising, rolling tide
The call of the captain's ring once more?
    And it well might be,
    So forlorn is she,
Where the weird winds sigh and wan birds soar.

The development of the most easily reached natural resources
was necessarily first.

The timber and fisheries were a boundless source of wealth

in evidence.

As early as 1847, a sawmill run with power afforded by the falls of the Des Chutes at Tumwater, furnished lumber to settlers as a means of profit.

The first cargo was taken by the brig *Orbit* in 1850, to San Francisco, she being the first American merchant vessel in the carrying trade of Puget Sound. The brig *George Emory* followed suit; each carried a return cargo of goods for trade with the settlers and Indians.

At first the forest-fallers had no oxen to drag the timbers, after they were hewn, to the water's edge, but rolled and hauled them by hand as far as practicable. It was in this manner that the brig *Leonesa* was loaded with piles at Alki in the winter of 1851-2, by the Dennys, Terry, Low, Boren and Bell.

Lee Terry brought a yoke of oxen to complete the work of loading, from Puyallup, on the beach, as there was no road through the heavy forest.

Several ships were loaded at Port Townsend, where the possession of three yoke of oxen gave them a decided advantage.

One ship, the *G. W. Kendall*, was sent from San Francisco to Puget Sound for ice. It is needless to say the captain did not get a cargo of that luxury; he reported that water did not freeze in Puget Sound and consoled the owner of the ship by returning with a valuable cargo of piles.

The cutting of logs to build houses and the grubbing of stumps to clear the land for gardens alternated with the cutting of piles. In the clearing of land, the Indians proved a great assistance; far from being lazy many of them were hard workers and would dig and delve day after day to remove the immense stumps of cedar and fir left after cutting the great trees. The settlers burned many by piling heaps of logs and brush on them, others by boring holes far into the wood and setting fire, while some were rent by charges of powder when it could be afforded.

The clearing of land in this heavily timbered country was an item of large expense if hired, otherwise of much arduous toil for the owner. The women and children often helped to pile brush and set fires and many a merry party turned out at night to "chunk up" the blazing heaps; after nightfall, their fire-lit figure flitting hither and yon against the purple darkness, suggested well-intentioned witches.

Cutting down the tall trees, from two hundred fifty to four hundred fifty feet, required considerable care and skill. Sometimes we felt the pathos of it all, when a huge giant, the dignified product of patient centuries of growth, fell crashing, groaning to the earth. This side of the subject, is presented in a poem "The Lone Fir Tree," not included in this volume.

When finally the small patches of land were cleared, planted and tended, the returns were astonishing, such marvelous vegetables, small fruits and flowers, abundant and luxuriant, rewarded the toiler. Nature herself, by her heaps of vegetation, had foreshown the immense productiveness of the soil.

In the river valleys were quite extensive prairies, which afforded superior stock range, but the main dependence of the people was in the timber.

In 1852 H. L. Yesler came, who built the first steam sawmill on Puget Sound, at Seattle. Other mills sprang up at Port Ludlow, Port Gamble, Port Madison and Port Blakely, making the names of Meigs, Pope, Talbot, Keller, Renton, Walker, Blinn and others, great in the annals of sawmilling on Puget Sound.

This very interesting account concerning Yesler's sawmill and those who worked in it in the early days was first published in a Seattle paper many years ago:

"The other day some of Parke's men at work on the foundation of the new Union Block on Front, corner of Columbia
Street, delving among ancient fragments of piles, stranded
logs and other debris of sea-wreck, long buried at that part
of the waterfront, found at the bottom of an excavation they
were making, a mass of knotted iron, corroded, attenuated
and salt-eaten, which on being drawn out proved to be a
couple of ancient boom-chains.

"The scribe, thinking he might trace something of the history of these ancient relics, hunted up Mr. Yesler, whom, after
considerable exploration through the mazes of his wilderness on Third and Jefferson Streets, he found, hose in hand,
watering a line of lilies, hollyhocks, penstemons, ageratums,
roses, et al.

"The subject of the interview being stated, Mr. Yesler proceeded to relate: 'Yes, after I got my mill started in 1853, the
first lot of logs were furnished by Dr. Maynard. He came to
me and said he wanted to clear up a piece on the spit, where
he wanted to lay out and sell some town lots. It was somewhere about where the New England and Arlington now
stand. The location of the old mill is now an indeterminate
spot, somewhere back of Z. C. Miles' hardware store. The
spot where the old cookhouse stood is in the intersection
of Mill and Commercial Streets, between the Colman Block
and Gard. Kellogg's drug store. Hillory Butler and Bill Gilliam
had the contract from Maynard, and they brought the logs
to the mill by hand—rolled or carried them in with handspikes. I warrant you it was harder work than Hillory or Bill
has done for many a day since. Afterwards, Judge Phillips,
who went into partnership with Dexter Horton in the store,
got out logs for me somewhere up the bay.

"'During the first five years after my mill was started, cattle teams for logging were but few on the Sound, and there were no steamboats for towing rafts until 1858. Capt. John S. Hill's *Ranger No. 2*, which he brought up from San Francisco, was the first of the kind, and George A. Meigs' little tug *Resolute*, which blew up with Capt. Johnny Guindon and his crew in 1861, came on about the same time. A great deal of the earliest logging on the Sound was done exclusively by hand, the logs being thrown into the water by handspikes and towed to the mill on the tide by skiffs.

"'In 1853 Hillory Butler took a contract to get me out logs at Smith's Cove. George F. Frye was his teamster. In the fall of 1854 and spring and summer of 1855, Edward Hanford and John C. Holgate logged for me on their claims, south of the townsite toward the head of the bay. T. D. Hinckley was their teamster, also Jack Harvey. On one occasion, when bringing in a raft to the mill, John lost a diary which he was keeping and I picked it up on the beach. The last entry it contained read: "June 5, 1855. Started with a raft for Yesler's mill. Fell off into the water." I remember I wrote right after "and drowned," and returned the book. I don't know how soon afterward John learned from his own book of his death by drowning.

"'The Indian war breaking out in the fall of '55 put a stop to their logging operations, as of all the rest.

"'The Indians killed or drove off all the cattle hereabouts and burned the dwellings of Hanford, Holgate and Bell on the borders of the town, besides destroying much other property throughout the country.

"'The logging outfits in those days were of the most primitive and meager description. Rafts were fastened together by ropes or light boom-chains. Supplies of hardware and other necessaries were brought up from San Francisco by the lumber vessels on their return trips as ordered by the loggers. I remember on one occasion Edmund Carr, John A. Strickler, F. McNatt and John Ross lost the product of a season's labor by their raft getting away from them and going to pieces while in transit between the mill and the head of the bay. My booming place was on the north side of the mill along the beach where now the foundations are going up for the Toklas & Singerman, Gasch, Melhorn and Lewis brick block. There being no sufficient breakwater thereabouts in those times, I used often to lose a great many logs as well as boom-chains and things by the rafts being broken up by storms.

"'My mill in the pioneer times before the Indian war furnished the chief resource of the early citizens of the place for a subsistence.

"'When there were not enough white men to be had for operating the mill, I employed Indians and trained them to do the work. George Frye was my sawyer up to the time he took charge of the *John B. Libby* on the Whatcom route. My engineers at different times were T. D. Hinckley, L. V. Wyckoff, John T. Moss and Douglass. Arthur A. Denny was screw-tender in the mill for quite a while; D. T. Denny worked at drawing in the logs. Nearly all the prominent old settlers at some time or other were employed in connection with the mill in some capacity, either at logging or as mill hands. I loaded some lumber for China and other foreign ports, as well as San Francisco.'"

The primitive methods, crude appliances and arduous toil in the early sawmills have given place to palaces of modern mechanical contrivance it would require a volume to describe, of enormous output, loading hundreds of vessels for unnumbered foreign ports, and putting in circulation millions of dollars.

As a forcible contrast to Mr. Yesler's reminiscence, this specimen is given of modern milling, entitled "Sawing Up a Forest," representing the business of but one of the great mills in later days (1896) at work on Puget Sound:

"The best evidence of the revival of the lumber trade of the Sound, is to be found at the great Blakeley mill, where four hundred thousand feet of lumber is being turned out every twenty-four hours, and the harbor is crowded with ships destined for almost all parts of the world.

"One of the mill officials said, 'We are at present doing a large business with South American and Australian ports, and expect with proper attention to secure the South African trade, which, if successful, will be a big thing. We have the finest lumber in the world, and there is no reason why we should not be doing five times the business that is being done on the Sound. Why, there is some first quality and some selected Norway lumber out there on the wharf, and it does not even compare with our second quality lumber.'

"The company has at present (1896) 350 men employed and between \$15,000.00 and \$20,000.00 in wages is paid out every month.

"The following vessels are now loading or are loaded and ready to sail:

"Bark *Columbia*, for San Francisco, 700,000 feet; ship *Aristomene*, for Valparaiso, 1,450,000 feet; ship *Earl Burgess*, for Amsterdam, 1,250,000 feet; bark *Mercury*, for San Francisco, 1,000,000 feet; ship *Corolla*, for Valparaiso, 1,000,000 feet; barkentine *Katie Flickinger*, for Fiji Islands, 550,000 feet; bark *Matilda*, for Honolulu, 650,000 feet; bark *E. Ramilla*, for Valparaiso, 700,000 feet; ship *Beechbank*, for Valparaiso, 2,000,000 feet.

"To load next week:

"Barkentine *George C. Perkins*, for Sidney, N. S. W., 550,000 feet; bark *Guinevere*, for Valparaiso, 850,000 feet.

"Those to arrive within the next two weeks:

"Bark *Antoinette*, for Valparaiso, 900,000 feet; barkentine *J. L. Stanford*, for Melbourne, 1,200,000 feet; ship *Saga*, for Valparaiso, 1,200,000 feet; bark *George F. Manson*, for Shanghai, China, 950,000 feet; ship *Harvester*, for South Africa, 1,000,000 feet."

Shingle making was a prominent early industry. The process was slow, done entirely by hand, in vivid contrast with the great facility and productiveness of the modern shingle mills of this region; in consequence of the slowness of manufacture they formerly brought a much higher price. It was an ideal occupation at that time. After the mammoth cedars were felled, sawn and rived asunder, the shingle-maker sat in the midst of the opening in the great forest, towering walls of green on all sides, with the blue sky overhead and fragrant wood spread all around, from which he shaped the thin, flat pieces by shaving them with a drawing knife.

Cutting and hewing spars to load ships for foreign markets began before 1856.

As recorded in a San Francisco paper:

"In 1855, the bark *Anadyr* sailed from Utsalady on Puget Sound, with a cargo of spars for the French navy yard at Brest. In 1857 the same ship took a load from the same place to an English navy yard.

"To China, Spain, Mauritius and many other places, went the tough, enduring, flexible fir tree of Puget Sound. The severe test applied have proven the Douglas fir to be without an equal in the making of masts and spars.

"In later days the *Fram*, of Arctic fame, was built of Puget Sound fir."

The discovery and opening of the coal mines near Seattle marks an epoch in the commerce of the Northwest.

As early as 1859 coal was found and mined on a small scale east of Seattle.

The first company, formed in 1866-7, was composed of old and well-known citizens: D. Bagley, G. F. Whitworth and Selucius Garfield, who was called the "silver-tongued orator." Others joined in the enterprise of developing the mines, which were found to be extensive and valuable. Legislation favored them and transportation facilities grew.

The names of McGilvra, Yesler, Denny and Robinson were prominent in the work. Tramways, chutes, inclines, tugboats, barges, coalcars and locomotives brought out the coal to deep water on the Sound, across Lakes Washington and Union, and three pieces of railroad. A long trestle at the foot of Pike Street, Seattle, at which the ship *Belle Isle,* among others, often loaded, fell in, demolished by the work of the teredo.

The writer remembers two startling trips up the incline, nine hundred feet long, on the east side of Lake Washington, in an empty coal car, the second time duly warned by the operatives that the day before a car load of furniture had been "let go" over the incline and smashed to kindlingwood long before it reached the bottom. The trips were made amidst an oppressive silence and were never repeated.

The combined coal fields of Washington cover an area of one thousand six hundred fifty square miles. Since the earliest developments great strides have been made and a large number of coal mines are operated, such as the Black Diamond, Gilman, Franklin, Wilkeson, the U. S. government standard, Carbonado, Roslyn, etc., with a host of underground workers and huge steam colliers to carry an immense output.

The carrying of the first telegraph line through the dense

forest was another step forward. Often the forest trees were pressed into service and insulators became the strange ornaments of the monarchs of the trackless wilderness.

Pioneer surveyors, of whom A. A. Denny was one, journalists, lawyers and other professional men, with the craftsmen, carpenters who helped to repair the *Decatur* and build the fort, masons who helped to build the old University of Washington, and other industrious workers brought to mind might each and every one furnish a volume of unique and interesting reminiscence.

The women pioneers certainly demand a work devoted to them alone.

Simultaneously with the commercial and political development, the educational and religious took place. The children of the pioneers were early gathered in schools and the parents preceded the teachers or supplemented their efforts with great earnestness. Books, papers and magazines were bountifully provided and both children and grown people read with avidity. For many years the mails came slowly, but when the brimming bags were emptied, the contents were eagerly seized upon, and being almost altogether eastern periodical literature, the children narrowly escaped acquiring the mental squint which O. W. Holmes speaks of having affected the youth of the East from the perusal of English literature.

The pioneer mail service was one of hardship and danger. The first mail overland in the Sound region was carried by A. B. Rabbeson in 1851, and could not have been voluminous, as it was transported in his pockets while he rode horseback.

A well known mail carrier of early days was Nes Jacob Ohm or "Dutch Ned," as every one called him. He, with his yellow dog and sallow cayuse, was regarded as an indispensable institution. All three stood the test of travel on the trail for many years. The yellow canine had quite a reputation as a panther dog, and no doubt was a needed protection in the dark wild forest, but he has long since gone where the good dogs go and the cayuse probably likewise.

"Ned" was somewhat eccentric though a faithful servant of the public. In common with other forerunners of civilization he was a little superstitious.

One winter night, grown weary of drowsing by his bright, warm fireplace in his little cabin, he began to walk back and forth in an absent-minded way, when suddenly his hair fairly stood on end; there were two stealthy shadows following him every where he turned. In what state of mind he passed the remainder of the night is unknown, but soon after he related the incident to his friends evincing much anxiety as to what it might signify. Probably he had two lights burning in different parts of the room or sufficiently bright separate flames in the fireplace.

Doubtless it remained a mystery unexplained to him, to the end of his days.

The pioneer merchants who traded with the Indians, and swapped calico and sugar for butter and eggs, with the settlers, pioneer steamboat men who ran the diminutive steamers between Olympia and Seattle, pioneer editors, who published tri-weeklies whose news did not come in daily, pioneer milliners who "did up" the hats of the other pioneer women with taste and neatness, pioneer legislators, blacksmiths, bakers, shoemakers, foundry men, shipbuilders, etc., blazed the trails of commerce where now there are broad highways.

CHAPTER IV

BUILDING OF THE TERRITORIAL UNIVERSITY

EARLY IN 1861, the University Commissioners, Rev. D. Bagley, John Webster and Edmund Carr, selected the site for the proposed building, ten acres in Seattle, described as a "beautiful eminence overlooking Elliott Bay and Puget Sound." A. A. Denny donated eight and a fraction acres, Terry and Lander, one and a fraction acres. The structure was fifty by eighty feet, two stories in height, beside belfry and observatory. There were four rooms above, including the grand lecture room, thirty-six by eighty feet, and six rooms below, beside the entrance hall of twelve feet, running through the whole building.

The president's house was forty by fifty, with a solid foundation of brick and cement cellar; the boarding house twenty-four by forty-eight, intended to have an extension when needed. A supply was provided of the purest spring water, running through one thousand four hundred feet of charred pump logs.

Buildings of such dimensions were not common in the Northwest in those days; materials were expensive and money was scarce.

It was chiefly through the efforts of John Denny that a large appropriation of land was made by Congress for the benefit of the new-born institution. Although advanced in years, his hair as white as snow, he made the long journey to Washington city and return when months were required to accomplish it.

By the sale of these lands the expense of construction and purchase of material were met. The land was then worth but one dollar and a half per acre, but enough was sold to amount to $30,400.69.

At that time the site lay in the midst of a heavy forest, through which a trail was made in order to reach it.

Of the ten-acre campus, seven acres were cleared of the tall fir and cedar trees at an expense of two hundred and seventy-five dollars per acre, the remaining three were worse, at three hundred and sixteen dollars per acre.

The method of removing these forest giants was unique and imposing. The workers partially grubbed perhaps twenty trees standing near each other, then dispatched a sailor aloft in their airy tops to hitch them together with a cable and descend to terra firma. A king among the trees was chosen whose downfall should destroy his companions, and relentlessly uprooting it, the tree-fallers suddenly and breathlessly withdrew to witness a grand sight, the whole group of unnumbered centuries' growth go crashing down at once. They would scarcely have been human had they uttered no shout of triumph at such a spectacle. To see but one great, towering fir tree go grandly to the earth with rush of boughs and thunderous sound is a thrilling, pathetic and awe-inspiring sight.

About the center of the tract was left a tall cedar tree to

which was added a topmast. The tree, shorn of its limbs and peeled clean of bark, was used for a flagstaff.

The old account books, growing yearly more curious and valuable, show that the majority of the old pioneers joined heartily in the undertaking and did valiant work in building the old University.

They dug, hewed, cleared land, hauled materials, exchanged commodities, busily toiled from morn to night, traveled hither and yon, in short did everything that brains, muscle and energy could accomplish in the face of what now would be deemed well nigh insurmountable obstacles. The president of the board of commissioners, the Rev. D. Bagley, has said that in looking back upon it he was simply foolhardy. "Why, we had not a dollar to begin with," said he; nevertheless pluck and determination accomplished wonders; many of the people took the lands at one dollar and a half an acre, in payment for work and materials.

Clarence B. Bagley, son of Rev. D. Bagley, is authority for the following statement, made in 1896:

"Forty-eight persons were employed on the work and nearly all the lumber for the building was secured from the mills at Port Blakeley and Port Madison, while the white pine of the finishing siding, doors, sash, etc., came from a mill at Seabeck, on Hood Canal. I have been looking over the books my father kept at that time and find the names of many persons whom all old-timers will remember. I found the entry relating to receiving 10,000 brick from Capt. H. H. Roeder, the price being $15.50 per thousand, while lime was $3 per barrel and cement $4.50 per barrel. Another entry shows that seven gross of ordinary wood screws cost in that early day $9.78. Capt. Roeder is now a resident of Whatcom County. The wages then were not very high, the ordinary workman receiving $2 and $2.25 per day and the carpenters and masons $4 per day.

"On the 10th of March, John Pike and his son, Harvey Pike, began to clear the ground for the buildings and a few days later James Crow and myself commenced. The Pikes cleared the acre of ground in the southeast corner and we cleared the acre just adjoining, so that we four grubbed the land on which the principal building now stands. All the trees were cut down and the land leveled off, and the trees which now grace the grounds started from seeds and commenced to grow up a few years later and are now about twenty-five years old. Among the men who helped clear the land were: Hillory Butler, John Carr, W. H. Hyde, Edward Richardson, L. Holgate, H. A. Atkins, Jim Hunt, L. B. Andrews, L. Pinkham, Ira Woodin, Dr. Josiah Settle, Parmelee & Dudley, and of that number that are now dead are Carr, Hyde, Holgate, Atkins and Parmelee and Dudley. Mr. Crow is now living at Kent and owns a good deal of property there. Mr. Carr was a relative of the Hanfords. Mr. Holgate was a brother of the Holgate who was killed in Seattle during the Indian war, being shot dead while standing at the door of the fort. He was an uncle of the Hanfords. Mr. Atkins was mayor of the town at one time.

"R. King, who dressed the flagstaff, is not among the living. The teamsters who did most of the hauling were Hillory Butler, Thomas Mercer and D. B. Ward, all of whom are still living. William White was blacksmith here then and did a good deal of work on the building. He is now living in California and is well-to-do, but his son is still a resident of Seattle. Thomas Russell was the contractor for putting up the frame of the university building. He died some time since and of his estate there is left the Russell House, and his family is well known. John Dodge and John T. Jordan did a good deal of the mason work, both of whom are now dead, but they have children who still live in this city. The stone for the foundation was secured from Port Orchard and the lime came from Victoria, being secured here at a large cost."

George Austin, who raised the flagstaff and put the top on, has been dead many years. Dexter Horton and Yesler, Denny & Co. kept stores in those days and furnished the nails, hardware and general merchandise. Mr. Horton's store was where the bank now stands and the store of Yesler, Denny & Co. was where the National Bank of Commerce now stands. L. V. Wyckoff, the father of Van Wyckoff, who was sheriff of the county for many years, did considerable hauling and draying. He also is dead. Frank Mathias was a carpenter and did a good deal of the finishing work. He died in California and his heirs have since been fighting for his estate.

H. McAlear kept a stove and hardware store and furnished the stoves for the building. He is now dead and there has been a contest over some of his property in the famous Hill tract in this city.

D. C. Beatty and R. H. Beatty, not relatives, were both carpenters. The former is now living on a farm near Olympia and the latter is in the insane asylum at Steilacoom. Ira Woodin is still alive and is the founder of Woodinville. In the early days Mr. Woodin and his father owned the only tannery in the country, which was located at the corner of South Fourth Street and Yesler Avenue, then Mill Street. O. J. Carr, whose name appears as a carpenter, lives at Edgewater. He was the postmaster of the town for many years.

O. C. Shorey and A. P. DeLin, as "Shorey & DeLin," furnished the desks for the several rooms and also made the columns that grace the front entrance to the building.

Plummer & Hinds furnished some of the materials used

in the construction. George W. Harris, the banker, auditor of the Lake Shore road, is a stepson of Mr. Plummer.

Jordan and Thorndyke were plasterers and both have been dead for many years.

David Graham, who did some of the grading, is still living in Seattle. A. S. Mercer did most of the grading with Mr. Graham. Mr. Mercer is a brother of Thomas Mercer, who brought out two parties of young ladies from the Atlantic Coast by sea, many of whom are married and are now living in Seattle. Harry Hitchcock, one of the carpenters, is now dead. Harry Gordon was a painter and was quite well known for some years. He finally went East, and I think is still living, although I have not heard from him for many years. Of the three who composed the board of university commissioners Mr. Carr and Mr. Webster are dead.

All the paint, varnishes, brushes, etc., were purchased in Victoria and the heavy duties made the cost very high; in fact, everything was costly in those days. An entry is made of a keg of lath nails which cost $15, and a common wooden wheelbarrow cost $7. The old bell came from the East, and cost, laid down in Seattle, $295. It cost $50 to put in position, and thus the whole cost was nearly $350. It is made of steel and was rung from the tower for the first time in March, 1862.

The only tinner in the place covered the cupola where hung the bell. Its widely reaching voice proclaimed many things beside the call to studies, fulfilling often the office of bell-buoy and fog-horn to distracted mariners wandering in fog and smoke, and giving alarm in case of fire. The succeeding lines set forth exactly historical facts as well as expressing the attachment of the old pupils to the bell and indeed to the university itself:

THE VOICE OF THE OLD UNIVERSITY BELL
A vibrant voice thrilled through the air,
Now here, now there, seemed everywhere;
My young thoughts stirred, laid away in a shroud,
And joyfully rose and walked abroad.
It was long ago in my youth and pride,
When my young thoughts lived and my young
    thoughts died,
And often and over all unafraid
They wander and wander like ghosts unlaid.

Through calm and storm for many a year,
I faithfully called my children dear,
And honest and urgent have been my tones
To hurry the laggard and hasten the drones,
But earnest and early or lazy and late
They toiled up the hill and entered the gate,
Across the campus they rushed pell-mell
At the call of the old University bell.

If danger menaced on land or sea,
The note of warning loud and free;
Or a joyous peal in the twilight dim
Of the New Year's dawn, after New Year's hymn.
If a ship in the bay floated out ablaze,
Or the fog-wreaths blinded the mariner's gaze,
Safe into port they steered them well,
Cheered by the old University bell.

When Lincoln the leader was stricken low,
O! a darker day may we never know,
A bitter wail from my heart was wrung
To float away from my iron tongue,
On storm-wing cast it traveled fast,
 Above me writhed the flag half-mast.
My children wept, their fathers frowned,
With clenched hands looked down to the ground,
For the saddest note that ever fell
From the throat of the old University bell.

But deep was the joy and wild was the clamor,
With leaping hot haste they hurried the hammer,
When the battles were fought and the war was all over,
O'er the North and the South did the peace angels hover;
My children sang sweetly and softly and low
"The Union forever, is safe now we know,"
The years they may come and the years they may go,
And hearts that were loyal will ever be so.

There's a long roll-call, I ring over all
That have harkened and answered in the old hall;
Adams and Andrews, (from A unto Z,
Alphabetic arrangement as any can see),
Bonney and Bagley and Mercer and Hays,
Francis and Denny in bygone days,
Hastings and Ebey, the Oregon Strongs,
And many another whose name belongs
To fame and the world, or has passed away
To realms that are bright with endless day.

The presidents ruled with a right good will,
Mercer and Barnard, Whitworth and Hill,
Anderson, Powell, Gatch and Hall,
Harrington now and I've named them all.
Witten and Thayer, Hansee and Lee,
The wise professors were fair to see,
They strictly commanded, did study compel
At the call of the old University bell.

Osborne, McCarty, Thornton and Spain,
With their companions in sunshine and rain,
Back in the seventies, might tell what befell
At the ring of the old University bell.
The eighties came on and the roll-call grew longer
Emboldened with learning, my voice rang the stronger;
The day of Commencement saw young men and maids
Proudly emerge from the classic shades
Where oft they had heard and heeded well
The voice of the old University bell.

> They bore me away to a shrine new and fine,
> Where the pilgrims of learning with yearning incline;
> Enwrapped they now seem, in a flowery dream,
> The stars of good fortune so radiant beam.
> Of the long roll call not one is forgot,
> If sorrow beset them or happy their lot;
> My wandering children all love me so well,
> Their life-work done, they'll wish a soft knell
> Might be tolled by the old University bell.

Such is the force of habit that it was many years before I could shake off the inclination to obey the imperative summons of the old University bell.

With other small children, I ran about on the huge timbers of the foundation, in the dusk when the workmen were gone, glancing around a little fearfully at the dark shadows in the thick woods, and then running home as fast as our truant feet could carry us.

The laying of the cornerstone was an imposing ceremony to our minds and a significant as well as gratifying occasion to our elders.

The speeches, waving of flags, salutes, Masonic emblems and service with the music rendered by a fine choir, accompanied by a pioneer melodeon, made it quite as good as a Fourth of July.

All the well-to-do ranchers and mill men sent their children from every quarter. The Ebeys of Whidby Island, Hays of Olympia, Strongs of Oregon, Burnetts of down Sound and Dennys of Seattle, beside the children of many other prominent pioneers, received their introduction to learning beneath its generous shelter. A cheerful, energetic crowd they were with clear brains and vigorous bodies.

The school was of necessity preparatory; in modern slang,

a University was rather previous in those days.

But all out-of-doors was greater than our books when it came to physical geography and natural history, to say nothing of botany, geology, etc. Observing eyes and quick wits discovered many things not yet in this year of grace set down in printed pages.

A curious thing, and rather absurd, was the care taken to instruct us in "bounding" New Hampshire, Vermont and all the rest of the Eastern states, while owing to the lack of local maps we were obliged to gain the most of our knowledge of Washington by traveling over it.

The first instruction given within its walls was in a little summer school taught by Mrs. O. J. Carr, which I attended.

Previous to this my mother was my patient and affectionate instructor, an experienced and efficient one I will say, as teaching had been her profession before coming west.

Asa Mercer was at the head of the University for a time, followed by W. E. Barnard, under whose sway it saw prosperous days. A careful and painstaking teacher with a corps of teachers fresh from eastern schools, and ably seconded in his efforts by his lovely wife, a very accomplished lady, he was successful in building up the attendance and increasing the efficiency of the institution. But after a time it languished, and was closed, the funds running low.

Under the Rev. F. H. Whitworth it again arose. It was then run with the common school funds, which raised such opposition that it finally came to a standstill.

D. T. Denny was a school director and county treasurer at the same time, but could not pay any monies to the University without an order from the county superintendent. On one occasion he was obliged to put a boy on horseback and send him eleven miles through the forest and back, making a twenty-two mile ride, to obtain the required order.

The children and young people who attended the University in the old times are scattered far and wide, some have attained distinction in their callings, many are worthy though obscure, and some have passed away from earthly scenes.

We spoke our "pieces," delivered orations, wrote compositions, played ball games of one or more "cats" and many old-fashioned games in and around the big building and often climbed up to the observatory to look out over the beautiful bay and majestic mountains. That glistening sheet of water often drew the eyes from the dull page and occasionally an unwary pupil would be reminded in a somewhat abrupt fashion to proceed with his researches.

One afternoon a boy who had been gazing on its changing surface for some minutes, caught sight of a government vessel rounding the point, and jumped up saying excitedly, "There's a war ship a-comin'!" to the consternation though secret delight of the whole school.

"Well, don't stop her," dryly said the teacher, and the boy subsided amid the smothered laughter of his companions.

Cupid sometimes came to school then, as I doubt not he does in these days, not as a learner but distracter—to those who were his victims.

It's my opinion, and I have it from St. Catherine, he should have been set on the dunce block and made to study Malthus.

Two notable victims are well remembered, one a lovely blonde young girl, a beautiful singer; the other as dark as a Spaniard, with melting black eyes and raven tresses. They did not wait to graduate but named the happy day. The blonde married a Democratic editor, well known in early journalism, the other a very popular man, yet a resident of Seattle.

The whole of the second story of the University consisted

of one great hall or assembly room with two small ante-rooms. Here the school exhibitions were held, lectures and entertainments given. Christmas trees, Sunday schools, political meetings and I do not know what else, although I think no balls were ever permitted in those days, a modern degeneration to my mind.

The old building has always been repainted white until within a few years and stood among the dark evergreen a thing of dignity and beauty, the tall fluted columns with Doric capitals being especially admired.

But changes will come; a magnificent, new, expensive and ornate edifice has been provided with many modern adjuncts—and the old University has been painted a grimy putty color!

The days of old, the golden days, will never be forgotten by the students of the old University, which, although perhaps not so comfortable or elegant nor of so elevated a curriculum as the new, compassed the wonderful beginnings of things intellectual, sowing the seed that others might harvest, planting the tree of knowledge from which others should gather the fruit.

CHAPTER V

A CHEHALIS LETTER, PENNED IN '52

Mound Prairie, Chehalis River, near
Mr. Ford's Tavern, Lewis County,
Oregon Territory. 14 Nov. 1852

M Y DEAR Elizabeth:
I believe this is the first letter I have addressed
to you since we removed from Wisconsin, and I feel
truly thankful to say that through the infinite mercy of God
both my family and self have been in the enjoyment of excellent, uninterrupted health.

The last letter we received from Wisconsin was from my
brother Thomas, complaining of our long silence. We found,
too, that Mr. James' long letter, containing an account of our
route—arrival in Oregon—our having made a claim on the
Clackamas, with description of it—and all our progress up
to February last, had been received. So here begins the next
chapter. About the middle of March we removed into our
new log house; here we found everything necessary to make
a homestead comfortable and even delightful—a beautiful

building spot on a pleasant knoll of considerable extent—a clear brook running along within a few yards of our door; and surrounded by the grandest mountain scenery—and more than that, decidedly healthy. Within walking distance of Oregon City and Milwaukee, and eight miles from Port- land. With all these advantages the boys could not reconcile themselves to it on account of the great lack of grass which prevails for twenty miles 'round.

Brush of all description, Hazel, Raspberry, Salal, Rose, Wil- low and Fern grow to a most gigantic size. And in February what appeared to us and others—a kind of grass—sprang up quickly over the ground and mountain side; nor was it 'till May, when it blossomed out, that we discovered what we hoped would be nourishment for our cattle, was nothing more than the grass Iris, and fully accounted for the straying of our cattle and the constant hunt that was kept up by our neighbors and selves after cattle and horses.

In fact we soon found that this was no place for cattle until it had been subdued and got into cultivation. To make the matter worse we were every now and then in the receipt of messages and accounts from our friends and acquaintances who were located, some in Umpqua, some in the Willamette Valley, some at Puget Sound. Those from Umpqua sent us word that there was grass enough all winter, on one claim for a thousand head of cattle. Mr. Lucas in the Callipooiah Mountains at the head of the Willamette, sent us pressing invitations to come up and settle by him, where he had grass as high as his knees in February. In the Willamette the first rate places were all taken up. Samuel and Billy joined in beg- ging their father to make a tour north or south to see some of these desirable places. Finally he was induced, though rather reluctantly (so well he liked our pleasant home and so confident was he of raising grass and grain) to visit one or the other after harvest. We finished our harvest in July and in August Mr. J., accompanied by Billy, set off on a journey of exploration to the north. The land route lay along the north bank of the Columbia for sixty miles to the mouth of the Cowlitz, then thirty miles up that river over Indian trails, all but impassable. This brought them into the beautiful prairies of Puget Sound, sixty or seventy miles through which brought them to that branch of the Pacific. They returned after an absence of between three and four weeks. So well were Mr. James and Billy pleased with the country that they made no delay on their return in selling out their improvements which they had an opportunity of doing immediately. We had milked but two cows during the summer, but even with the poor feed we had, I had kept the family in butter and sold $20 worth, but then I had fifty cents and five shillings per pound. As to my poultry, I obtained with some difficulty the favor of a pullet and a rooster for $2.00. In March I added another hen to my stock, and so rapidly did they increase, that in September I had, small and big, eighty. After keeping six pullets and a rooster for myself, I made $25.00 off the rest, so you may judge by a little what much will do in Oregon.

Well, it is time for me to take you on board the Batteaux, as I wish you all had been on the 16th of September, when we set sail down the Willamette from Milwaukee. After two days we entered the Columbia, one of the noblest of rivers. After three days, with a head wind all the time, we entered the mouth of the Cowlitz, a beautiful stream, but so swift that none but Indians can navigate it. We had to hire five Indians for $50.00 to take us up. Four days brought us to what is called the upper landing of the Cowlitz. Here ended our river travel—by far the most pleasant journey I ever made. There we met Samuel and Billy who with Tom had taken the cattle by the trail. We halted at a Mr. Jackson's, where we stopped for a fortnight, while Mr. J. and the boys journeyed away in search of adventures and a claim.

On the banks of the Chehalis, 30 miles north of where we stopped and 30 miles south of the Sound, they found a claim satisfactory in every respect to all parties, and what was not a little, we found a cabin a great deal better than the one we found last winter.

The Indians told us that *tennes* (white) Jack, who *momicked* (worked) it had *clatawawed* (traveled or went) to California in quest of *chicamun* (metal) and had never *chacooed* (come back), so we entered on *tennes* Jack's labours. As a farm and location, this certainly exceeds our most sanguine expectations. I often thought last year that we had bettered our conditions from what they were in Wisconsin, and now I think we have improved ours ten times beyond what we then were.

Our claim is along the banks of the Chehalis, a navigable river which empties into the Pacific at Grays Harbor, about 70 miles below us. A settlement is just commenced at the mouth of the river and a sawmill is erected 10 miles below us, or rather is building. These are all the settlements on the river below us, and our nearest neighbor above us is 6 miles up. A prairie of 10 miles long and varying in width from 2 to 4 miles stretched away to the north of us, watered with a beautiful stream of water and covered with grass at this time as green as in May.

A stream of water flows within a few yards of our house, so full of salmon that Tom and Johnny could with ease catch a barrel in an hour; they are from 20 to 30 lbs. in a fish. Besides which we have a small fish here very much resembling a pilchard.

We are blessed with the most beautiful springs of water, one of which will be enclosed in our door yard. As far as I can learn there are in the thickest settled parts of this portion of Oregon, about one family in a township—many towns are not so thickly settled. We are the only inhabitants of this great prairie except a few Indians who have a fishing station about a mile from us. These are on very friendly terms with us, supplying us with venison, wild fowl and mats at a very reasonable price, as we are the only customers and we in return letting them have what *sappalille* (flour) and molasses we can at a reasonable price, which they are always willing to pay. Soap is another article I am glad to see in request among them. And it affords them no little amusement to look at the plates of the Encyclopedia. But I fear it will be long before they will be brought to *momick* the *illahe* (earth). They are the finest and stoutest set of Indians we have seen.

We converse with them by means of a jargon composed of English, French and Chinook, and which the Indians speak fluently, and we are getting to *waw-waw* (speak) pretty well. My children, I am thankful to say, look better than I ever saw them in America; they have not had the least symptoms of any of the diseases that they were so much afflicted with in Wisconsin. And now, my dear Elizabeth, if wishing would bring you here, you should soon be here in what appears to me to be one of the most delightful portions of the globe. But then, ever since I have been in America I have regarded a mild climate as a "pearl of great price" in temporal things and felt willing to pay for it accordingly and I have not had the least reason to think I have valued it too high. Many and many a year has passed since I have enjoyed life as I have since I have been in Oregon.

I should have told you that the Chehalis is one of the most

beautiful rivers in Oregon. Our claim stretches a mile along the north bank of it. It flows through quite an elevated part of the country. Our house, though within a few rods of the river, has one of the finest views in Oregon, the prairie stretching away to the north like a fine lawn, skirted on each side by oak and maple, at this time in all the brilliant hues of Autumn; behind, on gently rising hills, forests of fir and cedar of most gigantic height and size; farther still to the northeast rises the ever snow-clad mountains of Rainier and St. Helens, on the opposite side to the southwest of the coast range, so near that we can see the trees on them. So magnificent are those immense snow mountains that none but those who have seen them can form any idea of it.

This prairie takes its name from a remarkable mound about a mile from our house; it stands in about 25 acres and is 100 feet high, with a pure spring half way up. The rest of the prairie is almost level without a spring except in the margin. The soil of the mound, as well as some of the margin, has just enough clay to make it a rich and excellent soil; the rest of the prairie is deficient in clay; it has a rich black mould overlaying two feet deep, resting on substratum of sand and gravel, which in some places is so mixed with the soil as to give it the name of a gravelly prairie. You might have the choice of fifty such prairies as this and some better on this river. Farmers were never better paid in the world, even my little dairy of two cows has for the month past turned me in, at least I have sold butter to the amount of two and a half bushels of wheat a day at Wisconsin prices of 30 cents, and have by me 26 pounds for which I shall have at least 60 cents or $1.00 per pound. I now milk three cows; we have four; and Mr. James means to add two more and a few sheep. Mr. J. sold the worst yoke of cattle he had for

$160.00. Cows are worth from $50.00 to $100.00; sheep are from $5.00 to $9.00; chickens, 60 cents to $1.00 each; eggs, 50 cents per dozen; dry goods and groceries just the same as in the states; wheat $3.00 per bushel. We left our wheat on the Clackamas to be threshed. They, Samuel and Billy, are now preparing to put in ten acres of fall wheat, potatoes are $2.00 per bushel. Indians easy to hire, both men and women, at reasonable wages. Extensive coal mines of excellent quality have been discovered within 15 miles of this place. But all these things are secondary in my estimation compared with the climate, which is allowed by all English to be superior to their native clime.

It makes me very sad to think how we are separated as a family, never to meet again (at least in all probability) under one roof. O, that we may all meet at least at the right hand of God, let this be our sole concern and our path will be made plain in temporals.

You have the advantage of us in schools, churches and society, but I feel quite patient to wait the arrival of those blessings in addition to those we enjoy. This letter will be accompanied by a paper to Mr. McNaves, *The Columbian*, published at Olympia, Puget Sound. Mr. James has just written an article for it, entitled the "Rainy Season." I wonder how Amy and Edward are getting on; how I wish they were here. Do you think they will ever come over? Should any of you (of course I include any old friends and acquaintances at Caledonia) determine on removing to this part, the instructions in my husband's letter are the best we can give.

There has been great suffering on the road this year. We have seen a great many families who came through in a very fair manner, some of them without even the loss of a single head of cattle; these were among the first trains; among the latter the loss of cattle and lives was awful. Some horrid murders were committed on the road, for which the murderers were tried and shot or hung on the spot. The papers say there will be fifteen thousand added to the population of Oregon by this year's emigration. It is in contemplation to open a road through from Grand Ronde on to Puget Sound, which will shorten the distance at least 300 miles and out of the very worst of the road. Samuel and Billy are determined to come to meet you on the new route with Jack and Dandy, and more if wanted. Now we are settled in earnest you shall hear from us oftener and hope we shall the same from you. Give my kindest and best love to Mother. One old lady, about her age, crossed the plains when we did; she was alive and well when we left the other side of the Columbia.

I must introduce to you an old acquaintance—the Rooks—caw! caw! caw! all around us. We have a rookery on our farm. It is now the 28th of Nov., a fortnight since I wrote the above, in hopes that it would be on its passage to Wisconsin ere this, but was disappointed of sending to the postoffice. Weather warm and sunshiny as May, two or three white frosts that vanished with the rising of the sun are all we have had, not the slightest prospect of sleighing nearer than the slopes of Mt. Rainier.

I have just asked all hands for the dark side of Oregon, not one could mention anything worth calling such. Mr. J. says the shades are so light as to be invisible. The grey squirrel on the south of the Columbia was the most formidable enemy to the farmer; more of that when I write next.

My kindest love to all the dear children; how I long to see them all again, particularly Anna; O, that she may be a very good girl. Richard and Allan often talk of writing to Avis and Lydia. How are Mr. and Mrs. Welch and family? How gladly would I welcome them to my humble cabin. I cannot help thinking, too, that Mrs. W. and I could enjoy ourselves here on the green sward and in looking at the beautiful evergreen shrubs and plants on the banks of the Chehalis, though we might be overtaken by a mild sprinkling. A canoe on the waters of that beautiful stream would help to compensate for the loss of a sleigh on the snows of Wisconsin, particularly when it can be enjoyed at the same season of the year. But I suppose I must look upon all this as a Utopian dream, as I expect few if any of you would barter your comfortable house for a log cabin; well, it is my home, and I hope I have not given you an exaggerated description of it. I wished my husband to write a more particular description of the soil and its productions than I could give, but he was in no writing mood. He says the prairies as far as he has seen are not equal to Iowa or Illinois, but for climate and health he thinks Oregon equals if not surpasses most parts of the world.

Well, I must bid you good-bye, with kind regards to Mr. and Mrs. Drummond, with all my other friends in Yorkville, Mr. Moyle and Susan, with all my friends and acquaintances in Caledonia. I will write again, all's well, about Christmas, and hope you will attend to the same rate and write once in a month. Farewell my dear sister. Yours in true affection,

A. M. James

P. S.—If Jane and Dick are married, I will risk saying that the best thing they can do is to come here. All the children send their love to you all. I should be thankful for a few flower seeds.

CHAPTER VI

SOME PIONEERS OF PORT TOWNSEND

I N PORT Townsend and Seattle papers of 1902 appeared the following items of history pertaining to settlers of Port Townsend:

"Port Townsend, Feb. 15, 1902.—On Friday, February 21, there is to be held in Port Townsend a reunion of old settlers to celebrate the fiftieth anniversary of the landing at this place of some of the first white families to settle on Puget Sound north of the little town of Steilacoom.

"Much interest is being manifested in the coming celebration among the old-timers on Puget Sound, many of whom have already responded to invitations that have been sent them. Most of these letters contain interesting anecdotes or references touching the past. One of them is from Judge E. D. Warbass, of San Juan county, who writes from 'Idlewild,' his country home, near Friday Harbor, under date of February 1. In his letter to J. A. Kuhn, whom he addresses as 'My Dear Ankutty Tillikum,' he says:

"'This is my birthday, born in A. D. 1825. Please figure up the time for yourself. I have just finished my breakfast and chores, and will get this letter off on the 9 o'clock mail. I am sincerely obliged for the honor of being invited to come to the Port Townsend celebration and to prepare and read some reminiscences of my experiences during all these years. I hope to be able to do so, and will, if I can, but you know I am no longer the same rollicking Ed, but quite an old man. However, I am willing to contribute my mite towards making your celebration a success, and weather and health permitting, will be there. Delate mika siam.'

"A. A. Plummer, Sr., and Henry Bacheller came to Port Townsend by sailing vessel from San Francisco, in the fall of 1851, and remained here during the winter. A few days after they arrived here, L. B. Hastings and F. W. Pettygrove came in overland from Portland, carrying their blankets on their backs. They soon decided to return to Portland and bring their families over. Mr. Hastings arranged with Plummer and Bacheller to build a cabin for him by the time he returned.

"He and Pettygrove went back to Portland, and soon afterward Mr. Hastings bought the schooner *Mary Taylor*. He made up a party of congenial people, and on February 9, 1852, the *Mary Taylor* sailed from the Columbia river with the following named persons, and their families, on board: L. B. Hastings, F. W. Pettygrove, Benjamin Ross, David Shelton, Thomas Tallentyre and Smith Hayes. The last named had no family.

"On February 19 the schooner passed in by Cape Flattery, and on the afternoon of the 20th came upon the Hudson Bay settlement on Vancouver Island, at Victoria. Present survivors of the trip, who were then children, recall how their fathers lifted them up to their shoulders and pointed out the little settlement, telling them at the same time that that country belonged to England, and of their own purpose of crossing over to the American side and there establishing a home for themselves. That night the schooner dropped anchor in Port Townsend bay.

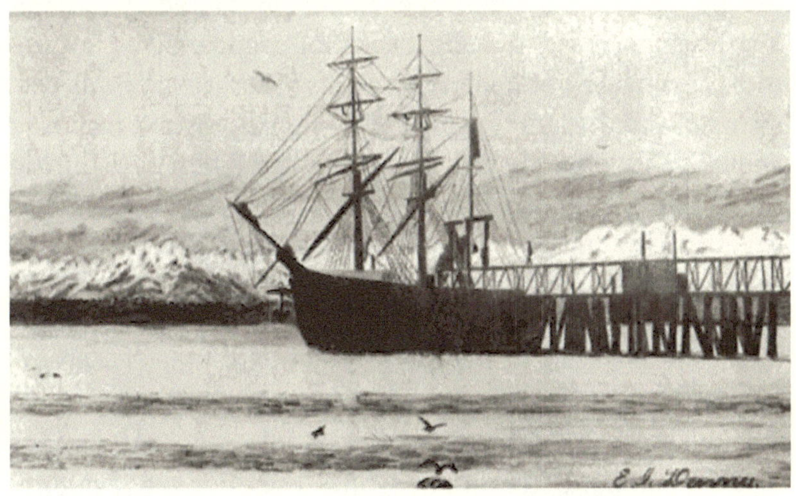

SHIP *BELLE ISLE* LOADING COAL, 1876

"Early next morning—February 21—the schooner was boarded by Quincy A. Brooks, deputy collector and inspector of customs. Mr. Brooks had arrived here only a few hours ahead of the *Mary Taylor*, coming from Olympia and bringing with him the following customs inspectors: A. M. Poe, H. C. Wilson and A. B. Moses. These men had been sent here by the collector of customs to investigate stories of smuggling being carried on between the Hudson Bay Company and Indians on the Sound. The customs officials were camped on the beach. With them were B. J. Madison and William Wilton, the former of whom later settled here. A. A. Plummer and Henry Bacheller were also camped on the beach here at the same time, having been here since their arrival from San Francisco in the preceding fall.

"Early in the forenoon of February 21 all on board the schooner *Mary Taylor* were landed on the beach and immediately began the work of carving out homes for themselves in what was then a wilderness thickly inhabited by Indians. Mr. Hastings found his cabin ready for occupancy, all but the roof, which had not been put on. A temporary roof was constructed and the family moved in. That night twelve inches of snow fell, it being the first snow that had fallen here during the entire winter. Mr. Hastings' schooner afterward made several trips between the Columbia river and the Sound, bringing additional families here.

"The present survivors of the *Mary Taylor's* passengers are the following: L. W. D. Shelton and his sister, Mary, Oregon C. Hastings, Frank W. Hastings, Maria Hastings Littlefield, Benj. S. Pettygrove and Sophia Pettygrove McIntyre. All but Mr. Shelton and his sister and Oregon C. Hastings are residents of Port Townsend.

"Oregon C. Hastings was born in Illinois in 1845, and crossed the plains in 1849 with his parents. He is living in Victoria.

"Benjamin S. Pettygrove is a native of Portland, Oregon, where he was born on September 30, 1846. He was the first white male child born in Portland.

"Frank W. Hastings was born in Portland on November 16, 1848.

"Sophia Pettygrove was born in Portland on November 17, 1848. She was married on her 17th birthday to Captain James McIntyre, who lost his life a few weeks ago in the wreck of the steamship *Bristol* in Alaskan waters.

"Judge J. A. Kuhn is the moving spirit in the matter of these pioneers' reunions and in the organization of Native Sons and Native Daughters lodges. He made a promise to G. Morris Haller of Seattle, as far back as 1877, he says, that he would take up the organizations referred to, in the interest of history and research. The matter remained dormant, however, till the year 1893, when, on March 2, of that year, he instituted in Port Townsend, Jefferson Camp No. 1, Native Sons of Washington, with 12 members present. The camp now has 118 members. On July 3, 1895, he instituted in Port Townsend, Lucinda Hastings Parlor No. 1, Native Daughters of Washington. There are now in the state nine camps of Native Sons and four parlors of Native Daughters.

"A. A. Plummer, Sr., now deceased, was one of the fathers of Port Townsend and was considered quite a remarkable man. He was born in the state of Maine, March 3, 1822, and was a veteran of the Mexican war. He fought under Col. Stevens in that conflict and at its close went to California, going from there to Portland by sailing vessel in 1850.

"Major Quincy A. Brooks was the second deputy collector of customs ever sworn into the service in the Puget Sound district. In January, 1852, he succeeded Elwood Evans as deputy collector for the district. The collector of customs was then Simpson P. Moses, of Cincinnati, Ohio, and the custom house was located at Olympia."

At the reunion on the 21st of February, 1902, many things were brought to light.

"Among the many stories of early days and reminiscences recalled at the pioneers' gathering one of the most interesting was Mr. Shelton's story of the trip of the *Mary Taylor* from Portland to Port Townsend. Mr. Shelton had committed his reminiscences to manuscript as follows:

"'Fifty years ago, some time about the first of February, the little 75-ton schooner *Mary Taylor* left Portland, Ore., for Puget Sound, having on board the families of L. B. Hastings, F. W. Pettygrove, David Shelton, Thomas Tallentyre,

Benjamin Ross and Smith Hayes. Mr. Hayes had no family here, but I think he had a family in the East. Mr. Ross had one son, about 20 years old.

"'Our little craft was navigated by Captain Hutchinson and a crew of four or five men. The families were all old acquaintances. Those of Hastings, Ross and Shelton crossed the plains together in 1847, and concluded to cast their fortunes together again in their last great move, which was to this country.

"'We lay at Astoria several days, waiting for a favorable opportunity to cross the bar. We made three trials before we ventured out to sea and were three or four days getting up to Cape Flattery, where we lay quite a while in a calm. We found here that we were in soundings, and some of the party commenced fishing, but all they could catch were dog fish, which we tried to eat, but we found that they were not the kind of fish that we cared about.

"'Our first sight of Indians in this part of the country was off Neah Bay. We were drifting near Waadah Island, when canoes came swarming out of their village in the bay. We had heard ugly stories about this tribe, and prepared for them by stacking our arms around the masts, to be handy in case of need. They were clamorous to come on board, but we thought that they were as well off in their canoes as they would be anywhere else. Some of our party sauntered along the deck with guns in their hands, in view of the Indians.

"'The Indians then wanted to trade fish for tobacco and trinkets. A few pieces of tobacco were thrown into their canoes and then they commenced throwing fish aboard, and such fish for a landsman to look at! There were bull-heads, rock-cod, kelp-fish, mackerel, fish as flat as your hand, and skates, and other monstrosities, the likes of which the most of our party had never seen before, and when our old cook dished them up for us at dinner we found that they were fine and delicious. There is where we made the acquaintance of sea-bass and rock-cod, and we have cultivated their acquaintance ever since. There were also mussels and clams among the lot, which we found to be very good. We were surrounded by another lot of Indians near Clallam Bay, with about the same performances and with the same results as at Neah Bay.'

"Another incident that I recall happened near Dungeness spit. A couple of canoes filled with Indians came alongside and as there was only a few of them they were allowed to come on board. The tyee of the crowd introduced himself as Lord Jim. He wore a plug hat, a swallowtailed coat, a shirt and an air of immense importance. I suppose he had secured his outfit as a '*cultus potlatch*' from persons he had met. He had evidently met several white people in his time, as he had a number of testimonials as to his character as a good Indian. I remember of hearing one of his testimonials read and it impressed me as having come from one who had studied the Indian character to some effect. It read something like this:

"'To whom it may concern: This will introduce Lord Jim, a noted Indian of this part of the country. Look out for him or he will steal the buttons off your coat.' A further acquaintance with Lord Jim seemed to inspire the belief that the confidence of the writer was not misplaced.

"Shortly after we left Lord Jim we sailed along Protection Island, one of the beauty spots of the Strait of Juan de Fuca. Somewhere along here another thing happened—trivial in its nature—the memory of which has stayed with me all these years. Mr. Pettygrove was walking the deck in a meditative manner, when he happened to feel that he needed a cigar. He called to his son, Ben, about six years old, and told him to bring him some cigars. Ben wanted to know how many he should get. His father told him to get as many as he had fingers on both hands. Ben, proud of his commission, darted away and soon returned with eight cigars. His father looked at them a moment and said: 'How is this; you have only brought me eight cigars?' 'Well,' said Ben, 'that is all the fingers I have.' 'No,' said his father, 'you have ten on both your hands.' 'Why, no I haven't,' said Ben, 'two of them are thumbs,' and I guess Ben was right.

"The next morning, after passing Dungeness Spit, we found our vessel anchored abreast of what is now the business part of Port Townsend, which was then a large Indian village. That was February 21, 1852, fifty years ago today. How it stirs the blood and quickens the memory to look back over those eventful years—eventful years for our state, our Pacific Coast and our entire country—and these years have been equally eventful for the little band that landed here that day so full of hope and energy.

"Our fathers and mothers are all gone to their well-earned rest and reward. Of the thirteen children that were with them at that time nine are still living, and I am proud of the fact that they are all respectable citizens of the community in which they live. They have seen all the history of this part of the country that amounts to much and in their humble way have helped to make it. They have helped conquer the wilderness and the savages and have done their share in laying the foundation of what will be one of the greatest states of our Union. Their fathers were men of honesty and more than ordinary force of character, as their deeds and labors in behalf of their country and families show, and the mothers of blessed memory—their children never realized the power for good they were in this world until they were grown and had families of their own, but they know it now. They know now how they encouraged their husbands when dark days came; how they cheerfully shared the trials and hardships incident to those early pioneer days, and when brighter fortunes came they exercised the same helpful guiding influence in their well ordered, comfortable homes that they did in their first log cabins in the wilderness."

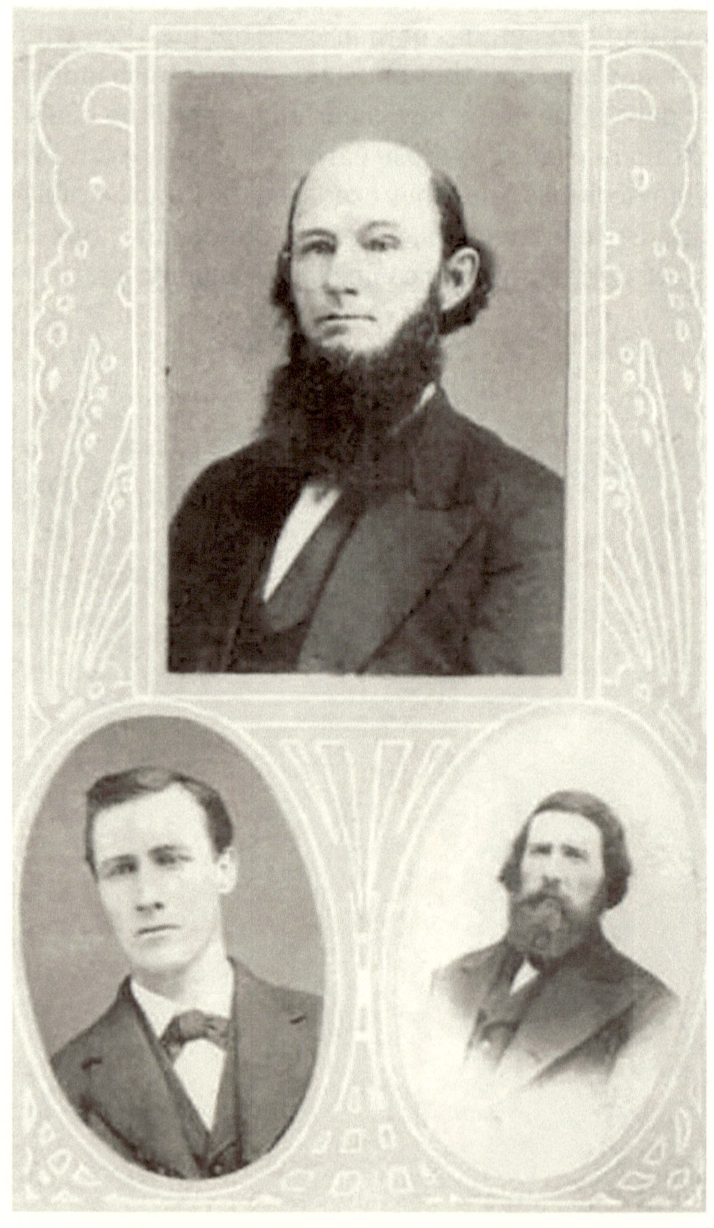

REV. D. E. BLAINE, WILLIAM R.
BOREN, CARSON D. BOREN

PERSONNEL OF THE PIONEER ARMY

A LONG ROLL of honor I might call of the brave men and women who dared and strove in the wild Northwest of the long ago. If I speak of representative pioneers, those unnamed might be equally typical of the bold army of "forest-felling kings," "forest-fallers" as well as "fighters," like those Northland men of old.

There are the names of Denny, Yesler, Phillips, Terry, Low, Boren, Butler, Bell, Mercer, Maple, Van Asselt, Horton, Hanford, McConaha, Smith, Maynard, Frye, Blaine and others who felled the forest and laid foundations at and near Seattle; Briggs, Hastings, Van Bokkelin, Hammond, Pettygrove with others founded Port Townsend, while Lansdale, Crockett, Alexander, Cranney, Kellogg, Hancock, Izett, Busby, Ebey and Coupe, led the van for Whidby Island; Eldridge and Roeder at Bellingham Bay; toward the head of navigation, McAllister, Bush, Simmons, Packwood, Chambers, Shelton, are a few of those who blazed the way.

The blows of the sturdy forest-felling kings rang out from many a favored spot on the shores of the great Inland Sea, cheerful signals for the thousands to come after them.

These, and the long list of the Here Unnamed, waged the warfare of beginnings, which required such large courage, independence, persistence, faith and uncompromising toil, as the velvet-shod aftercomers can scarcely conceive of.

Simultaneously with the early subjugation of the country, the political, educational, commercial and social initiatory movements were made of whose present development the people of Puget Sound may well be proud.

Since the organization of the Washington Pioneer Association in October, 1883, the old pioneers and their children have met year by year in the lavish month of June to recount their adventures, toils and privations, and enjoy the sympathy begotten of similar experiences, in the midst of modern ease and plenty.

A concourse of this kind in Seattle evoked the following words of appreciation:

"No organization, no matter what its nature might be, could afford the people of Seattle more gratification by holding its assemblage in their midst than is afforded them by the action of the Pioneers' Association of Washington Territory in holding its annual gathering in this city. Unlike conventions and gatherings in which only a portion of the community is interested, the meeting of the pioneers is interesting to all. To some, of course, the event is of more importance than to others, but all have an interest in the Pioneers' Association, all have a pride in the achievement of its members, and all can feel that they are the beneficiaries of the struggle and hardships of which the pioneers tell.

"The reminiscences of the pioneers from the history of the first life breathings of our commonwealth—of a commonwealth which, though in its infancy, is grand indeed, and which gives promise of attaining greatness in the full maturity of its powers of which those who laid the foundations of the state scarcely dreamed. The pioneers are the fathers of the commonwealth; their struggles and their hardships were the struggles and the hardships of a state coming into being. They cleared the forests, not for themselves alone, but for posterity and for all time. As they subdued a wild and rugged land and prepared it to sustain and support its share of the people of the earth, each blow of their ax was a blow destined to resound through all time, each furrow turned by their ploughshares that the earth might yield again and again to their children's children so long as man shall inhabit the earth. No stroke of work done in the progress of that great labor was done in vain. None of the mighty energy was lost. Each tree that fell, fell never to rise. Each nail driven in a settler's hut was a nail helping to bind together the fabric of the community. Each day's labor was given to posterity more surely than if it had been sold for gold to be buried in the earth and brought forth by delighted searchers centuries hence.

"It is for this that we honor the pioneers. It is for this that we are proud and happy to have them meet among us. We are their heirs. Our inheritance is the fruit of their labor, the reward of their fortitude, the recompense of their hardships. The home of today, the center of comfort and contentment, the very soul of the state, could not have been but for the log cabins of forty years ago. The imposing edifice of learning, the complete system of education, could not have been but for the crude school house of the past. The churches and religious institutions of today are the result of the untiring and unselfish labors of the itinerant preacher who wandered back and forth, now painfully picking his way through the forest, now threading with his frail canoe the silver streams, now gliding over the calm waters of the Sound, ever laying broad and deep the true foundations of the grand civilization that was to be. The flourishing cities, the steel rails that bind us to the world, the stately steamers that, behemoth-like, journey to and fro in our waters,—these things could not be but for the rude straggling hamlets, the bridle path cut with infinite labor through the most impenetrable of forests, and the canoe which darted arrow-like through gloomy passages, over bright bays and up laughing waters.

"All honor to the pioneers—all honor and welcome. We say it who are their heirs, we whose homes are on the land which they reclaimed from the forests, we who till the fields that they first tilled, we whose pride and glory is the grand land-locked sea on which they gazed delighted so many years ago. Welcome to them, and may they come together again and again as the years pass away. When their eyes are dim with age and their hair is as white as the snows that cover the mountains they love, may they still see the land which they created the home of a great, proud people, a people loving the land they love, a people honoring and obeying the laws that they have honored and obeyed so long, a people honoring, glorying in, the flag which they bore over treeless plains, over lofty mountains, over raging torrents, through suffering and danger, always proudly, always confidently, always hopefully, until they planted it by the shore of the Western sea in the most beautiful of all lands. May each old settler, as he journeys year by year toward the shoreless sea, over whose waters he must journey away, feel that the flag which he carried so far and so bravely will wave forever in the soft southwestern breeze, which kisses his furrowed brow and toys with his silvery hair. May he feel, too, that the

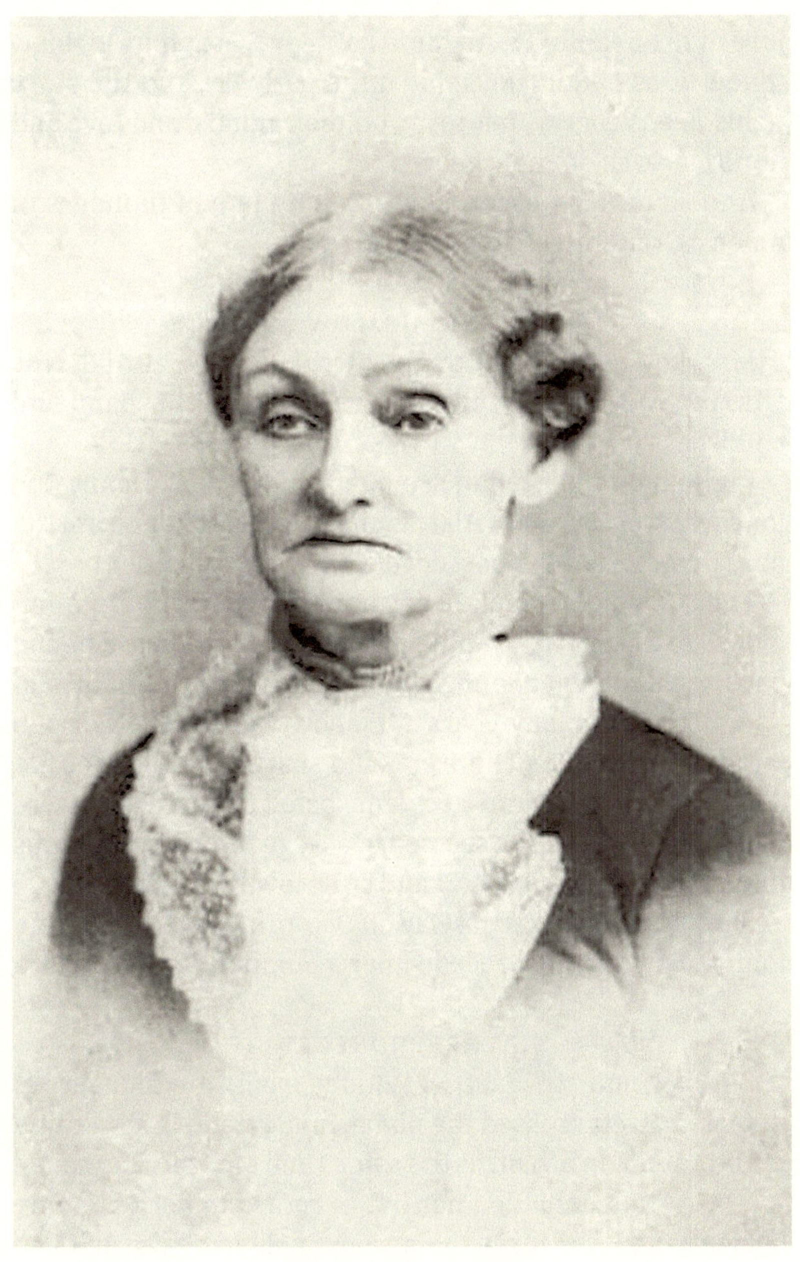

MRS. LYDIA C. LOW

love of the people is with him, that they watch him, lovingly, tenderly, as he journeys down the pathway, and the story of his deeds is graven forever on their minds, and love and honor forever on their hearts."

And so do I, a descendent of a long line of pioneers in America, reiterate, "Honor the Pioneers."

LYDIA C. LOW

Mrs. Low was one of the party that landed at Alki, Nov. 13th, 1851, having crossed the plains with her husband and children.

I have heard her tell of seeing my father, D. T. Denny, the lone white occupant of Alki, as she stepped ashore from the boat that carried the passengers from the schooner.

The Lows did not make a permanent settlement there, but moved to a farm back of Olympia, thence to Sonoma, Cal., and back again to Puget Sound, where they made their home at Snohomish for many years. Mrs. Low was the mother of a large family of nine children, who shared her pioneer life. Some died in childhood, accidents befell others, a part were more fortunate, yet she seemed in old age serene, courageous, undaunted as ever, faithful and true, lovely and beloved.

She passed from earth away on Dec. 11th, 1901, her husband, John D. Low, having preceded her a number of years before.

OTHER PIONEERS

Both Mr. and Mrs. Izett of Whidby Island are pioneers of note. Mrs. Izett crossed the plains in 1847, and in 1852 came to the Sound on a visit, at the same time Mr. Izett happened to arrive. He persuaded her not to return to her old home. Mr. Izett in 1850 went to India from England by way of Cape Horn, and two years later came to Seattle. For four years he secured spars for the British government at Utsalady. In 1859 he built the first boat of any size to be constructed on Puget Sound. This was a 100-ton schooner, and she was built at Oak Harbor. In 1862 he framed two of the first Columbia river steamers. Mrs. Izett is a sister of Mrs. F. A. Chenoweth, whose husband was a judge, with four associates, of the first Washington territorial tribunal. Another of the members was Judge McFadden. Mr. Izett knew well Gen. Isaac I. Stevens, the first governor of the territory. He came to Washington in the fall of 1859, and issued his first proclamation as governor the following February. The legislature met soon after.

J. W. MAPLE

John Wesley Maple was not only one of the oldest settlers of this (King) county, but he was one of its most prominent men. He figured to some extent in political life, but during the last few years had retired to the homestead by the Duwamish, where his father had settled after crossing the plains nearly fifty years ago, and where he himself met his death yesterday. (In March of 1902.)

He was born in Guernsey county, Ohio, January 1, 1840. As a little boy he spent his childhood days near the farm of the McKinleys, and often during his later years he was fond of relating apple stealing expeditions in which he indulged as a little boy, and for which the father of the late President McKinley often chastised him. From Ohio his father, Jacob Maple, moved to Keokuk, Ia., where he lived near the farm on which Mayor Humes, of Seattle, was reared.

In 1856, Jacob Maple, the father, and Samuel Maple, the brother of John W., came to Puget Sound. In 1862 the rest of the family followed them. In crossing the plains John W. Maple was made captain of the four wagon trains which were united in the expedition. He guided them to Pendleton, Ore., where they separated. Thence he came to the Duwamish river, where his father and brother had settled.

Later Mr. Maple and Samuel Snyder took up a homestead on Squak slough. A few years after that Mr. Maple went to Ellensburg. He finally returned to spend the rest of his life on the homestead.

HELD MANY OFFICES

In the early days he was several times elected to county offices. He was at one time supervisor for the road district extending from Yesler way to O'Brien station and to Renton. In 1896 he was elected treasurer of King county on the Populist ticket. He furnished a bond of $1,600,000. At the end of his term a shortage was found. Every cent of this was finally made good by him to those who stood on his bond.

In 1897 Mr. Maple received a complimentary vote on the part of several members of the state legislature for the office of United States senator. For this office his neighbors indorsed him, and August Toellnor, of Van Asselt, was sent by them to Olympia to see what could be done to further the candidacy. Since the end of his term as treasurer Mr. Maple has held no office, save that of school director in his district. Only a week ago Mr. Maple announced to his friends that he had left the Populist party and had returned to the Republican party, to which he had belonged prior to the wave of Populism which swept over the West in the early nineties.

During all of his life he was an ardent student of literature, and he possessed one of the finest libraries in the state. He was known as a strong orator, and was during his younger days an exhorter in the Methodist Protestant church, of which he was a member.

Mr. Maple was married twice. His first wife, who died more than twenty years ago, was Elizabeth Snyder, a daughter of Samuel Snyder, one of the oldest residents of the Duwamish valley. Six children were the fruit of this union, Charles, Alvin B., Cora, now Mrs. Frank Patten; Dora, now Mrs. Charles Norwich; Bessie, now dead, and Clifford J. Maple. His second wife was Minnie Borella. Three children were born to her, Telford C., Lelah and Beulah Maple.

Of his brothers and sisters the following are living: Mrs. Katherine Van Asselt and Mr. Eli B. Maple, of this city; Mrs. Jane Cavanaugh, of California; Mrs. Elvira Jones and Mrs. Ruth Smith, of Kent, and Aaron Maple, who now lives on the old Maple homestead in Iowa.

CHARLES PROSCH AND THOMAS PROSCH

"The summer in which the gold excitement broke out in the Colville country, in 1855," said Thomas Prosch, "several members of a party of gold hunters from Seattle were massacred by the Indians in the Yakima Valley while on their way to the gold fields. The party went through Snoqualmie Pass in crossing the mountains. The territorial legislature sent word to Washington and the government undertook to punish the guilty tribes by a detachment of troops under Maj. Haller. This was defeated and war followed for several years. It was most violent in King county in 1855 and 1856, and in Eastern Washington in 1857 and 1858. The principal incidents in the West were the massacre of the whites in 1855 and the attack upon Seattle the following year. In 1857 Col. Steptoe sustained a memorable defeat on the Eastern side of the mountains, and the hostilities were terminated by the complete annihilation of the Indian forces in the same locality the following year by Col. Wright. He killed 1,000 horses and hanged many of the Indians besides the frightful carnage of the battlefield."

Mr. Prosch and his father, Charles Prosch, with several other members of his family, arrived in the state and in Seattle between the years 1849 and 1857. Gen. M. M. Carver, the founder of Tacoma, who was Mrs. Thomas Prosch's father, came to the territory in 1843 with Dr. Whitman, who was massacred, with Applegate and Nesmith.

Time and strength would fail me did I attempt to obtain and record accounts of many well known pioneers; I must leave them to other more capable writers. However, I will briefly mention some who were prominent during my childhood.

The Hortons, Dexter Horton and Mrs. Horton, the latter a stout, rosy-cheeked matron whose house and garden, particularly the dahlias growing in the yard, elicited my childish admiration. I remember how certain little pioneer girls were made happy by a visit from her, at which time she fitted them with her own hands some pretty grey merino dresses trimmed with narrow black velvet ribbon. Also how one of them was impressed by the sorrow she could not conceal, the tears ran down her cheeks as she spoke of a child she had lost.

One family have never forgotten the Santa Claus visit to their cottage home, the same being impersonated by Dexter Horton, who departed after leaving some substantial tokens of his good will.

The pioneer ministers of the Gospel were among the most fearless of foundation builders. Reverends Wm. Close, Alderson, Franklin, Doane, Bagley, Whitworth, Belknap, Greer, Mann, Atwood, Hyland, Prefontaine, and others; of Rev. C. Alderson, who often visited my father and mother, Hon. Allen Weir has this to say:

"I remember very clearly when, during the 'sixties,' Brother Alderson used to visit the settlement in which my father's family lived at Dungeness, in Clallam county, Washington Territory. He was then stationed at White River, twelve miles or more south of Seattle. There was no Tacoma in those days. To reach Dungeness, Brother Alderson had to walk over a muddy road a dozen miles or more to Seattle, then by the old steamer *Eliza Anderson* to Port Townsend, and then depend upon an Indian canoe twenty-five miles to the old postoffice at Elliot Cline's house. After his arrival it would require several days to get word passed around among the neighbors so as to get a preaching announcement circulated. Sometimes he would preach at Mr. Cline's house, sometimes at Alonzo Davis', and sometimes at my father's. He was literally blazing the trail where now is an highway. The first announcement of these services in the Dungeness river bottom was when a bearded, muddy-booted old bachelor from Long Prairie stopped to halloo to father and interrupt log piling and stump clearing long enough to say: 'H-a-y! Mr. Weir! The's a little red-headed Englishman goin' to preach at Cline's on Sunday! Better go an' git your conschense limbered up.' Everybody knew the road to Cline's. At each meeting the audience was limited to the number of settlers within a dozen miles. All had to attend or proclaim themselves confirmed heathen. The preacher, who came literally as the 'Voice of one crying in the wilderness,' was manifestly not greatly experienced at that time in his work—but he was intensely earnest, courageous, outspoken, a faithful messenger; and under his ministrations many were reminded of their old-time church privileges 'back in old Mizzoory,' in 'Kentuck,' or in 'Eelinoy,' or elsewhere. I remember that to my boyish imagination it seemed a wonderful amount of 'grit' was required to carry on his gospel work. He made an impression as an honest toiler in the vineyard, and was accepted at par value for his manly qualities. He was welcomed to the hospitable homes of the people. If we could not always furnish yellow-legged chickens for dinner we always had a plentiful supply of bear meat or venison.

"After Brother Alderson returned to Oregon I never met him again, except at an annual conference in Albany (in 1876, I think it was), but I always remembered him kindly as a sturdy soldier of the Cross who improved his opportunities to administer reproof and exhortation. The memory is a benediction."

Of agreeable memory is Mrs. S. D. Libby, to whom the pioneer women were glad to go for becoming headgear—and the hats were very pretty, too, as well as the wearers, in those days. Good straw braids were valued and frequently made over by one who had learned the bleacher's and shaper's art in far Illinois.

A little pioneer girl used often to rip the hats to the end that the braids might be made to take some new and fashionable form.

"The beautiful Bonney girls," Emmeline, Sarah and Lucy, afterward well known as Mrs. Shorey, Mrs. G. Kellogg and Mrs. Geo. Harris, might each give long and interesting accounts of early times. Others I think of are the John Ross family, whose sons and daughters are among the few native white children of pioneer families of Seattle (the Ross family were our nearest neighbors for a long time, and good neighbors they were, too); the Peter Andrews family, the Maynards, who were among the earliest and most prominent settlers; Mrs. Maynard did many a kindness to the sick; the Samuel Coombs family, of whom "Sam Coombs," the patriarch, known to all, is a great lover and admirer of pioneers; Ray Coombs, his son, the artist, and Louisa, his daughter, one of the belles of early times; the L. B. Andrews family; Mr. Andrews was a friend of Grandfather John Denny, and himself a pioneer of repute; his fair, pleasant, blue-eyed daughter was my schoolmate at the old U., then new; the Hanfords, valued citizens, now so distinguished and so well known; Mrs. Hanford's account of the stirring events of early days was recognized and drawn from by the historian Bancroft in compiling his great work; the De Lins; the Burnetts, long known and much esteemed; the Sires family; the Harmons, Woodins, Campbells, Plummers, Hinds, Weirs of Dungeness, later of Olympia, of whom Allen Weir is well known and distinguished; yes, and Port Gamble, Port Madison, Steilacoom and Olympia people, what volumes upon volumes might have been, might be written—it will take many a basket to hold the chips to be picked up after their and our *Blazing the Way*.

HAIL, AND FAREWELL

Heroic Pioneers!
Of kings and conquerors fully peers;
Well may the men of later day
Proclaim your deeds, crown you with bay;
Forest-fallers, reigning kings,
In that far time that memory brings.
Nor savage beast, nor savage man,
Majestic forests' frowning ban,
Could palsy arms or break the hearts,
Till wilds gave way to busy marts;
You served your time and country well,
Let tuneful voices paeans swell!

O, steadfast Pioneers!
Bowed 'neath the snows of many years,
Your patient courage never fails,

Your strong true prayers arise,
E'en from the heavenly trails
To "mansions in the skies."
To noble ones midst daily strife,
And those who've crossed the plains of life,
Far past the fiery, setting sun,
The dead and living loved as one,
(Tolls often now the passing bell)
We greeting give and bid farewell.

O Mother Pioneers!
We greet you through our smiles and tears;
You laid foundations deep,
Climbed oft the sun-beat rocky steep
Of sorrow's mountain wild,
Descended through the shadowy vales
Led by the little child.
Within, without your cabins rude
As toiling builders well you wrought,
With busy hands and constant hearts,
And eager children wisdom taught;
Long be delayed the passing bell,
Long be it ere we say "Farewell!"

Beloved Pioneers!
Whom glory waits in coming years,
You planted here with careful hand
The youngest scion in our land
Cut from the tree of Liberty;
To fullest stature it shall grow,
With fruitful branches bending low,
Your worth then shall the people know.
When all your work on earth is done,
Your marches o'er and battles won,
(No more will toll the passing bell)
They'll watch and wait at Heaven's gate
To bid you Hail! and nevermore, Farewell!

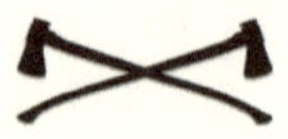

ABOUT THE AUTHOR

Emily Inez Denny (1853-1918) was the daughter of Seattle pioneers David Denny and Louisa Boren Denny. She attended classes at the territorial university (University of Washington) and became a renowned artist and writer whose work documented the experiences of the pioneers who built Seattle. A longtime member of the Women's Century Club, she was an advocate for women's rights and equal suffrage.

www.ingramcontent.com/pod-product-compliance
Lightning Source LLC
Chambersburg PA
CBHW021221060726

47590CB00005B/1589

* 9 7 8 0 5 7 8 9 3 3 8 2 5 *